JOHN DONNE

Selected Poems

With an Introduction and Notes by
ILONA BELL

PENGUIN BOOKS

PENGUIN CLASSICS

Published by the Penguin Group
Penguin Books Ltd, 80 Strand, London WC2R ORL, England
Penguin Group (USA) Inc., 375 Hudson Street, New York, New York 10014, USA
Penguin Group (Canada), 90 Eglinton Avenue East, Suite 700, Toronto, Ontario, Canada M4P 2Y3
(a division of Pearson Penguin Canada Inc.)
Penguin Ireland, 25 St Stephen's Green, Dublin 2, Ireland
(a division of Penguin Books Ltd)
Penguin Group (Australia), 250 Camberwell Road, Camberwell, Victoria 3124, Australia
(a division of Pearson Australia Group Pty Ltd)
Penguin Books India Pvt Ltd, 11, Community Centre, Panchsheel Park, New Delhi – 110 017, India
Penguin Books (NZ), cnr Airborne and Rosedale Roads, Albany, Auckland 1310, New Zealand
(a division of Pearson New Zealand Ltd)
Penguin Books (South Africa) (Pty) Ltd, 24 Sturdee Avenue, Rosebank, Johannesburg 2196, South Africa

Penguin Books Ltd, Registered Offices: 80 Strand, London WC2R ORL, England

www.penguin.com

This selection first published in Penguin Classics 2006

019

Editorial material copyright © Ilona Bell, 2006
All rights reserved

The moral right of the editor has been asserted

Set in 10.25/12.25 pt PostScript Adobe Sabon
Typeset by Rowland Phototypesetting Ltd, Bury St Edmunds, Suffolk
Printed in England by Clays Ltd, St Ives plc

ISBN-13: 978-0-140-42440-9

www.greenpenguin.co.uk

Contents

EPIGRAMS

ELEGIES

THE EPITHALAMIONS OR MARRIAGE SONGS

SATIRES

LETTERS

FUNERAL ELEGIES

DIVINE POEMS

Acknowledgements

First of all, I want to thank Christopher Ricks for convincing me to undertake this edition of John Donne's poetry; it has been an even greater joy than I could have imagined. Years of teaching and writing brought me very close to Donne; editing brought me even closer. Both Ricks and Laura Barber, my editor at Penguin, read and commented on the text with great insight and exquisite attention to the smallest details.

Donne has been blessed with superb modern editors. From text to annotations, this edition is everywhere indebted to their labours, knowledge and judgement.

Thanks to Williams College and the Mellon Foundation, I have had three extraordinary editorial assistants, Eliza Segell, Elizabeth DiMenno and Margaret Gilmore. Their contributions have been indispensable at every stage of the process. For their critical intelligence, their careful attention to every word, their indefatigable labours and constant good cheer, even when I said yet again, 'Thou hast not done, / For I have more,' I owe them each a great, great debt.

I first fell in love with Donne's poetry in Anne Ferry's brilliant graduate-school seminar; she has been a model teacher, mentor and friend. C. A. Patrides was wonderfully supportive when I first began to write about Donne. John Shawcross, Ted-Larry Pebworth and Claude Summers have generously shared their great knowledge for many years.

Amanda Bell, Robert Bell, Zelda Bradburd, Elizabeth DiMenno, Dennis Flynn, Margaret Gilmore, M. Thomas Hester, Judith Isaacson, Christopher Pye, Lawrence Raab and the Fellows at the Oakley Center for the Humanities and Social

Sciences all read the introduction with great care, and made invaluable, thoughtful suggestions.

I am indebted to M. Thomas Hester for giving me permission to use his wonderful Latin translation of Donne's epitaph on Anne More, and to Dennis Flynn for sharing his vast knowledge of Donne's life.

The librarians at Sawyer Library could not have been more responsive to my requests. Robert L. Volz, Wayne G. Hammond and Elaine Yanow were extremely generous in enabling me to take full advantage of Chapin Library's remarkable rare book collection, with its two fine copies of the 1633 Donne.

Robert Bell provided a patient and attentive ear, a critical eye, astute counsel and loving encouragement throughout.

Though I have done everything I could to avoid the errors that have animated my nightmares, whatever mistakes remain are entirely my own.

Finally I wish to dedicate this my work

> *to Kaitlin and Amanda*
> *Fæminæ Lectissimæ, dilectissimæque*
> *Women most choice/select/read,*
> *most beloved/loving/well-read.*

Chronology

1572 Born between 24 January and 19 June, son of John and Elizabeth Donne.

1576 Father dies; mother marries Dr John Symmings.

1584 Matriculates at Hart Hall (later part of Hertford College), Oxford.

Anne More born, 27 May.

1585 Probably travels to the Continent with Henry Stanley, Earl of Derby.

1588 Stepfather dies.

Defeat of Spanish Armada.

1589 Probably travels abroad.

1590–91 Mother marries Richard Rainsford.

1592 Studies law at Lincoln's Inn until 1595 or 1596.

1593 Master of the Revels at Lincoln's Inn.

Receives part of his inheritance.

Brother Henry dies in Newgate Prison after being incarcerated for making confession to a Catholic priest.

1594 Receives further share of his and Henry's inheritance.

1596 Joins the Earl of Essex's military expedition to Cadiz, on the southern tip of Spain.

1597 Participates in Essex's military expedition to the Azores islands.

Enters service of Sir Thomas Egerton, Lord Keeper of the Great Seal.

Elizabeth Wolley marries Egerton, and brings her niece, Anne More, to York House, Egerton's London mansion.

1600 Lady Egerton dies, 20 January.

1601 Member of Parliament for Brackley, Northampton.
   Given lease of his cousin John Heywood's lands until 1605.
   Secretly marries Anne More shortly before Christmas.
1602 Reveals his marriage, imprisoned briefly, and dismissed
   from Egerton's service.
   Marriage declared legal by the Court of Audience, Canter-
   bury, 27 April.
   Moves to Pyrford, near Guildford in Surrey, home of Anne's
   cousin Francis Wolley.
1603 First child, Constance, born.
   Death of Queen Elizabeth; accession of James I (James VI of
   Scotland).
1604 Second child, John, born.
1605 Travels to France and Italy.
   Third child, George, born.
1606 Returns to England; moves family to Mitcham in Surrey.
   Around this time begins to receive £20 a quarter from Anne's
   father, Sir George More.
1607 Fourth child, Francis, born.
   Takes lodging in the Strand, London.
   Prefatory Latin poem published in Ben Jonson's *Volpone*.
1608 Fifth child, Lucy, born.
1609 Sixth child, Bridget, born.
   'The Expiration' published in Alfonso Ferrabosco the Youn-
   ger's *Airs*.
1610 Publishes *Pseudo-Martyr*, a prose treatise arguing that
   English Catholics should take the Oath of Allegiance, and
   that those who refused should not be considered martyrs.
   Receives honorary MA from Oxford University.
1611 Seventh child, Mary, born.
   Ignatius his Conclave and *An Anatomy of the World (The
   First Anniversary)* published.
   Accompanies Sir Robert Drury to the Continent; wife and
   children on the Isle of Wight.
1612 During his absence, eighth child stillborn.
   Returns to England; moves family to house at Sir Robert
   Drury's town house in London.
   The First and Second Anniversaries published.

'Break of Day' published in William Corkine's *Second Book of Airs*.

1613 Ninth child, Nicholas, born; dies within a year.

Elegy on Prince Henry published in the third edition of Joshua Sylvester's *Lachrymae Lachrymarum*.

1614 Daughter Mary and son Francis die.

Member of Parliament for Taunton, Somerset.

1615 Tenth child, Margaret, born.

Takes Anglican Orders, becomes deacon and priest at St Paul's Cathedral, London.

Appointed Royal Chaplain.

Made honorary Doctor of Divinity by Cambridge University.

1616 Eleventh child, Elizabeth, born.

Vicar at Keyston, Huntingdon, and Sevenoaks, Kent.

Reader in Divinity at Lincoln's Inn.

George More's quarterly payments end around this time.

1617 Anne Donne dies, 15 August, seven days after the stillbirth of their twelfth child.

1619 Serves as chaplain to Viscount Doncaster's embassy to Germany.

1621 Becomes dean of St Paul's Cathedral, 22 November.

The Anniversaries republished.

1622 Rector of Blunham, Bedfordshire.

Justice of the Peace for Kent and Bedford.

Publishes first sermon.

Honorary member of the Virginia Company, a joint-stock corporation, formed in 1606 with a charter from King James I, to settle Virginia.

1623 Gravely ill, writes *Devotions upon Emergent Occasions*.

Publishes *Three Sermons upon Special Occasions*.

1624 *Devotions* published.

Becomes vicar of St Dunstan's-in-the-West, London.

1625 Death of James I; Charles I succeeds.

1627 Daughter Lucy dies.

1630 Mortally ill, writes his will.

1631 Dies in London, 31 March, survived by six children.

Buried at St Paul's Cathedral, 3 April.

1633 First edition of Donne's poems published.

Introduction

Around 1618 Ben Jonson predicted that John Donne 'for not being understood would perish'. Since we might think the passage of time has made Donne's poetry difficult, it is telling to hear this from Donne's contemporary, a learned poet who 'esteemeth John Donne the first poet in the world in some things'. As Jonson foresaw, the next century failed to appreciate Donne's bold individuality, irregular metre and jarring disjunctions. The neoclassical poet John Dryden protested that Donne 'affects the metaphysics' and 'perplexes the minds of the fair sex with nice speculations of philosophy, when he should engage their hearts, and entertain them with the softnesses of love'. Samuel Johnson, the great eighteenth-century man of letters, also objected: 'The most heterogeneous ideas are yoked by violence together.'[1]

The nineteenth century was both more understanding and more critical. The romantic poet Samuel Taylor Coleridge found Donne's poems – 'where the writer *thinks*, and expects the reader to do so' – electrifying: 'Wit! – wonder – exciting vigour, intenseness and peculiarity of thought . . . this is the wit of Donne!'[2] The most popular Victorian anthology omitted Donne's poems because, as Alexander Grosart, who published *The Complete Poems of John Donne* in 1872, explained, 'It takes courage to print the poetry of Dr John Donne in our age.' On the subject of Donne's poems the Victorians were divided. 'Few are good for much,' Henry Hallam wrote in the late 1830s: 'the conceits have not even the merit of being intelligible, and it would perhaps be difficult to select three passages that we should care to read again.' Yet Robert Browning was so fond of quoting the love poems in his own love letters to Elizabeth Barrett that she referred to Donne as 'your Donne'.[3]

By the late nineteenth and early twentieth century, with Sir Edmund Gosse's and Sir Herbert Grierson's seminal editions of 1899 and 1912 and T. S. Eliot's oracular modernist essays of 1921, the originality, contrariety and rugged strength of Donne's poetry were widely recognized as the mark of his peculiar genius.[4] Yet it was not until the end of the twentieth century that his religious marginalization and sexual daring were openly discussed.

English Renaissance poetry is rooted in convention, and Donne writes in well-established genres and verse forms: elegy, epigram, satire, love lyric, epithalamion or marriage song, verse epistle, sonnet and hymn.[5] Yet Donne constantly turns conventional poetic forms to unpredictable ends. An avid reader, who, like the speaker in Satire I, preferred the 'constant company' of his books to gadding about town, Donne frequently invokes the classics, the Bible, medieval philosophy, and earlier English, French and Italian Renaissance poets, only to distance himself from them. He mocks the futility of the conventional Petrarchan lover, stuck in a stock conceit and frozen in a static love for an inaccessible, heavenly mistress: 'Alas, alas, who's injured by my love? / What merchant's ships have my sighs drowned?' the speaker asks in 'The Canonization'.[6] In an era deluged by love sonnets, Donne's love lyrics, although known as Songs and Sonnets, contain not even one formal sonnet: fourteen lines of iambic pentameter verse that follow a conventional rhyme scheme. Donne saved those gems for God.

Ben Jonson complained 'that Donne for not keeping of accent deserved hanging'. Yet Donne's lines do scan; as Coleridge realized, 'the sense must be understood in order to ascertain the metre.'[7] Like most English poets until the twentieth century, Donne writes iambic verse, which is comprised of successive feet with one unstressed and one stressed beat (–'). Yet his iambic rhythms are loosened by an unusually high number of substitutions and elisions, which unfetter and intensify the verse, capturing the rugged unpredictability of passionate, col-

loquial speech. 'Holy Sonnet XIV', for example, derives its
explosive energy from a preponderance of caesurae, or pauses
(//), and spondees, or double stresses (''):

Báttēr /mȳ heárt, // thrée-pér/sōned Gód; // fōr Yóu
Ās yét/ būt knóck, // bréathe, //shíne, // ānd séek /tō ménd.

Unlike his immediate predecessors and contemporaries –
most notably Sir Philip Sidney, Edmund Spenser and William
Shakespeare – Donne does not deploy elaborate descriptions of
symbolic natural landscapes, classical myths or female beauty.
He can luxuriate in a lovely natural image – 'Gentle love deeds,
as blossoms on a bough / From love's awakened root do bud
out now' ('Love's Growth') – but not often, and not for long.
He prefers shockingly unpoetic images that dazzle the mind
and penetrate the skin. 'The Flea' turns a pesky little louse (a
conventional trope of libertine poets) into something marvel-
lous: 'and this / Our marriage bed, and marriage temple is; / . . .
we'are met / And cloistered in these living walls of jet.' 'The
Relic' imagines 'A bracelet of bright hair about the bone' of a
corpse.
Suspicious of decorative language, Donne dramatizes the
movement of thoughts shifting and unfolding as one line or
stanza turns to the next. The first stanza of 'The Good Morrow'
concludes with resounding (but conventional) abstractions
about love and beauty, punctuated, though not quite punc-
tured, by a joke about the speaker's prior sexual experiences:
'If ever any beauty I did see, / Which I desired, and got, 'twas
but a dream of thee.' The next stanza starts anew, making the
revelation of exalted, sexually consummated love seem as fresh
and natural as waking up in the morning: 'And now good
morrow to our waking souls.'
Donne reinvigorates poetic language with 'new-made idiom'
(to borrow a phrase from 'Valediction of the Book') drawn
from science and from everyday life: construction, medicine,
law, trade, finance, astronomy, geography, astrology. Con-
structing metaphors as craftsmen make globes, he wields conti-
nents and oceans, ranging from 'the Indias of spice and mine'

to the bed where he is lying with his lover ('The Sun Rising'). Like his contemporaries, Donne sees man as a microcosm of the universe; his vision of the world is at once global ('Let sea-discoverers to new worlds have gone') and intensely private: 'Let us possess one world, each hath one, and is one' ('The Good Morrow'). 'The First Anniversary' heralds the latest scientific discoveries and practices: the revolution of the earth around the sun; newly found stars and planets; anatomical dissection of corpses. Very much a man of his time, yet forward-looking, Donne worries about insoluble scientific problems: 'Of longitudes, what other way have we, / But to mark when and where the dark eclipses be?' ('Valediction of the Book').[8] Donne sounds remarkably modern when the 'new philosophy calls all in doubt', dissolving the stable, hierarchical worldview: 'all in pieces, all coherence gone' ('The First Anniversary').[9] What's left? The body in all its corporeality, the 'muscle, sinew,'and vein / Which tile this house' ('A Valediction of my Name in the Window').

Donne is less an idealist or an aesthete than a builder, an explorer, a sceptic, a sensualist. In his witty, irreverent elegies he writes with remarkable frankness about sex: the pressure of an erection, the delights of foreplay and the clitoris ('the centric part' ('Elegy: Love's Progress')), the pleasure of sexual orgasm, the let-down of post-coital sadness.[10] 'To His Mistress Going to Bed' dramatizes the exciting discovery of undressing a lover in a society where people were almost never naked: 'O my America, my new-found-land'. 'The Comparison' contrasts his friend's aggressive, unsatisfying sexual encounters with the mutual satisfaction the speaker and his mistress enjoy by paying careful, knowing attention to one another's bodies. 'Sappho to Philænis' adopts the persona of the Greek lesbian poet Sappho, who masturbates as she looks into a mirror, imagining that she is touching and speaking to her absent female lover, Philænis.[11] If this arouses male voyeurs, it also gives female creativity and female sexual pleasure a voice that vies with the 'masculine persuasive force' that Donne exerts in 'Elegy: On His Mistress'.[12]

Donne is impatient with set patterns, suspicious of ready-made answers. In the epigrams, as in many of the lyrics, the witty turn of the ending sends us back to the beginning to rethink what we thought we understood. The famously knotty satires mock stupidity, deride self-indulgence, and attack corruption.[13] They also seek the one true Church. Donne came of age during a time when religious belief was passionately debated and politically fraught. Within two generations the government had abandoned Roman Catholicism under Henry VIII (r. 1509–1547) and institutionalized the Protestant Reformation under Edward VI (r. 1547–53) only to return to Catholicism with Queen Mary (r. 1553–58) and back again to Protestantism with Queen Elizabeth (r. 1558–1603). The law required monthly attendance at the services of the Church of England, but dissent was widespread. Donne's third satire scorns the fictitious Graius for accepting the state Church simply because

> Some preachers, vile ambitious bawds, and laws,
> Still new like fashions, bid him think that she
> Which dwells with us is only perfect.

Donne's search for the one true Church soon turns into a search for truth itself, a pursuit so rigorous that it requires the fearless perseverance of a mountain climber:

> On a huge hill,
> Cragged and steep, Truth stands, and he that will
> Reach her, about must, and about must go;
> And what the'hill's suddenness resists, win so.
>   ('Satire III')

For Donne the road to knowledge, whether secular or religious, is always a 'strange way', circuitous but rigorous.[14]

The great twentieth-century scholar C. S. Lewis once complained that 'Donne's poetry is too simple to satisfy. It's complexity is all on the surface.'[15] Yet Donne's poems are not riddles that can be solved once and for all. In 'A Hymn to God the Father', Donne anticipates his own death and recalls his

sins, especially his earthly love for Anne More. In the witty but
haunting refrain, Donne puns obsessively on his own name and
his wife's maiden name: 'When Thou hast done, Thou hast not
done, / For I have more.' Donne is quibbling with God (quib-
bling with God!), but he is also talking to those of us who think
our task is easily done – and to those of us who fear our task
will never be done.

Even at the most sombre moments Donne's language yields
puns and multiple meanings – chasms where the flat verbal
surface doubles over and splits apart, leaving us on the edge of
an interpretative divide. In 'A Nocturnal upon St Lucy's Day',
stability dissolves, and Donne is 're-begot / Of absence, dark-
ness, death, things which are not' – and naught. In 'Holy Sonnet
XIX' obscurity, uncertainty, and confusion release the free play
of thought and language:

> O, to vex me, contraries meet in one;
> Inconstancy unnaturally hath begot
> A constant habit, that when I would not
> I change in vows and in devotion.

Contrariety and 'inconstancy' meet in Donne's vexed repre-
sentations of women. At times the poems echo familiar stereo-
types and deeply entrenched patriarchal attitudes: women are
creatures of the body rather than the intellect; they are uncon-
stant; they should be subordinate to and governed by men. A
joke about women's mindlessness can still get a laugh (as when
the speaker in John Updike's short story 'A & P' comments,
'Do you really think it's a mind in there or just a little buzz like
a bee in a glass jar?').[16] Donne's jibe 'Hope not for mind in
women' ('Love's Alchemy') may still amuse some readers, but
it also makes one all the more mindful of 'Valediction of the
Book', where Donne constructs a tradition of women writers
reaching back to classical antiquity and ending with his wonder-
fully intellectual mistress. The book he urges her to write, a
compendium of all practical and theoretical knowledge 'in
cipher writ, or new-made idiom', will elude and expose the
mistaken presumptions of powerful, narrow-minded men.

Similarly, the gender stereotyping of 'Song ("Go and catch a falling star")' – 'Nowhere / Lives a woman true, and fair' – is proved weak or untrue by the following poem, 'Woman's Constancy', where it is impossible to determine whether the speaker is male or female. When the witty about-face reveals the speaker to be just as inconstant (or not) as the listener, the conclusion prompts us to read the poem again, re-examining the reasons why we think certain qualities are masculine or feminine.

If, as some critics believe, 'Elegy: To His Mistress Going to Bed' subjugates the woman – 'My kingdom, safeliest when with one man manned' – 'The Anniversary' offers a bold new answer to the ideological problems posed by Queen Elizabeth's presence on the throne: 'Here upon earth, we'are kings, and none but we / Can be such kings, nor of such subjects be.' The lovers' reign redistributes sexual and political power equally – and is all the more prized because it is unparalleled. In 'The Undertaking' Donne repudiates conventional sex roles altogether: 'And dare love that, and say so too, / And forget the he and she.'

During Donne's day, literature, especially lyric poetry, was still very close to the oral tradition. Reading was generally vocal rather than silent. Printed books were becoming more widely available, but short poems were recited, read aloud, sung, and passed about in handwritten manuscripts.[17] Donne's poems were not intended for the general public. Rather, they were addressed to an exclusive private audience, a coterie comprised of his lover, a group of irreverent male wits, close friends, fellow poets or literati, potential or valued patrons (both male and female) and God. Donne published only a few of his poems, and regretted doing so almost immediately. He sent poems to a few faithful friends, but made them promise not to make copies. A few of his songs were known, and two were published, but most of Donne's poems did not circulate even in manuscript until years after they were written. When they began to escape the confines of his closely guarded private circle, in the 1620s, the poems were highly sought after, as the extraordinary number of existing manuscript copies attests.

In early modern England, plays and printed books were subject to government censorship. Donne could speak more openly about sex, morality, religion and politics by writing for a carefully chosen private audience. His religious poems, like his love lyrics, are constantly pushing the limits – enacting resistance, seeking answers, risking outrage.

In 'Holy Sonnet XIV' Donne turns all his poetic force and personal charm to wooing God: 'Yet dearly'I love You,'and would be loved fain.' The conclusion is brilliantly original and startling: 'I, / Except You'enthrall me, never shall be free, / Nor ever chaste, except You ravish me.' 'Ravish' is one of those characteristically Donnean words with two very different, almost contradictory meanings: fill with rapture or spiritual exaltation; but also seize and carry away by force, violate, rape. By imagining himself simultaneously as a mystic and as a victim of sexual violence, Donne tries to move beyond simple binaries – beyond reason. The shocking expression of masochistic desire dramatizes what the poem discovers: that divine love requires a violently wrenching leap of faith and an inexplicable, incomprehensible gift of grace.

Of course, we have no idea how God responded, but that is the point. The Holy Sonnets have all the intimacy, intensity and expectation of a private lyric dialogue that yearns for and depends upon an answering response that the poem does not and cannot contain. Donne's divine poems are filled with images of erotic, secular love, just as his love poems are permeated with references to exalted spiritual love, because the dynamic is strikingly similar: Donne's love lyrics can no more force his friend or mistress to affirm his poetic persuasions than his religious lyrics can force God to offer His love, grant His grace, 'and make me new' ('Holy Sonnet XIV').

A large number of Donne's poems were written for a specific reader or a select subset of readers. The opening lines typically provide clues designating the original, intended audience – clues that help explain the premises with which the poem begins and the persuasive thrust with which it ends. 'Satire V', which attacks judicial corruption, is addressed to Donne's boss, Sir Thomas Egerton, and Egerton's boss, the Queen. But there is no indication that Donne imagined Egerton, or Queen Elizabeth – or God – overhearing poems not addressed to them, such as the elegies or the love poems. Donne's occasional poems are at once highly wrought literary artefacts and acts of personal communication rooted in an immediate historical context.

Each of the verse letters is addressed to someone whom Donne knew, sometimes intimately, sometimes more formally. They actively engage with a situation or set of circumstances well known to both the poet and the addressee but only partially discernible by us – something that is equally true and important but less obvious in many poems written in other genres. For example, the verse letters to Sir Henry Wotton describe Wotton's retreat to the country when his lord, Robert Devereux, 2nd Earl of Essex, was at odds with the Queen in 1598–1600. The poems do not explain that Wotton's political ambitions were thwarted by the events at court, because that was already understood by Donne and Wotton themselves.[18] Donne's verse letters anxiously await Wotton's intervening letters. Worried that their missives could easily miscarry, Donne warns Wotton to be discreet. The verse letters to Wotton and to T. W. acknowledge what poems written in less overtly autobiographical genres only imply: events and verbal exchanges outside the poem provoke, interpenetrate and respond to observations and developments inside the poem, and vice versa.

In the epistles to female patrons, as in the Epithalamions and 'The First Anniversary', elaborate tropes, ambiguous, inverted syntax, and abstract philosophical language ease Donne's discomfort at seeking financial reward in exchange for poetic praise.[19] Yet there is always an appealing personal note as well: a reference to a poem that Lucy Russell, Countess of Bedford, wrote and showed Donne on an earlier visit; memories of the Countess of Huntingdon as a young bride, when Donne was serving her new stepfather and secretly courting Anne More. My favourite is a playful tale about Lady Magdalen Herbert hoarding and kissing letters (although this we must infer) from her fiancé, Sir John Danvers, who was a friend of Donne's.

Donne expected his readers and listeners to be attentive and astute enough to disentangle his intricate syntax, to visualize

and conceptualize his metaphors, to tease out his witty, para-
doxical wordplay, and in some cases, but not all, to understand
his abstruse, allusive language. As the notes to this edition
explain, some of Donne's most perplexing and enigmatic
poems, such as 'The Undertaking', 'The Flea' and 'The Curse',
sustain two completely contradictory readings, meaning one
thing to Donne's mistress or male confidant and something
quite different to his derisive male peers.[20]

'Dark texts need notes', Donne writes to Lucy, Countess of
Bedford, in 'You have refined me', reminding her (and us)
that private manuscript poetry depends on a store of topical
knowledge and shared experiences that the poems intimate but
do not explain. Donne was well aware that his listeners' and
readers' responses would be shaped by the expectations they
brought to the poem. Knowing that many of his contemporaries
would disapprove, in 'The Canonization' and 'The Ecstasy'
Donne imagines an ideal lyric audience, 'some lover such as
we', capable of fully understanding his private lyric dialogue
with his mistress. 'The Undertaking' consciously conceals his
most private meaning 'from profane men / which will no faith
on this bestow, / Or, if they do, deride'.

Donne is generally seen as an egotist, given to self-analysis,
self-fashioning and self-advertisement. He is often cocky and
full of himself, strutting his brilliant wit. Yet no one's poems
are more profoundly and persistently dialogic, more attuned
to a reader's or listener's answering response, than Donne's.
Critics have described the woman in Donne's poems (both
admiringly and disapprovingly) as a blank, an excuse for
similes, a reflection of male desire, but that is a misconception,
based on a failure to understand that she is his primary lyric
audience. When he is writing and speaking *to* her (and remem-
ber this is a period when poems were still regularly performed
and read aloud), there is no need to describe her. He is not
trying to flatter her by cataloguing her physical beauty from
head to toe; rather, he is trying to convince her that it is worth
taking an extraordinary risk to defend and preserve their
love.

Some of the Songs and Sonnets contain veiled hints that

Donne's original, private audience was Anne More. In 'A Val-
ediction of My Name in the Window' Donne's name magically
merges with More's: ''Tis more, that it shows thee to thee, /
And clear reflects thee to thine eye.' Although the love lyrics,
unlike the verse letters, do not explicitly name Donne's lyric
audience, they nonetheless create the impression of a private
conversation by combining the rhetorical strategies of drama
and epistolary verse. Some, like 'Song ("Go and catch a falling
star")', are bravura performances, calculated to provoke a
knowing laugh from Donne's male peers. Most are one side of
a private lyric dialogue, a 'dialogue of one' ('The Ecstasy'); they
question, argue, cajole, plead and, above all, refer to, elicit and
eagerly, anxiously, await an answering response. They often
begin with bold assertions, but they generally end with con-
ditionals, double meanings or alternatives that only the listener
or reader can resolve. Donne's love poems invite dialogue and
seek reciprocity because, unlike Petrarchan poets, he believes
'it cannot be / Love, till I love her that loves me' ('Love's Deity').

In 'A Valediction Forbidding Mourning' Donne's speaker is
going on a journey, and urges his mistress not to cry openly lest
her tears 'tell the laity our love'. Donne's seventeenth-century
biographer Izaak Walton thought Donne wrote this poem to
his wife before journeying to the Continent with Sir Robert
Drury in 1611–12. Yet Donne's anxiety about revealing her
feelings to 'the laity' (or laymen) hints at a clandestine love
affair. Throughout, the intimacy of tone, the distressing, ines-
capable imminence of the journey, and the persuasive pressure
to keep their love alive when he is away make us feel the implied
presence of a private female lyric audience. Donne offers a
series of consoling analogies: their separation is as inevitable as
a soul leaving the body for heaven, as 'innocent' as the move-
ment of the heavenly spheres; their relationship is as malleable
and precious as 'gold to airy thinness beat'. He quickly drops
one analogy after another as he realizes that his rhetorical
flourishes evade, but do not dispel, her concerns. At one point
he boldly announces, 'Our two souls therefore, which are
one . . .' But then he is not so sure. As the Book of Common
Prayer and all three of Donne's Epithalamions point out, only

holy matrimony can transform two into one. A qualification
follows almost immediately: 'If they be two, they are two so /
As stiff twin compasses are two . . .'

This two-legged compass (the kind used to draw circles) is
not exactly the sort of image you expect in a love poem, but
it works. The compass, Donne's most famous metaphysical
conceit, has been criticized for shifting direction: pulling apart,
circling, drawing together again. Yet that adaptability is pre-
cisely what makes the image so brilliantly responsive to his
journey and so solicitous of his lover's feelings. Unlike the
preceding more distant and reductive analogies, the image of
the compass delineates the complex interactions that simul-
taneously link and separate the lovers. Right away, it acknowl-
edges *her* emotional concern and *her* spiritual yearning. Even
before he leaves, they must pull apart. That is the hard part,
especially if it is a clandestine affair, since she cannot be present
at his departure or return. When he roams, her soul 'leans, and
hearkens' after him. Her soul is 'the fixed foot' because she is
stuck at home. Yet she is nonetheless instrumental. As anyone
who has used such a compass knows, her role is actually the
more difficult to execute. Only if she exerts a determinedly
steadfast force can he complete his perfect circle: 'Thy firmness
makes my circle just, / And makes me end where I begun.' He
circles around her because he feels linked to her – even when
he is away. When he returns, she 'grows erect as that [circling
foot] comes home'. The pun, referring ever so discreetly to *her*
sexual arousal, sanctions her passionate desire for his safe
return and inscribes her power to divert or direct his course –
and his metaphors.

Donne's poems reveal a lifelong preoccupation with divinity,
love and social connections – the three great shaping forces on
his life. Born in 1572 into an ancient Catholic family, John
Donne grew up during a time when punitive measures against
Catholics were intensifying. Donne left university before taking
the Oath of Allegiance to the Church of England, and travelled
on the Continent. He returned to study law at Lincoln's Inn
in 1592. The following year Donne's brother Henry died in

Newgate Prison after being incarcerated for making confession to a Catholic priest.[21] In 1596 and 1597 Donne volunteered to fight with the Earl of Essex in military expeditions to Cadiz, in southern Spain, and the Azores. Upon returning later in 1597 he became secretary to Sir Thomas Egerton, the Lord Keeper of the Great Seal.

While Donne was serving the Lord Keeper, Egerton married his second wife, Elizabeth Wolley, who brought her niece, Anne More, to York House, Egerton's London mansion, to continue her education and be introduced to society. John Donne and Anne More fell in love. Fearing the disapproval of her father, Sir George More, an active anti-Papist, they took great pains to conceal their love affair. At some point rumours reached Anne's father, and the lovers were separated, but only after they had made a clandestine marriage contract that could not be broken without loss of honour. In 1601 Anne accompanied her father from his Surrey home to London for the opening of Parliament. Shortly before Christmas, the seventeen-year-old Anne More and the twenty-nine-year-old John Donne were secretly married, after which Anne returned to her father's home in Surrey.

Most marriages in the upper echelons were arranged by parents and guardians, who controlled dowries, lands and in-heritance. Yet once a young woman reached the age of twelve, and a young man the age of fourteen, they were legally free to marry without parental permission. It was not until more than a month afterwards that Donne finally wrote to Anne's father to reveal the marriage, saying, 'we adventured equally', affirming the freely chosen, egalitarian love he celebrates in 'The Anniversary' and elsewhere. Announcing with his characteristic but not particularly politic wit that 'it is irremediably done', Donne begged Sir George not to direct his anger at his daughter, and pointed out how easily he could ensure their happiness.[22] No such luck. Donne and two of the friends who performed and witnessed the wedding were thrown in jail. Worse yet, Donne lost his position as Egerton's secretary. Donne continued to write pleas to his father-in-law and his former boss, and he also took his case to court. There were judicial hearings in

January 1602, but it was not until 27 April that the Court of Audience, in Canterbury, declared the marriage legal.

Donne won a wife he loved, but in so doing he sacrificed his professional aspirations. The couple moved to the country, where their family grew apace, a child appearing almost annually. Donne obtained patronage from a number of aristocratic supporters whom he courted in poetry, but he failed to gain professional stability until, after much soul-searching, he was finally persuaded by King James to become an Anglican minister. In 1616 he was appointed first Reader in Divinity at Lincoln's Inn. The following year, fifteen years after their clandestine marriage, Anne Donne died, seven days after the stillbirth of their twelfth child. In 1621 Donne became dean of St Paul's, the great London cathedral, where he preached brilliant, witty, dramatic sermons. Donne wrote a few poems after his wife's death in 1617 and a few hymns to God in contemplation of his own death, but most of his energy and literary talent went into religious meditations and sermons. He died on 31 March 1631 at the age of fifty-nine, survived by six of his twelve children. The first collected edition of his poems appeared in 1633. It sold so well that an expanded second edition appeared two years later.

Donne sharpened his poetic skills in an era when harbouring a Catholic priest could cost you your life, in a world where wooing, seducing and marrying a young heiress could either secure your future or land you in prison and destroy your career, and in a patronage culture where writing brilliant, delicately veiled poems of praise could win valuable support. Together, Donne's Catholic upbringing, clandestine courtship and financial exigencies bred habits of mind and uses of language that are ingrained in his poetry – verbal and syntactical ambiguity, allegorical figures of speech, enigma, irony, amphibology (saying one thing and meaning another) and equivocation (saying one thing that could be taken to mean the opposite) – and that make reading his poetry as intriguing and challenging today as it was in his own time.

There is no greater, or more daring, writer of love poems or religious lyrics in the English language. Donne extols 'Lovers'

Infiniteness', but he is constantly wishing for more – 'If yet I have not all thy love, / Dear, I shall never have it all / . . . / Yet I would not have all yet, / He that hath all can have no more.' 'Can have no more' – more verbal play, more emotional and spiritual intensity, more sexual pleasure, more recognition of his poetry's persuasive force, more palpable signs of God's grace, more of the woman he loved most (and whose name he loved to pun upon). Yet he is also constantly on the lookout for intellectual challenges, emotional tensions, problematic potential interpretations – for more of the ifs, ors and buts that make his poems so dialogic and so difficult.

Donne would, I expect, be amused to learn that there is now a John Donne Society, a *John Donne Journal*, an annual John Donne conference, and that his poetry is discussed in class-rooms, conferences and journals around the world by teachers and scholars eager to secure their own academic patronage. He would certainly be pleased to hear that his poems are still read by lovers wooing each other, by friends conversing in a pub, by inquiring minds and aspiring souls struggling with ego, uncertainty and self-doubt. There is now little danger that Donne's poems will perish for not being understood; it is above all their complexity and difficulty that make them so compelling and endlessly fascinating.

NOTES

1. Quoted from *John Donne: The Critical Heritage*, ed. A. J. Smith (London: Routledge, 1975), vol. 1, pp. 70, 69, 151, 218.

2. Ibid., p. 275.

3. Kathleen Tillotson, 'Donne's Poetry in the Nineteenth Century (1800–72)', *Elizabethan and Jacobean Studies Presented to Frank Percy Wilson in Honour of his Seventieth Birthday* [ed. Herbert Davis and Helen Gardner] (Oxford: Clarendon Press, 1959), pp. 322, 317, 325.

4. Edmund Gosse (ed.), *The Life and Letters of John Donne* (New York: Dodd, Mead & Co.; London: William Heinemann, 1899); Herbert J. C. Grierson (ed.), *The Poems of John Donne*, 2 vols. (Oxford: Oxford University Press, 1912); T. S. Eliot, 'The

Metaphysical Poets [1921]', in *Selected Essays* (1932; New York: Harcourt Brace, 1960), pp. 241–50. For a fuller account, see Deborah Aldrich Larson, *John Donne and Twentieth-Century Criticism* (Rutherford, NJ: Fairleigh Dickinson University Press, 1989).

5. On Donne's genres, see *Renaissance Genres: Essays on Theory, History, and Interpretation*, ed. Barbara Kiefer Lewalski, Harvard English Studies 14 (Cambridge, Mass.: Harvard University Press, 1986), and *Donne and the Resources of Kind*, ed. A. D. Cousins and Damian Grace (Madison, NJ: Fairleigh Dickinson University Press; London: Associated University Presses, 2002).

6. Donne's relation to lyric tradition is explored in Heather Dubrow, *Echoes of Desire: English Petrarchism and its Counter-discourses* (Ithaca, NY: Cornell University Press, 1995), pp. 203–48, and Anne Ferry, *All in War with Time: Love Poetry of Shakespeare, Donne, Jonson, Marvell* (Cambridge, Mass.: Harvard University Press, 1975), pp. 65–125.

7. *Donne: The Critical Heritage*, ed. Smith, pp. 69, 266.

8. See Dava Sobel, *Longitude: The True Story of a Lone Genius Who Solved the Greatest Scientific Problem of his Time* (New York: Walker, 1995).

9. See Charles Monroe Coffin, *John Donne and the New Philosophy* (New York: Columbia University Press, 1937), and William Empson, *Essays on Renaissance Literature*, vol. 1: *Donne and the New Philosophy*, ed. John Haffenden (Cambridge: Cambridge University Press, 1993).

10. On the prevalence of post-coital sadness, see Christopher Ricks, *Essays in Appreciation* (Oxford: Clarendon Press, 1996; New York: Oxford University Press, 1998), 'John Donne: "Farewell to Love"', pp. 19–50. For a historical account of the renewed interest in the clitoris, see Katherine Park, 'The Rediscovery of the Clitoris: French Medicine and the Tribade, 1570–1620', in *The Body in Parts: Fantasies of Corporeality in Early Modern Europe*, ed. David Hillman and Carla Mazzio (New York: Routledge, 1997), pp. 170–93.

11. The poem has provoked widely disparate responses; a good place to start is Janel Mueller, 'Lesbian Erotics: The Utopian Trope of Donne's "Sapho to Philænis"', *Journal of Homosexuality* 23 (1992), pp. 103–34.

12. See Achsah Guibbory, '"Oh, Let Mee Not Serve So": The Politics of Love in Donne's Elegies', and Stanley Fish, 'Masculine Persuasive Force: Donne and Verbal Power', both in *John Donne*, ed.

Andrew Mousley (New York: St Martin's Press, 1999), pp. 25–44 and 157–81 respectively.

13. See M. Thomas Hester, *Kinde Pitty and Brave Scorn: John Donne's Satyres* (Durham, NC: Duke University Press, 1982).

14. On the interpenetration of religion, ethics and poetry, see Theresa M. DiPasquale, *Literature and Sacrament: The Sacred and the Secular in John Donne* (Pittsburgh: Duquesne University Press, 1999); Meg Lota Brown, *Donne and the Politics of Conscience in Early Modern England* (Leiden: E. J. Brill, 1995), and *John Donne's Religious Imagination: Essays in Honor of John T. Shawcross*, ed. Raymond-Jean Frontain and Frances M. Malpezzi (Conway, Ark: UCA Press, 1995).

15. C. S. Lewis, 'Donne and Love Poetry in the Seventeenth Century', in *John Donne: A Collection of Critical Essays*, ed. Helen Gardner (Englewood Cliffs, NJ: Prentice Hall, 1965), p. 96.

16. John Updike, *The Early Stories 1953–1975* (New York: Alfred A. Knopf, 2003), p. 597.

17. Manuscript circulation and Donne's coterie audience are discussed in Arthur F. Marotti, *John Donne, Coterie Poet* (Madison, Wis.: University of Wisconsin Press, 1986); Ted-Larry Pebworth, 'John Donne, Coterie Poetry, and the Text as Performance', *Studies in English Literature* 29 (1989), pp. 61–75; Dennis Flynn, 'Donne and a Female Coterie', *Lit: Literature, Interpretation, and Theory* 1 (1989), pp. 127–36; David Novarr, *The Disinterred Muse: Donne's Texts and Contexts* (Ithaca, NY: Cornell University Press, 1980).

18. Ted-Larry Pebworth and Claude J. Summers reconstruct the political events underlying Donne's and Wotton's poetic exchange in ' "Thus Friends Absent Speake": The Exchange of Verse Letters between John Donne and Henry Wotton', *Modern Philology* 81 (1984), pp. 361–77.

19. For two quite different approaches to Donne's female patrons, see Margaret Maurer, 'John Donne's Verse Letters', *Modern Language Quarterly* 37 (1976), pp. 234–59, and David Aers and Gunther Kress, ' "Darke texts need notes": Versions of Self in Donne's Verse Epistles', in *John Donne*, ed. Mousley, pp. 122–34.

20. For a fuller account of how and why these poems sustain contradictory readings, see Ilona Bell, 'Courting Anne More', *John Donne Journal* 19 (2000), pp. 59–86, and ' "If it be a shee": The Riddle of Donne's "Curse" ', in *John Donne's 'Desire of More': The Subject of Anne More Donne in his Poetry*, ed. M. Thomas

Hester (Newark, Del.: University of Delaware Press; London: Associated University Presses, 1996), pp. 106–139.

21. The impact of Donne's Roman Catholicism is explored in John Carey, *John Donne: Life, Mind, and Art* (London: Faber and Faber; New York: Oxford University Press, 1981), and Dennis Flynn, *John Donne and the Ancient Catholic Nobility* (Bloomington, Ind.: Indiana University Press, 1995).

22. *John Donne's Marriage Letters in the Folger Shakespeare Library*, ed. M. Thomas Hester, Robert Parker Sorlien and Dennis Flynn (Washington: Folger Shakespeare Library, 2005), pp. 35, 36.

Further Reading

EDITIONS

Patrides, C. A. (ed.), *The Complete English Poems of John Donne* (London: Dent, 1985)

Shawcross, John T. (ed.), *The Complete Poetry of John Donne* (Garden City, NY: Anchor-Doubleday, 1967)

REFERENCE GUIDES

Roberts, John R., *John Donne: An Annotated Bibliography of Modern Criticism*, 2 vols. (Columbia, Mo., and London: University of Missouri Press, 1973, 1982)

—, *John Donne: An Annotated Bibliography of Modern Criticism, 1979–1995* (Pittsburgh: Duquesne University Press, 2004)

BIOGRAPHIES

Bald, R. C., *John Donne: A Life* (Oxford and New York: Oxford University Press, 1970)

Edwards, David Lawrence, *John Donne: Man of Flesh and Spirit* (London: Continuum, 2001)

Le Comte, Edward, *Grace to a Witty Sinner: A Life of Donne* (New York: Walker, 1965)

CRITICAL STUDIES

Baumlin, James S., *John Donne and the Rhetorics of Renaissance Discourse* (Columbia, Mo., and London: University of Missouri Press, 1991)

Bell, Ilona, 'The Role of the Lady in Donne's Songs and Sonets', *Studies in English Literature* 23 (1983), pp. 113–29

Bloom, Harold (ed.), *John Donne: Comprehensive Research and Study Guide* (Broomall, Pa.: Chelsea House, 1999)

Corthell, Ronald, *Ideology and Desire in Renaissance Poetry: The Subject of Donne* (Detroit: Wayne State University Press, 1997)

DiPasquale, Theresa M., *Literature and Sacrament: The Sacred and the Secular in John Donne* (Pittsburgh: Duquesne University Press, 1999)

Docherty, Thomas, *John Donne, Undone* (London: Methuen, 1986). A deconstructive reading of the poems.

Empson, William, *Essays on Renaissance Literature*, vol. 1: *Donne and the New Philosophy*, ed. John Haffenden (Cambridge: Cambridge University Press, 1993)

Ferry, Anne, *The 'Inward' Language: Sonnets of Wyatt, Sidney, Shakespeare, Donne* (Chicago: University of Chicago Press, 1983). Analyses the language used to explore the inner self in the Holy Sonnets.

Fiore, Peter Amadeus, *Just So Much Honor: Essays Commemorating the Four-hundredth Anniversary of the Birth of John Donne* (University Park, Pa., and London: Pennsylvania State University Press, 1972). A collection of essays by eminent Renaissance scholars.

Gardner, Helen (ed.), *John Donne: A Collection of Critical Essays* (Englewood Cliffs, NJ: Prentice-Hall, 1962). Traces changing twentieth-century attitudes towards Donne.

Guibbory, Achsah (ed.), *The Cambridge Companion to John Donne* (Cambridge: Cambridge University Press, 2006). Broad-ranging essays offering an introduction and overview of topics central to Donne's writing.

Hester, M. Thomas (ed.), *John Donne's 'desire of more': The*

Subject of Anne More Donne in his Poetry (Newark, Del.: University of Delaware Press; London: Associated University Presses, 1996)

—, and R. V. Young, Jr (eds.), *John Donne Journal: Studies in the Age of Donne,* 1982–

Kermode, Frank, *John Donne* (New York: Longmans, Green, 1957). An introduction to Donne's life and works.

Leishman, J. B., *The Monarch of Wit: An Analytical and Comparative Study of the Poetry of John Donne* (London: Hutchinson, 1951)

Marotti, Arthur F., *John Donne, Coterie Poet* (Madison, Wis., and London: University of Wisconsin Press, 1986). A study of manuscript circulation, with readings of poems in their biographical and socio-historical contexts.

— (ed.), *Critical Essays on John Donne* (New York: G. K. Hall, 1994)

Mousley, Andrew (ed.), *John Donne* (Houndsmills, NY: Palgrave, 1999). A collection of critical essays using historicist, feminist, psychoanalytic and deconstructive approaches.

Nutt, Joe, *John Donne: The Poems* (Houndmills, NY: Macmillan, 1999). Critical analyses of the entire range of Donne's poetry.

Pinka, Patricia Garland, *This Dialogue of One: The Songs and Sonnets of John Donne* (University, Ala.: University of Alabama Press, 1982). A study of the speaker's thoughts and feelings.

Roberts, John R. (ed.), *Essential Articles for the Study of John Donne's Poetry* (Hamden, Conn.: Archon Books, 1975)

Sanders, Wilbur, *John Donne's Poetry* (Cambridge: Cambridge University Press, 1971). Close readings of numerous poems.

Stein, Arnold Sidney, *John Donne's Lyrics: The Eloquence of Action* (Minneapolis: University of Minnesota Press, 1962). Readings that stress the unity of imaginative form.

Summers, Claude J., and Ted-Larry Pebworth (eds.), *The Eagle and the Dove: Reassessing John Donne* (Columbia, Mo.: University of Missouri Press, 1986). A collection of essays on a variety of topics.

Warnke, Frank J., *John Donne* (Boston: Twayne, 1987). A concise, comprehensive overview of Donne the man and artist.

Winny, James, *A Preface to Donne* (London: Longman, 1970). An introduction for new readers seeking critical guidance.

A Note on the Texts

Although this is a selected edition of Donne's poems, it contains his most important and widely read poems, as well as a substantial selection of poems from every genre: all the Songs and Sonnets, Epigrams, Epithalamions, Holy Sonnets and Hymns; a majority of the Elegies and Letters; 'The First Anniversary'. It omits several long poems ('The Litany', 'Metempsychosis', 'Satire IV', a number of Funeral Elegies) in order to make space for a larger number of shorter poems.

Donne published only a handful of poems during his lifetime, and he immediately regretted doing so. 'The fault that I acknowledge in myself, is to have descended to print anything in verse,' Donne wrote to a friend after publishing *The Anniversaries*. 'I confess I wonder how I declined to it, and do not pardon myself.' Astonishingly, he did not even keep copies of his own poems. In 1614, when he was thinking about printing some of his verse, 'not for much public view, but at mine own cost, a few copies', he wrote to another friend asking to borrow that 'old book', a manuscript collection of poems, saying it 'cost me more to seek them, than it did to make them'.[1]

Only one poem exists definitively in Donne's handwriting, a verse letter to Lady Carey and Mistress Essex Rich, written in late 1611 from Amiens; it is printed here with Donne's punctuation unaltered.[2] In all other cases, we do not know exactly what Donne wrote. A few poems are dated in the manuscripts: 'To Mr Henry Wotton' ("Here's no more news than virtue")' 20 July 1598; 'Metempsychosis' 16 August 1600; 'La Corona' July 1607; 'Goodfriday, 1613. Riding Westward'. 'The First Anniversary', 'A Funeral Elegy' and 'The Second

Anniversary' were published with Donne's approval in 1611 and 1612, shortly after they were written.[3] Dates for the remaining poems are more or less conjectural. The Elegies, the Satires and most of the Epigrams were written in the 1590s, when Donne was studying at Lincoln's Inn or serving as secretary to the Lord Keeper. 'The Storm', 'The Calm' and a few of the Epigrams were written during the Azores expedition of 1597. Most of the Songs and Sonnets were written before Donne's marriage in 1601, 'The Curse' most likely in 1599 and 'Lecture upon the Shadow' in January 1601. Dates for individual Epithalamions and Letters appear in the Notes. The Latin 'Epitaph on Anne Donne' and 'Holy Sonnet XVII ("Since she whom I loved")', were written after his wife's death in 1617, 'Hymn to God my God, in my Sickness' and 'A Hymn to God the Father' probably in 1623, when Donne was mortally ill.

Despite the paucity of autograph manuscripts, *The Variorum Edition* has assembled over 5,000 transcriptions of some 225 poems.[4] Some of the variants may suggest that Donne was in the habit of revising his poems. Many of the manuscripts were made during his lifetime, and may therefore be closer to what he wrote than the first edition, which was published two years after his death. Yet most of the extant manuscripts were copied from other manuscripts, and often the original copy no longer exists, so it can be difficult to know which copy is earlier or most authoritative.

This edition uses the first published seventeenth-century edition of each poem as its copy-text. Thus the copy-text of 'The First Anniversary' is the first edition of 1611, which Donne probably saw into print; the text is emended according to the errata slip found in one copy of the 1612 reprint, which was probably compiled by Donne himself.[5] Most of the poems were published for the first time in 1633; more were added in 1635, a few as late as the seventh printing of 1669. Only when a poem was not published by 1669 has a manuscript been used as the copy-text for this volume.

Texts have been emended with variants from manuscripts or subsequent seventeenth-century editions when there is a

compelling reason to do so: when the copy-text contains obvi-
ous misspellings, grammatical mistakes, miscopied or miscon-
strued words; when the *Variorum* text offers a significant
improvement; when a particular variant simply makes much
better sense.[6] These emendations are listed in the Notes, along
with a few especially interesting variants. Since there are so
many Donne manuscripts, and since most reliable variants
appear in several manuscripts, specific manuscripts are not
cited.[7]

Spelling and punctuation were not standardized during
Donne's day, and have changed since; for example, the first
edition regularly uses a colon where we expect a comma, and
a word or name was often spelled several ways, even within a
single piece of writing. Since (with one exception) we do not
have Donne's manuscripts, and since copyists and printers
freely changed spelling and punctuation, this edition mod-
ernizes the spelling and capitalization, except where the old
spelling contains apt double meanings ('travail', for example,
generally means both to travel and to labour). Pronouns refer-
ring to God and Christ have been capitalized for the sake of
clarity. The punctuation has been modernized very delicately,
to eliminate false leads that make reading Donne's poems more
difficult than necessary, but to preserve meaningful syntactical
ambiguities. Syllables that are elided (or run together) to create
the correct number of syllables for the metre are marked with
an apostrophe ('find'st'). Quotation marks are not used, since
they did not exist during Donne's day.

The order of the poems poses another problem. The 1633
first edition groups poems by genre, but is not consistent; for
example, Songs and Sonnets is interrupted by 'The First Anni-
versary', 'A Funeral Elegy' and 'The Second Anniversary'.
Consequently, this edition follows the 1635 order, which not
only includes more poems but also has more consistent generic
groupings. The exception is 'The Flea', which begins Songs and
Sonnets in 1635. It appears here before 'The Curse', which is
its position both in 1633 and in five out of six Group I manu-
scripts,[8] because 'The Good Morrow' makes a much better

beginning for Songs and Sonnets. 'Sappho to Philænis', which often appears among the elegies in modern editions, appears here among the verse letters, as it did in 1635. Poems not included in 1635 are added to the appropriate genre.

The notes do not explain what a poem means; rather, they provide definitions and information so that readers can reach their own interpretation. Definitions are drawn primarily from *The Oxford English Dictionary* (Oxford University Press, 2005, http://www.oed.com), although Donne's usage regularly pre-dates the earliest examples given there. For glossing Donne's pervasive sexual double meanings, Eric Partridge, *Shakespeare's Bawdy: A Literary and Psychological Essay and a Comprehensive Glossary* (New York: E. P. Dutton, 1948), and Frankie A. Rubinstein, *Dictionary of Shakespeare's Sexual Puns and their Significance* (London: Macmillan Press, 1984), provide valuable supplements to the *OED*. Biblical quotations are from the King James Bible (1611). Birth and death dates are primarily from *The Oxford Dictionary Online* (Oxford University Press, 2005, http://dictionary.oed.com).

The annotations gloss words unfamiliar to readers today, but, equally important, they note familiar words that meant something quite different in Donne's day. Since the poems regularly incorporate a variety of possible definitions to thicken and complicate the meaning, and in some cases to create multiple meanings for the poem as a whole, the notes often contain several, sometimes seemingly contradictory, choices.

There are numerous excellent editions of Donne's poems, which readers can consult for further information: *The Variorum Edition of the Poetry of John Donne*, ed. Gary A. Stringer et al. (Bloomington, Ind.: Indiana University Press, 1995–); *The Complete Poetry of John Donne*, ed. John T. Shawcross (Garden City, NY: Anchor-Doubleday, 1967); *The Poems of John Donne*, ed. Herbert J. C. Grierson, 2 vols. (Oxford: Clarendon Press, 1912, 1963); *The Complete English Poems of John Donne*, ed. C. A. Patrides (London: Dent, 1985); *John Donne: The Complete English Poems*, ed. A. J. Smith (Harmondsworth: Penguin, 1971, 1983); *John Donne*, ed. John Carey (Oxford and New York: Oxford University Press, 1990);

Songs and Sonets of John Donne, ed. Theodore Redpath (London: Methuen, 1956; New York: St Martin's Press, 1983); *John Donne: The Elegies, and the Songs and Sonnets*, ed. Helen Gardner (Oxford: Clarendon Press, 1965) and *The Divine Poems*, ed. Gardner (Oxford: Clarendon Press, 1952, 1969); *John Donne: The Anniversaries*, ed. Frank Manley (Baltimore: Johns Hopkins Press, 1963); *The Epithalamions, Anniversaries, and Epicedes*, ed. W. Milgate (Oxford and New York: Clarendon Press, 1978) and *The Satires, Epigrams and Verse Letters*, ed. Milgate (Oxford: Clarendon Press, 1967).

NOTES

1. John Donne, *Letters to Severall Persons of Honour*, ed. M. Thomas Hester (1651; Delmar, NY: Scholars' Facsimiles & Reprints, 1977), pp. 238, 197.
2. The Loseley manuscript of Donne's epitaph upon his wife's death may also be in Donne's handwriting. See *John Donne's Marriage Letters in the Folger Shakespeare Library*, ed. M. Thomas Hester, Robert Parker Sorlien and Dennis Flynn (Washington: Folger Shakespeare Library, 2005).
3. Other poems published during Donne's lifetime are listed in the Chronology.
4. *The Variorum Edition of the Poetry of John Donne*, ed. Gary A. Stringer et al. (Bloomington, Ind.: Indiana University Press, 1995–), II, xlix. The manuscripts are listed in II, xxxii–xxxvii; the poems in II, xix–xxv.
5. The introduction to *John Donne: The Anniversaries*, ed. Frank Manley (Baltimore: Johns Hopkins University Press, 1963) explains Donne's responsibility for the 1611 text and the list of errata.
6. Only volumes 2, 6 and 8 of *The Variorum Edition* were available when this edition went to press.
7. The abbreviation 'ms' is used whether the variant appears in one or several manuscripts. For more information on which manuscripts contain specific variants, readers should consult *The Variorum Edition* and editions by Shawcross, Grierson, etc. cited at the end of this Note on the Texts.
8. The Group I manuscripts contain the largest number of well-

grouped Donne poems. They are listed in *The Variorum Edition*,
II, xliii, and in *A Bibliography of Dr John Donne, Dean of Saint
Paul's*, ed. Geoffrey Keynes (Oxford: Clarendon Press, 1973),
p. 185. The Donne Variorum website (http://donnevari-
orum.com) includes a first-line index to seventeenth-century edi-
tions and the most important manuscript collections, including
the Group I manuscripts. For descriptions of specific manu-
scripts, see *Index of English Literary Manuscripts*, ed. Peter Beal
(London: Mansell; New York: R. R. Bowker, 1980), I, 243–61.

Selected Poems

The Good Morrow

I wonder by my troth, what thou and I
Did, till we loved. Were we not weaned till then?
But sucked on country pleasures, childishly?
Or snorted we in the'seven sleepers' den?
'Twas so; but this, all pleasures fancies be.
If ever any beauty I did see,
Which I desired, and got, 'twas but a dream of thee.

And now good morrow to our waking souls,
Which watch not one another out of fear,
For love, all love of other sights controls,   10
And makes one little room an everywhere.
Let sea-discoverers to new worlds have gone,
Let maps to others, worlds on worlds have shown,
Let us possess one world, each hath one, and is one.

My face in thine eye, thine in mine appears,
And true plain hearts do in the faces rest;
Where can we find two better hemispheres
Without sharp North, without declining West?
What ever dies was not mixed equally;
If our two loves be one, or thou and I   20
Love so alike, that none do slacken, none can die.

Song

Go and catch a falling star,
   Get with child a mandrake root,
Tell me where all past years are,
   Or who cleft the Devil's foot,

Teach me to hear mermaids singing,
Or to keep off envy's stinging,
     And find
     What wind
Serves to advance an honest mind.

If thou be'est born to strange sights,
  Things invisible to see,
Ride ten thousand days and nights,
  Till age snow white hairs on thee,
Thou, when thou return'st, wilt tell me
All strange wonders that befell thee,
     And swear
     Nowhere
Lives a woman true, and fair.

If thou find'st one, let me know,
  Such a pilgrimage were sweet;
Yet do not, I would not go,
  Though at next door we might meet;
Though she were true when you met her,
And last till you write your letter,
     Yet she
     Will be
False, ere I come, to two, or three.

Woman's Constancy

Now thou hast loved me one whole day,
Tomorrow when thou leav'st, what wilt thou say?
Wilt thou then antedate some new-made vow?
    Or say that now
We are not just those persons which we were?
Or, that oaths made in reverential fear
Of Love, and his wrath, any may forswear?

Or, as true deaths, true marriages untie,
So lovers' contracts, images of those,
Bind but till sleep, death's image, them unloose? 10
  Or, your own end to justify,
For having purposed change and falsehood, you
Can have no way but falsehood to be true?
Vain lunatic, against these 'scapes I could
  Dispute, and conquer, if I would,
   Which I abstain to do,
For by tomorrow, I may think so too.

The Undertaking

I have done one braver thing
 Than all the Worthies did,
And yet a braver thence doth spring,
 Which is, to keep that hid.

It were but madness now t'impart
 The skill of specular stone,
When he which can have learned the art
 To cut it can find none.

So, if I now should utter this,
 Others (because no more   10
Such stuff to work upon, there is,)
 Would love but as before.

But he who loveliness within
 Hath found, all outward loathes,
For he who colour loves, and skin,
 Loves but their oldest clothes.

If, as I have, you also do
 Virtue'attired in woman see,
And dare love that, and say so too,
 And forget the he and she, 20

And if this love, though placed so,
    From profane men you hide,
Which will no faith on this bestow,
    Or, if they do, deride,

Then you have done a braver thing
    Than all the Worthies did.
And a braver thence will spring
    Which is, to keep that hid.

The Sun Rising

Busy old fool, unruly Sun,
    Why dost thou thus,
Through windows and through curtains call on us?
Must to thy motions lovers' seasons run?
    Saucy pedantic wretch, go chide
    Late schoolboys and sour prentices,
  Go tell court-huntsmen that the King will ride,
  Call country ants to harvest offices;
Love, all alike, no season knows, nor clime,
Nor hours, days, months, which are the rags of time.

Thy beams, so reverend and strong,
    Why should'st thou think?
I could eclipse and cloud them with a wink,
But that I would not lose her sight so long:
    If her eyes have not blinded thine,
    Look, and tomorrow late, tell me
  Whether both the Indias of spice and mine
  Be where thou left'st them, or lie here with me.
Ask for those kings whom thou saw'st yesterday,
And thou shalt hear, All here in one bed lay.

> She's all states, and all princes I,
> Nothing else is.
> Princes do but play us; compared to this,
> All honour's mimic, all wealth alchemy;
> Thou Sun art half as happy'as we,
> In that the world's contracted thus.
> Thine age asks ease, and since thy duties be
> To warm the world, that's done in warming us.
> Shine here to us, and thou art everywhere;
> This bed thy centre is, these walls, thy sphere. 30

The Indifferent

I can love both fair and brown,
Her whom abundance melts, and her whom want
    betrays,
Her who loves loneness best, and her who masks and
    plays,
Her whom the country formed, and whom the town,
Her who believes, and her who tries,
Her who still weeps with spongy eyes,
And her who is dry cork, and never cries;
I can love her, and her, and you and you,
I can love any, so she be not true.

Will no other vice content you? 10
Will it not serve your turn to do as did your mothers?
Or have you all old vices spent, and now would find
    out others?
Or doth a fear, that men are true, torment you?
O we are not, be not you so,
Let me, and do you, twenty know.
Rob me, but bind me not, and let me go.
Must I, who came to travail thorough you,
Grow your fixed subject, because you are true?

Venus heard me sigh this song,
And by love's sweetest part, variety, she swore,
She heard not this till now; and that it should be so
    no more.
She went, examined, and returned ere long,
And said, alas, some two or three
Poor heretics in love there be,
Which think to 'stablish dangerous constancy.
But I have told them, since you will be true,
You shall be true to them, who'are false to you.

Love's Usury

For every hour that thou wilt spare me now,
        I will allow,
Usurious God of Love, twenty to thee,
When with my brown, my grey hairs equal be;
Till then, Love, let my body reign, and let
Me travel, sojourn, snatch, plot, have, forget,
Resume my last year's relict: think that yet
        We'had never met.

Let me think any rival's letter mine,
        And at next nine
Keep midnight's promise; mistake by the way
The maid, and tell the lady'of that delay;
Only let me love none, no, not the sport;
From country grass, to comfitures of court,
Or city's quelque-choses, let report
        My mind transport.

This bargain's good; if when I'am old, I be
        Inflamed by thee,
If thine own honour, or my shame, or pain,
Thou covet most, at that age thou shalt gain.

Do thy will then, then subject and degree,
And fruit of love, Love I submit to thee;
Spare me till then, I'll bear it, though she be
   One that loves me.

The Canonization

For God's sake hold your tongue, and let me love,
   Or chide my palsy, or my gout,
My five grey hairs, or ruined fortune flout,
   With wealth your state, your mind with arts improve,
      Take you a course, get you a place,
      Observe his honour, or his grace,
Or the King's real, or his stamped face
   Contemplate, what you will, approve,
   So you will let me love.

Alas, alas, who's injured by my love?   10
   What merchant's ships have my sighs drowned?
Who says my tears have overflowed his ground?
   When did my colds a forward spring remove?
      When did the heats which my veins fill
      Add one more to the plaguy bill?
Soldiers find wars, and lawyers find out still
   Litigious men, which quarrels move,
   Though she and I do love.

Call us what you will, we'are made such by love;
   Call her one, me another fly,   20
We'are tapers too, and at our own cost die,
   And we in us find the'eagle and the dove.
      The phoenix riddle hath more wit
      By us, we two being one, are it.
So to one neutral thing both sexes fit.
   We die and rise the same, and prove
   Mysterious by this love.

We can die by it, if not live by love,
   And if unfit for tombs and hearse
Our legend be, it will be fit for verse;
   And if no piece of chronicle we prove,
     We'll build in sonnets pretty rooms;
     As well a well-wrought urn becomes
The greatest ashes, as half-acre tombs,
   And by these hymns, all shall approve
   Us canonized for love.

And thus invoke us: you whom reverend love
   Made one another's hermitage,
You, to whom love was peace, that now is rage,
   Who did the whole world's soul contract, and
       drove
     Into the glasses of your eyes
     So made such mirrors, and such spies,
That they did all to you epitomize,
   Countries, towns, courts, beg from above
   A pattern of your love.

The Triple Fool

   I am two fools, I know,
For loving, and for saying so
   In whining poetry;
But where's that wiseman that would not be I,
   If she would not deny?
Then as th'earth's inward narrow crooked lanes
Do purge seawater's fretful salt away,
   I thought, if I could draw my pains
Through rhyme's vexation, I should them allay;
Grief brought to numbers cannot be so fierce,
For he tames it, that fetters it in verse.

But when I have done so,
Some man, his art and voice to show,
  Doth set and sing my pain,
And by delighting many, frees again
  Grief, which verse did restrain.
To love and grief tribute of verse belongs,
But not of such as pleases when 'tis read,
  Both are increased by such songs,
For both their triumphs so are published,   20
And I, which was two fools, do so grow three;
Who are a little wise, the best fools be.

Lovers' Infiniteness

If yet I have not all thy love,
Dear, I shall never have it all;
I cannot breathe one other sigh to move,
Nor can entreat one other tear to fall.
And all my treasure, which should purchase thee,
Sighs, tears, and oaths, and letters, I have spent.
Yet no more can be due to me,
Than at the bargain made was meant.
If then thy gift of love were partial,
That some to me, some should to others fall,   10
  Dear, I shall never have thee all.

Or if then thou gavest me all,
All was but all which thou had'st then;
But if in thy heart, since, there be or shall
New love created be by other men,
Which have their stocks entire, and can in tears,
In sighs, in oaths, and letters, outbid me,
This new love may beget new fears,
For this love was not vowed by thee,
And yet it was, thy gift being general,   20
The ground, thy heart, is mine; what ever shall
  Grow there, dear, I should have it all.

Yet I would not have all yet,
He that hath all can have no more,
And since my love doth every day admit
New growth, thou should'st have new rewards in store;
Thou canst not every day give me thy heart,
If thou canst give it, then thou never gavest it;
Love's riddles are, that though thy heart depart,
30   It stays at home, and thou with losing savest it;
But we will have a way more liberal
Than changing hearts, to join them, so we shall
    Be one, and one another's all.

Song

Sweetest love, I do not go
    For weariness of thee,
Nor in hope the world can show
    A fitter love for me,
        But since that I
Must die at last, 'tis best
To use myself in jest,
    Thus by feigned deaths to die.

Yesternight the sun went hence,
10   And yet is here today;
He hath no desire nor sense,
    Nor half so short a way;
        Then fear not me,
But believe that I shall make
Speedier journeys, since I take
    More wings and spurs than he.

O how feeble is man's power,
    That if good fortune fall,
Cannot add another hour,
20   Nor a lost hour recall?

But come bad chance,
And we join to it our strength,
And we teach it art and length,
    Itself o'er us to'advance.

When thou sigh'st, thou sigh'st not wind,
    But sigh'st my soul away;
When thou weep'st, unkindly kind,
    My life's blood doth decay.
        It cannot be
That thou lov'st me, as thou say'st,   30
If in thine my life thou waste;
    Thou art the best of me.

Let not thy divining heart
    Forethink me any ill;
Destiny may take thy part,
    And may thy fears fulfil;
        But think that we
Are but turned aside to sleep;
They who one another keep
    Alive, ne'er parted be.   40

The Legacy

When I died last, and, dear, I die
As often as from thee I go,
Though it be but an hour ago,
And lovers' hours be full eternity,
I can remember yet, that I
Something did say, and something did bestow;
Though I be dead, which sent me, I should be
Mine own executor and legacy.

I heard me say, tell her anon,
10 That myself (that's you, not I)
Did kill me,'and when I felt me die,
I bid me send my heart, when I was gone,
But I alas could there find none,
When I had ripped me,'and searched where hearts
        did lie;
It killed me'again, that I who still was true,
In life, in my last will should cozen you.

Yet I found something like a heart,
But colours it, and corners had,
It was not good, it was not bad,
20 It was entire to none, and few had part.
As good as could be made by art
It seemed, and therefore for our losses sad,
I meant to send this heart instead of mine,
But O, no man could hold it, for 'twas thine.

A Fever

O do not die, for I shall hate
    All women so, when thou art gone,
That thee I shall not celebrate,
    When I remember, thou wast one.

But yet thou canst not die, I know;
    To leave this world behind is death,
But when thou from this world wilt go,
    The whole world vapours with thy breath.

Or if, when thou, the world's soul, goest,
10   It stay, 'tis but thy carcass then,
The fairest woman, but thy ghost,
    But corrupt worms, the worthiest men.

O wrangling schools, that search what fire
    Shall burn this world, had none the wit
Unto this knowledge to aspire,
    That this her fever might be it?

And yet she cannot waste by this,
    Nor long bear this torturing wrong,
For much corruption needful is
    To fuel such a fever long.   20

These burning fits but meteors be,
    Whose matter in thee is soon spent.
Thy beauty,'and all parts, which are thee,
    Are unchangeable firmament.

Yet 'twas of my mind, seizing thee,
    Though it in thee cannot persevere.
For I had rather owner be
    Of thee one hour, than all else ever.

Air and Angels

Twice or thrice had I loved thee,
Before I knew thy face or name;
So in a voice, so in a shapeless flame,
Angels affect us oft, and worshipped be;
    Still when, to where thou wert, I came,
Some lovely glorious nothing I did see;
    But since, my soul, whose child love is,
Takes limbs of flesh, and else could nothing do,
    More subtle than the parent is,
Love must not be, but take a body too,   10
    And therefore what thou wert, and who
        I bid Love ask, and now
That it assume thy body, I allow,
And fix itself in thy lip, eye, and brow.

Whil'st thus to ballast love, I thought,
And so more steadily to have gone,
With wares which would sink admiration,
I saw I had love's pinnace overfraught,
    Ev'ry thy hair for love to work upon
Is much too much, some fitter must be sought;
    For nor in nothing, nor in things
Extreme and scatt'ring bright can love inhere;
    Then as an angel, face and wings
Of air, not pure as it, yet pure doth wear,
    So thy love may be my love's sphere;
        Just such disparity
As is twixt air and angels' purity
'Twixt women's love and men's will ever be.

Break of Day

'Tis true, 'tis day, what though it be?
O wilt thou therefore rise from me?
Why should we rise because 'tis light?
Did we lie down because 'twas night?
Love, which in spite of darkness brought us hither,
Should in despite of light keep us together.

Light hath no tongue, but is all eye;
If it could speak as well as spy,
This were the worst that it could say,
That, being well, I fain would stay,
And that I loved my heart and honour so,
That I would not from him, that had them, go.

Must business thee from hence remove?
O, that's the worst disease of love,
The poor, the foul, the false, love can
Admit, but not the busied man.
He which hath business, and makes love, doth do
Such wrong as when a married man doth woo.

The Anniversary

All kings and all their favourites,
   All glory'of honours, beauties, wits,
The sun itself, which makes times, as they pass,
Is elder by a year, now, than it was
When thou and I first one another saw.
All other things to their destruction draw,
   Only our love hath no decay;
This no tomorrow hath, nor yesterday;
Running it never runs from us away,
But truly keeps his first, last, everlasting day.   10

Two graves must hide thine and my corpse;
   If one might, death were no divorce.
Alas, as well as other princes, we
(Who prince enough in one another be)
Must leave at last in death, these eyes and ears,
Oft fed with true oaths, and with sweet salt tears;
   But souls where nothing dwells but love
(All other thoughts being inmates) then shall prove
This, or a love increasèd there above,
When bodies to their graves, souls from their   20
      graves remove.

And then we shall be throughly blest,
   But we no more than all the rest;
Here upon earth, we'are kings, and none but we
Can be such kings, nor of such subjects be;
Who is so safe as we, where none can do
Treason to us, except one of us two?
   True and false fears let us refrain,
Let us love nobly,'and live, and add again
Years and years unto years, till we attain
To write threescore: this is the second of our reign.   30

A Valediction of My Name in the Window

I

My name engraved herein
Doth contribute my firmness to this glass,
   Which, ever since that charm, hath been
   As hard as that which graved it was;
Thine eye will give it price enough to mock
    The diamonds of either rock.

II

'Tis much that glass should be
As all-confessing, and through-shine as I;
   'Tis more, that it shows thee to thee,
   And clear reflects thee to thine eye.
But all such rules love's magic can undo,
    Here you see me, and I am you.

III

As no one point, nor dash,
Which are but accessories to this name,
   The showers and tempests can outwash,
   So shall all times find me the same;
You this entireness better may fulfil,
    Who have the pattern with you still.

IV

Or if too hard and deep
This learning be for a scratched name to teach,
   It as a given death's head keep,
   Lovers' mortality to preach,
Or think this ragged bony name to be
    My ruinous anatomy.

V

Then, as all my souls be
Emparadised in you (in whom alone
  I understand, and grow and see),
  The rafters of my body, bone,
Being still with you, the muscle, sinew,'and vein,
    Which tile this house, will come again.   30

VI

Till my return repair
And recompact my scattered body so,
  As all the virtuous powers which are
  Fixed in the stars, are said to flow
Into such characters as graved be
    When these stars have supremacy,

VII

So, since this name was cut
When love and grief their exaltation had,
  No door 'gainst this name's influence shut;
  As much more loving, as more sad,   40
'Twill make thee; and thou should'st, till I return,
    Since I die daily, daily mourn.

VIII

When thy'inconsiderate hand
Flings ope this casement, with my trembling name,
  To look on one, whose wit or land
  New batt'ry to thy heart may frame,
Then think this name alive, and that thou thus
    In it offend'st my genius.

IX

And when thy melted maid,
Corrupted by thy lover's gold and page,
   His letter at thy pillow'hath laid,
   Disputed it, and tamed thy rage,
And thou begin'st to thaw towards him, for this,
     May my name step in, and hide his.

X

And if this treason go
To'an overt act, and that thou write again,
   In superscribing, this name flow
   Into thy fancy from the pane.
So, in forgetting thou rememb'rest right,
     And unaware to me shalt write.

XI

But glass and lines must be
No means our firm substantial love to keep;
   Near death inflicts this lethargy,
   And this I murmur in my sleep;
Impute this idle talk to that I go,
     For dying men talk often so.

Twicknam Garden

Blasted with sighs, and surrounded with tears,
   Hither I come to seek the spring,
   And at mine eyes, and at mine ears,
Receive such balms, as else cure everything;
   But O, self traitor, I do bring
The spider love, which transubstantiates all,
   And can convert manna to gall;
And that this place may thoroughly be thought
   True paradise, I have the serpent brought.

50

60

'Twere wholesomer for me that winter did   10
   Benight the glory of this place,
   And that a grave frost did forbid
These trees to laugh and mock me to my face;
   But that I may not this disgrace
Endure, nor yet leave loving, Love let me
   Some senseless piece of this place be;
Make me a mandrake, so I may grow here,
   Or a stone fountain weeping out my year.

Hither with crystal vials, lovers come,
   And take my tears, which are love's wine,   20
   And try your mistress' tears at home,
For all are false that taste not just like mine;
   Alas, hearts do not in eyes shine,
Nor can you more judge woman's thoughts by tears,
   Than by her shadow what she wears.
O perverse sex, where none is true but she,
   Who's therefore true, because her truth kills me.

Valediction of the Book

I'll tell thee now, dear love, what thou shalt do
   To anger Destiny, as she doth us,
   How I shall stay, though she eloign me thus,
And how posterity shall know it too,
     How thine may out-endure
     Sibyl's glory, and obscure
     Her who from Pindar could allure,
   And her through whose help Lucan is not lame,
And her whose book (they say) Homer did find, and
     name.

Study our manuscripts, those myriads   10
   Of letters, which have past twixt thee and me,
   Thence write our annals, and in them will be,
To all whom love's subliming fire invades,

Rule and example found;
There, the faith of any ground
No schismatic will dare to wound,
That sees how Love this grace to us affords,
To make, to keep, to use, to be these his records.

This book, as long-lived as the elements,
    Or as the world's form, this all-gravèd tome
    In cipher writ, or new-made idiom;
We for Love's clergy only'are instruments.
        When this book is made thus,
        Should again the ravenous
        Vandals and the Goths invade us,
    Learning were safe; in this our universe
Schools might learn sciences, spheres music, angels
        verse.

Here Love's divines (since all divinity
    Is love or wonder) may find all they seek,
    Whether abstract spiritual love they like,
Their souls exhaled with what they do not see,
        Or loath so to amuse
        Faith's infirmity, they choose
        Something which they may see and use;
    For though mind be the heaven where love doth sit,
Beauty'a convenient type may be to figure it.

Here more than in their books may lawyers find,
    Both by what titles mistresses are ours,
    And how prerogative these states devours,
Transferred from Love himself to womankind,
        Who, though from heart and eyes
        They exact great subsidies,
        Forsake him who on them relies,
    And for the cause, honour or conscience give –
Chimeras, vain as they, or their prerogative.

Here statesmen (or of them, they which can read)
   May of their occupation find the grounds:
   Love and their art alike it deadly wounds,
If to consider what 'tis, one proceed,
     In both they do excel   50
     Who the present govern well,
     Whose weakness none doth, or dares, tell;
   In this thy book, such will their nothing see,
As in the Bible some can find out alchemy.

Thus vent thy thoughts; abroad I'll study thee,
   As he removes far off that great heights takes;
   How great love is, presence best trial makes,
But absence tries how long this love will be;
     To take a latitude,
     Sun, or stars, are fitliest viewed   60
     At their brightest, but to conclude
   Of longitudes, what other way have we,
But to mark when and where the dark eclipses be?

Community

   Good we must love, and must hate ill,
   For ill is ill, and good, good still,
     But these are things indifferent
   Which we may neither hate, nor love,
   But one, and then another prove,
     As we shall find our fancy bent.

   If then at first wise nature had
   Made women either good or bad,
     Then some we might hate, and some choose,
   But since she did them so create   10
   That we may neither love nor hate,
     Only this rests, all, all may use.

If they were good it would be seen,
Good is as visible as green,
    And to all eyes itself betrays;
If they were bad, they could not last,
Bad doth itself and others waste,
    So they deserve nor blame, nor praise.

But they are ours as fruits are ours,
He that but tastes, he that devours,
    And he that leaves all, doth as well;
Changed loves are but changed sorts of meat,
And when he hath the kernel eat,
    Who doth not fling away the shell?

Love's Growth

I scarce believe my love to be so pure
    As I had thought it was,
    Because it doth endure
Vicissitude, and season, as the grass;
Methinks I lied all winter, when I swore
My love was infinite, if spring make'it more.
But if this medicine, love, which cures all sorrow
With more, not only be no quintessence,
But mixed of all stuffs paining soul or sense,
And of the sun his working vigour borrow,
Love's not so pure and abstract as they use
To say which have no mistress but their muse,
But as all else, being elemented too,
Love sometimes would contemplate, sometimes do.

And yet no greater but more eminent,
    Love by the spring is grown;
    As in the firmament,
Stars by the sun are not enlarged, but shown,
Gentle love deeds, as blossoms on a bough,
From love's awakened root do bud out now.

If, as in water stirred more circles be
Produced by one, love such additions take,
Those, like so many spheres, but one heaven make,
For they are all concentric unto thee;
And though each spring do add to love new heat,
As princes do in times of action get
New taxes, and remit them not in peace,
No winter shall abate the spring's increase.

Love's Exchange

Love, any devil else but you,
Would for a given soul give something too.
At court your fellows every day,
Give th'art of rhyming, huntsmanship, and play,
For them who were their own before;
Only'I have nothing which gave more,
But am, alas, by being lowly, lower.

I ask no dispensation now
To falsify a tear, or sigh, or vow,
I do not sue from thee to draw   10
A *non obstante* on nature's law,
These are prerogatives, they inhere
In thee and thine; none should forswear
Except that he Love's minion were.

Give me thy weakness, make me blind,
Both ways, as thou and thine, in eyes and mind;
Love, let me never know that this
Is love, or that love childish is.
Let me not know that others know
That she knows my pain, least that so   20
A tender shame make me mine own new woe.

If thou give nothing, yet thou'art just,
Because I would not thy first motions trust;
Small towns which stand stiff, till great shot
Enforce them, by war's law condition not.
Such in love's warfare is my case:
I may not article for grace,
Having put Love at last to show this face.

This face, by which he could command
And change the'idolatry of any land,
This face, which wheresoe'er it comes,
Can call vowed men from cloisters, dead from
    tombs,
And melt both poles at once, and store
Deserts with cities, and make more
Mines in the earth, than quarries were before.

For this, Love is enraged with me,
Yet kills not; if I must example be
To future rebels; if th'unborn
Must learn, by my being cut up, and torn:
Kill, and dissect me, Love; for this
Torture against thine own end is,
Racked carcasses make ill anatomies.

Confined Love

Some man unworthy to'be possessor
Of old or new love, himself being false or weak,
  Thought his pain and shame would be lesser,
If on womankind he might his anger wreak,
      And thence a law did grow,
      One might but one man know,
      But are other creatures so?

Are sun, moon, or stars by law forbidden,
To'smile where they list, or lend away their light?
    Are birds divorced, or are they chidden   10
If they leave their mate, or lie abroad a night?
        Beasts do no jointures lose
        Though they new lovers choose,
        But we are made worse than those.

    Whoe'er rigged fair ship to lie in harbours,
And not to seek new lands, or not to deal withal?
    Or built fair houses, set trees, and arbours,
Only to'lock up, or else to let them fall?
        Good is not good unless
        A thousand it possess,   20
        But doth waste with greediness.

The Dream

Dear love, for nothing less than thee
Would I have broke this happy dream;
      It was a theme
For reason, much too strong for fantasy,
Therefore thou wak'dst me wisely; yet
My dream thou brok'st not, but continued'st it;
Thou art so truth, that thoughts of thee suffice
To make dreams truths, and fables histories;
Enter these arms, for since thou thought'st it best
Not to dream all my dream, let's act the rest.   10

As lightning, or a taper's light,
Thine eyes, and not thy noise, waked me;
      Yet I thought thee
(For thou lovest truth) an angel, at first sight,
But when I saw thou sawest my heart,
And knew'st my thoughts, beyond an angel's art,

When thou knew'st what I dreamt, when thou knew'st
          when
Excess of joy would wake me, and cam'st then,
I must confess, it could not choose but be
Profane to think thee anything but thee.

Coming and staying showed thee, thee,
But rising makes me doubt that now
          Thou art not thou.
That love is weak, where fear's as strong as he;
'Tis not all spirit, pure and brave,
If mixture it of fear, shame, honour, have.
Perchance, as torches which must ready be,
Men light and put out, so thou deal'st with me,
Thou cam'st to kindle, goest to come; then I
Will dream that hope again, but else would die.

A Valediction of Weeping

          Let me pour forth
My tears before thy face, whil'st I stay here,
For thy face coins them, and thy stamp they bear,
And by this mintage they are something worth,
          For thus they be
          Pregnant of thee,
Fruits of much grief they are, emblems of more;
When a tear falls, that thou falls which it bore,
So thou and I are nothing then, when on a diverse
          shore.

          On a round ball
A workman that hath copies by can lay
An Europe, Afric, and an Asia,
And quickly make that, which was nothing, all;
          So doth each tear,
          Which thee doth wear,

A globe, yea world, by that impression grow,
Till thy tears mixed with mine do overflow
This world, by waters sent from thee, my heav'n
            dissolvèd so.

       O more than Moon,
Draw not up seas to drown me in thy sphere,   20
Weep me not dead in thine arms, but forbear
To teach the sea what it may do too soon;
       Let not the wind
       Example find
To do me more harm than it purposeth;
Since thou and I sigh one another's breath,
Whoe'er sighs most is cruellest, and hastes the other's
          death.

Love's Alchemy

Some that have deeper digged Love's mine than I,
Say where his centric happiness doth lie:
     I'have loved, and got, and told,
But should I love, get, tell, till I were old,
I should not find that hidden mystery;
     O, 'tis imposture all:
And as no chemic yet th'elixir got,
     But glorifies his pregnant pot,
     If by the way to him befall
Some odoriferous thing, or medicinal,   10
  So, lovers dream a rich and long delight,
  But get a winter-seeming summer's night.

Our ease, our thrift, our honour, and our day,
Shall we, for this vain bubble's shadow pay?
     Ends love in this, that my man,
Can be as happy as I can; if he can

Endure the short scorn of a bridegroom's play?
    That loving wretch that swears,
'Tis not the bodies marry, but the minds,
    Which he in her angelic finds,
    Would swear as justly, that he hears,
In that day's rude hoarse minstrelsy, the spheres.
    Hope not for mind in women; at their best,
    Sweetness and wit they'are, but mummy possessed.

The Flea

Mark but this flea, and mark in this,
How little that which thou deny'st me is;
It sucked me first, and now sucks thee,
And in this flea, our two bloods mingled be;
Thou know'st that this cannot be said
A sin, nor shame, nor loss of maidenhead;
    Yet this enjoys before it woo,
    And pampered swells with one blood made of two,
    And this, alas, is more than we would do.

O stay, three lives in one flea spare,
Where we almost, yea more than married are.
This flea is you and I, and this
Our marriage bed, and marriage temple is;
Though parents grudge, and you, we'are met
And cloistered in these living walls of jet.
    Though use make you apt to kill me,
    Let not to that, self-murder added be,
    And sacrilege, three sins in killing three.

Cruel and sudden, hast thou since
Purpled thy nail in blood of innocence?
Wherein could this flea guilty be,
Except in that drop which it sucked from thee?

Yet thou triumph'st, and say'st that thou
Find'st not thyself, nor me, the weaker now;
   'Tis true; then learn how false, fears be;
   Just so much honour, when thou yield'st to me,
   Will waste, as this flea's death took life from thee.

The Curse

Whoever guesses, thinks, or dreams he knows
Who is my mistress, wither by this curse;
   His only,'and only'his purse
   May some dull heart to love dispose,
And she yield then to all that are his foes;
   May he be scorned by one, whom all else scorn,
   Forswear to others, what to her he'hath sworn,
   With fear of missing, shame of getting, torn;

Madness his sorrow, gout his cramp, may he
Make, by but thinking who hath made him such;   10
   And may he feel no touch
   Of conscience, but of fame, and be
Anguished, not that 'twas sin, but that 'twas she;
   In early and long scarceness may he rot,
   For land which had been his, if he had not
   Himself incestuously an heir begot;

May he dream treason, and believe that he
Meant to perform it, and confess, and die,
   And no record tell why;
   His sons, which none of his may be,   20
Inherit nothing but his infamy;
   Or may he so long parasites have fed,
   That he would fain be theirs, whom he hath bred,
   And at the last be circumcised for bread;

The venom of all stepdames, gamsters' gall,
What tyrants and their subjects interwish,
    What plants, mines, beasts, fowl, fish
    Can contribute, all ill which all
Prophets or poets spake; and all which shall
30   Be'annexed in schedules unto this by me,
    Fall on that man; for if it be a she,
    Nature beforehand hath out-cursèd me.

The Message

Send home my long strayed eyes to me,
Which (O) too long have dwelt on thee,
Yet since there they have learned such ill,
    Such forced fashions,
    And false passions,
      That they be
      Made by thee
Fit for no good sight, keep them still.

Send home my harmless heart again,
10   Which no unworthy thought could stain,
Which if'it be taught by thine
    To make jestings
    Of protestings,
      And break both
      Word and oath,
Keep it, for then 'tis none of mine.

Yet send me back my heart and eyes,
That I may know, and see thy lies,
And may laugh and joy, when thou
20   Art in anguish
      And dost languish
        For someone
        That will none,
Or prove as false as thou art now.

A Nocturnal upon St Lucy's Day, Being the Shortest Day

'Tis the year's midnight, and it is the day's,
Lucy's, who scarce seven hours herself unmasks;
    The sun is spent, and now his flasks
    Send forth light squibs, no constant rays;
       The world's whole sap is sunk;
The general balm th'hydroptic earth hath drunk,
Whither, as to the bed's-feet, life is shrunk,
Dead and interred; yet all these seem to laugh,
Compared with me, who am their epitaph.

Study me then, you who shall lovers be   10
At the next world, that is, at the next spring,
    For I am every dead thing,
    In whom love wrought new alchemy.
       For his art did express
A quintessence even from nothingness,
From dull privations, and lean emptiness;
He ruined me, and I am re-begot
Of absence, darkness, death, things which are not.

All others, from all things, draw all that's good,
Life, soul, form, spirit, whence they being have;   20
    I, by love's limbeck, am the grave
    Of all that's nothing. Oft a flood
       Have we two wept, and so
Drowned the whole world, us two; oft did we grow
To be two chaoses, when we did show
Care to aught else; and often absences
Withdrew our souls, and made us carcasses.

But I am by her death (which word wrongs her),
Of the first nothing the elixir grown;
    Were I a man, that I were one   30
    I needs must know; I should prefer,

        If I were any beast,
Some ends, some means; yea plants, yea stones, detest,
And love; all, all, some properties invest;
If I an ordinary nothing were,
As shadow,'a light and body must be here.

But I am none; nor will my sun renew.
You lovers, for whose sake the lesser sun
    At this time to the Goat is run
      To fetch new lust, and give it you,
        Enjoy your summer all;
Since she enjoys her long night's festival,
Let me prepare towards her, and let me call
This hour her vigil, and her eve, since this
Both the year's and the day's deep midnight is.

Witchcraft by a Picture

I fix mine eye on thine, and there
    Pity my picture burning in thine eye,
My picture drowned in a transparent tear,
    When I look lower I espy;
      Had'st thou the wicked skill
By pictures made and marred, to kill,
How many ways might'st thou perform thy will?

But now I'have drunk thy sweet salt tears,
    And though thou pour more I'll depart;
My picture vanished, vanish fears
    That I can be endamaged by that art;
      Though thou retain of me
One picture more, yet that will be,
Being in thine own heart, from all malice free.

The Bait

Come live with me, and be my love,
And we will some new pleasures prove
Of golden sands, and crystal brooks,
With silken lines, and silver hooks.

There will the river whispering run
Warmed by thy eyes more than the sun.
And there the'enamoured fish will stay,
Begging themselves they may betray.

When thou wilt swim in that live bath,
Each fish, which every channel hath,   10
Will amorously to thee swim,
Gladder to catch thee, than thou him.

If thou, to be so seen, beest loath,
By sun, or moon, thou dark'nest both,
And if myself have leave to see,
I need not their light, having thee.

Let others freeze with angling reeds,
And cut their legs with shells and weeds,
Or treacherously poor fish beset,
With strangling snare, or windowy net: 20

Let coarse, bold hands from slimy nest
The bedded fish in banks out-wrest,
Or curious traitors, sleave-silk flies,
Bewitch poor fishes' wand'ring eyes.

For thee, thou need'st no such deceit,
For thou thyself art thine own bait;
That fish, that is not catched thereby,
Alas, is wiser far than I.

The Apparition

When by thy scorn, O murd'ress, I am dead,
    And that thou think'st thee free
From all solicitation from me,
Then shall my ghost come to thy bed,
And thee, feigned vestal, in worse arms shall see;
Then thy sick taper will begin to wink,
And he, whose thou art then, being tired before,
Will, if thou stir, or pinch to wake him, think
    Thou call'st for more,
10   And in false sleep will from thee shrink,
And then poor aspen wretch, neglected thou
Bathed in a cold quicksilver sweat wilt lie
    A verier ghost than I;
What I will say, I will not tell thee now,
Lest that preserve thee;'and since my love is spent,
I'had rather thou should'st painfully repent,
Than by my threat'nings rest still innocent.

The Broken Heart

He is stark mad whoever says
    That he hath been in love an hour,
Yet not that love so soon decays,
    But that it can ten in less space devour;
Who will believe me if I swear
That I have had the plague a year?
    Who would not laugh at me if I should say
    I saw a flask of powder burn a day?

Ah, what a trifle is a heart
10   If once into Love's hands it come?
All other griefs allow a part
    To other griefs, and ask themselves but some;

They come to us, but us Love draws,
He swallows us, and never chews:
    By him, as by chained shot, whole ranks do die;
    He is the tyrant pike, our hearts the fry.

If 'twere not so, what did become
    Of my heart when I first saw thee?
I brought a heart into the room,
    But from the room I carried none with me;   20
If it had gone to thee, I know
Mine would have taught thine heart to show
    More pity unto me: but Love, alas,
    At one first blow did shiver it as glass.

Yet nothing can to nothing fall,
    Nor any place be empty quite,
Therefore I think my breast hath all
    Those pieces still, though they be not unite;
And now as broken glasses show
A hundred lesser faces, so   30
    My rags of heart can like, wish, and adore,
    But after one such love, can love no more.

A *Valediction Forbidding Mourning*

As virtuous men pass mildly'away,
    And whisper to their souls to go,
Whil'st some of their sad friends do say,
    The breath goes now, and some say, no,

So let us melt, and make no noise,
    No tear-floods, nor sigh-tempests move,
'Twere profanation of our joys
    To tell the laity our love.

Moving of th'earth brings harms and fears,
 Men reckon what it did and meant,
But trepidation of the spheres,
 Though greater far, is innocent.

Dull sublunary lovers' love
 (Whose soul is sense) cannot admit
Absence, because it doth remove
 Those things which elemented it.

But we by'a love so much refined
 That ourselves know not what it is,
Inter-assurèd of the mind,
 Care less, eyes, lips, and hands to miss.

Our two souls therefore, which are one,
 Though I must go, endure not yet
A breach, but an expansion,
 Like gold to airy thinness beat.

If they be two, they are two so
 As stiff twin compasses are two:
Thy soul, the fixed foot, makes no show
 To move, but doth, if the'other do.

And though it in the centre sit,
 Yet when the other far doth roam,
It leans, and hearkens after it,
 And grows erect as that comes home.

Such wilt thou be to me, who must,
 Like th'other foot, obliquely run.
Thy firmness makes my circle just,
 And makes me end where I begun.

The Ecstasy

Where, like a pillow on a bed,
  A pregnant bank swelled up to rest
The violet's reclining head,
  Sat we two, one another's best.
Our hands were firmly cemented
  With a fast balm, which thence did spring;
Our eye-beams twisted, and did thread
  Our eyes upon one double string;
So to'intergraft our hands as yet
  Was all the means to make us one,   10
And pictures in our eyes to get
  Was all our propagation.
As 'twixt two equal armies, Fate
  Suspends uncertain victory,
Our souls (which to advance their state
  Were gone out) hung 'twixt her and me.
And whil'st our souls negotiate there,
  We like sepulchral statues lay;
All day, the same our postures were,
  And we said nothing all the day.   20
If any, so by love refined
  That he souls' language understood,
And by good love were grown all mind,
  Within convenient distance stood,
He (though he knows not which soul spake
  Because both meant, both spake, the same)
Might thence a new concoction take,
  And part far purer than he came.
This ecstasy doth unperplex
  (We said) and tell us what we love;   30
We see by this, it was not sex;
  We see, we saw not what did move;

But as all several souls contain
   Mixture of things, they know not what,
Love these mixed souls doth mix again,
   And makes both one, each this and that.
A single violet transplant,
   The strength, the colour, and the size
(All which before was poor, and scant)
   Redoubles still, and multiplies.
When love, with one another so
   Interanimates two souls,
That abler soul, which thence doth flow,
   Defects of loneliness controls.
We then, who are this new soul, know
   Of what we are composed and made,
For th'atomies of which we grow,
   Are souls, whom no change can invade.
But O, alas, so long, so far
   Our bodies why do we forbear?
They'are ours, though they're not we; we are
   The'intelligences, they the spheres.
We owe them thanks because they thus
   Did us to us at first convey,
Yielded their sense's force to us,
   Nor are dross to us, but allay.
On man heaven's influence works not so,
   But that it first imprints the air,
For soul into the soul may flow,
   Though it to body first repair.
As our blood labours to beget
   Spirits as like souls as it can,
Because such fingers need to knit
   That subtle knot which makes us man,
So must pure lovers' souls descend
   T'affections and to faculties,
Which sense may reach and apprehend,
   Else a great prince in prison lies.

To'our bodies turn we then, that so
    Weak men on love revealed may look;   70
Love's mysteries in souls do grow,
    But yet the body is his book.
And if some lover such as we
    Have heard this dialogue of one,
Let him still mark us; he shall see
    Small change, when we'are to bodies gone.

Love's Deity

I long to talk with some old lover's ghost,
    Who died before the god of love was born,
I cannot think that he who then loved most
    Sunk so low as to love one which did scorn.
But since this god produced a destiny,
And that vice-nature, custom, lets it be,
    I must love her that loves not me.

Sure, they which made him god meant not so
      much,
    Nor he, in his young godhead, practised it;
But when an even flame two hearts did touch,   10
    His office was indulgently to fit
Actives to passives. Correspondency
Only his subject was; it cannot be
    Love, till I love her that loves me.

But every modern god will now extend
    His vast prerogative as far as Jove.
To rage, to lust, to write to, to commend,
    All is the purlieu of the god of love.
O were we wakened by this tyranny
To'ungod this child again, it could not be,   20
    I should love her who loves not me.

Rebel and atheist too, why murmur I,
    As though I felt the worst that love could do?
Love may make me leave loving, or might try
    A deeper plague, to make her love me too,
Which, since she loves before, I'am loath to see;
Falsehood is worse than hate, and that must be
    If she whom I love should love me.

Love's Diet

To what a cumbersome unwieldiness
And burdenous corpulence my love had grown,
    But that I did, to make it less,
    And keep it in proportion,
Give it a diet, made it feed upon
That which love worst endures, discretion.

Above one sigh a day I'allowed him not,
Of which my fortune and my faults had part;
    And if sometimes by stealth he got
    A she-sigh from my mistress' heart,
And thought to feast on that, I let him see
'Twas neither very sound, nor meant to me.

If he wrung from me'a tear, I brined it so
With scorn or shame, that him it nourished not;
    If he sucked hers, I let him know
    'Twas not a tear which he had got,
His drink was counterfeit, as was his meat;
For eyes which roll towards all, weep not, but sweat.

Whatever he would dictate, I writ that,
But burnt my letters; when she writ to me,
    And that that favour made him fat,
    I said, if any title be
Conveyed by this, ah, what doth it avail
To be the fortieth name in an entail?

Thus I redeemed my buzzard love, to fly
At what, and when, and how, and where I choose;
   Now negligent of sports I lie,
   And now as other falconers use,
I spring a mistress, swear, write, sigh and weep,
And the game killed or lost, go talk, and sleep.   30

The Will

Before I sigh my last gasp, let me breathe,
Great Love, some legacies; here I bequeath
Mine eyes to Argus, if mine eyes can see;
If they be blind, then Love, I give them thee;
My tongue to Fame; to'ambassadors mine ears;
   To women or the sea, my tears;
Thou, Love, hast taught me heretofore
By making me serve her who'had twenty more,
That I should give to none but such as had too much
    before.

My constancy I to the planets give;   10
My truth to them who at the court do live;
Mine ingenuity and openness
To Jesuits; to'buffoons my pensiveness;
My silence to'any who abroad hath been;
   My money to a Capuchin.
Thou, Love, taught'st me, by'appointing me
To love there where no love received can be,
Only to give to such as have an incapacity.

My faith I give to Roman Catholics;
All my good works unto the schismatics   20
Of Amsterdam; my best civility
And courtship to an university;

My modesty I give to soldiers bare;
  My patience let gamesters share.
Thou, Love, taught'st me, by making me
Love her that holds my love disparity,
Only to give to those that count my gifts indignity.

I give my reputation to those
Which were my friends; mine industry to foes;
To schoolmen I bequeath my doubtfulness;
My sickness to physicians, or excess;
To Nature, all that I in rhyme have writ;
  And to my company my wit.
Thou, Love, by making me adore
Her who begot this love in me before,
Taught'st me to make as though I gave, when I did but
      restore.

To him for whom the passing bell next tolls,
I give my physic books; my written rolls
Of moral counsels, I to Bedlam give;
My brazen medals unto them which live
In want of bread; to them which pass among
  All foreigners, mine English tongue.
Thou, Love, by making me love one
Who thinks her friendship a fit portion
For younger lovers, dost my gifts thus disproportion.

Therefore I'll give no more; but I'll undo
The world by dying, because love dies too.
Then all your beauties will be no more worth
Than gold in mines where none doth draw it forth,
And all your graces no more use shall have
  Than a sun-dial in a grave.
Thou, Love, taught'st me, by making me
Love her who doth neglect both me and thee,
To'invent, and practise, this one way, to'annihilate all
      three.

The Funeral

Whoever comes to shroud me, do not harm
    Nor question much
That subtle wreath of hair which crowns my arm;
The mystery, the sign, you must not touch,
    For 'tis my outward soul,
Viceroy to that, which unto heaven being gone,
    Will leave this to control
And keep these limbs, her provinces, from dissolution.

For if the sinewy thread my brain lets fall
    Through every part,   10
Can tie those parts, and make me one of all,
Those hairs which upward grew, and strength and art
    Have from a better brain,
Can better do'it; except she meant that I
    By this should know my pain,
As prisoners then are manacled, when they'are
        condemned to die.

What ere she meant by'it, bury it by me,
    For since I am
Love's martyr, it might breed idolatry,
If into others' hands these relics came;   20
    As 'twas humility
To'afford to it all that a soul can do,
    So, 'tis some bravery,
That since you would have none of me, I bury some of
        you.

The Blossom

Little think'st thou, poor flower,
   Whom I have watched six or seven days,
And seen thy birth, and seen what every hour
Gave to thy growth, thee to this height to raise,
And now dost laugh and triumph on this bough,
         Little think'st thou
That it will freeze anon, and that I shall
Tomorrow find thee fall'n, or not at all.

Little think'st thou, poor heart,
   That labours yet to nestle thee,
And think'st by hovering here to get a part
In a forbidden or forbidding tree,
And hop'st her stiffness by long siege to bow,
         Little think'st thou
That thou tomorrow, ere that sun doth wake,
Must with this sun and me a journey take.

But thou which lov'st to be
   Subtle to plague thyself, wilt say,
Alas, if you must go, what's that to me?
Here lies my business, and here I will stay;
You go to friends, whose love and means present
         Various content
To your eyes, ears, and tongue, and every part.
If then your body go, what need you'a heart?

Well then, stay here; but know,
   When thou hast stayed and done thy most,
A naked thinking heart, that makes no show,
Is to a woman but a kind of ghost;
How shall she know my heart, or, having none,
         Know thee for one?
Practice may make her know some other part,
But take my word, she doth not know a heart.

Meet me at London, then,
Twenty days hence, and thou shalt see
Me fresher, and more fat, by being with men,
Than if I had stayed still with her and thee.
For God's sake, if you can, be you so too;
I will give you
There to another friend whom we shall find
As glad to have my body as my mind.   40

The Primrose

Upon this primrose hill
Where, if heav'n would distill
A shower of rain, each several drop might go
To his own primrose, and grow manna so;
And where their form, and their infinity
Make a terrestrial galaxy,
As the small stars do in the sky,
I walk to find a true love; and I see
That 'tis not a mere woman that is she,
But must, or more or less than woman be.   10

Yet know I not which flower
I wish, a six or four;
For should my true-love less than woman be,
She were scarce anything; and then, should she
Be more than woman, she would get above
All thought of sex, and think to move
My heart to study'her and not to love;
Both these were monsters; since there must reside
Falsehood in woman, I could more abide,
She were by art, than Nature, falsified.   20

Live primrose then, and thrive
With thy true number, five;
And women, whom this flower doth represent,
With this mysterious number be content;

Ten is the farthest number; if half ten
    Belongs unto each woman, then
    Each woman may take half us men;
Or, if this will not serve their turn, since all
Numbers are odd, or even, and they fall
First into this five, women may take us all.

30

The Relic

When my grave is broke up again
Some second guest to entertain
(For graves have learned that woman-head,
To be to more than one a bed),
    And he that digs it spies
A bracelet of bright hair about the bone,
    Will he not let'us alone,
And think that there a loving couple lies,
Who thought that this device might be some way
To make their souls, at the last busy day,
Meet at this grave, and make a little stay?

10

If this fall in a time or land
Where mis-devotion doth command,
Then he that digs us up will bring
Us to the bishop and the king
    To make us relics; then
Thou shalt be'a Mary Magdalen, and I
    A something else thereby;
All women shall adore us, and some men;
And since at such time miracles are sought,
I would have that age by this paper taught
What miracles we harmless lovers wrought.

20

First, we loved well and faithfully,
Yet knew not what we loved, nor why;
Difference of sex no more we knew
Than our guardian angels do;

　　　　　Coming and going, we
Perchance might kiss, but not between those meals;
　　　　　Our hands ne'er touched the seals
Which nature, injured by late law, sets free.　　　　　30
These miracles we did, but now, alas,
All measure, and all language, I should pass,
Should I tell what a miracle she was.

The Damp

When I am dead, and doctors know not why,
　　　　　And my friends' curiosity
Will have me cut up to survey each part,
When they shall find your picture in my heart,
　　　　　You think a sudden damp of love
　　　　　Will through all their senses move,
And work on them as me, and so prefer
Your murder to the name of massacre.

Poor victories; but if you dare be brave,
　　　　　And pleasure in your conquest have,　　　　　10
First kill th'enormous giant, your Disdain,
And let th'enchantress Honour, next be slain,
　　　　　And like a Goth and Vandal rise,
　　　　　Deface records and histories
Of your own arts and triumphs over men,
And without such advantage kill me then.

For I could muster up as well as you
　　　　　My giants and my witches too,
Which are vast Constancy and Secretness,
But these I neither look for, nor profess;　　　　　20
　　　　　Kill me as woman, let me die
　　　　　As a mere man; do you but try
Your passive valour, and you shall find then,
In that you'have odds enough of any man.

The Dissolution

She'is dead; and all which die
    To their first elements resolve;
And we were mutual elements to us,
    And made of one another.
My body then doth hers involve,
And those things whereof I consist, hereby
In me abundant grow and burdenous,
    And nourish not, but smother.
My fire of passion, sighs of air,
Water of tears, and earthly sad despair,
            Which my materials be
(But ne'r worn out by love's security),
She, to my loss, doth by her death repair;
    And I might live long wretched so,
But that my fire doth with my fuel grow.
        Now, as those active kings,
    Whose foreign conquest treasure brings,
Receive more, and spend more, and soonest break,
This (which I am amazed that I can speak),
        This death hath with my store
            My use increased.
And so my soul, more earnestly released,
Will outstrip hers; as bullets flown before
A latter bullet may o'ertake, the powder being more.

A Jet Ring Sent

Thou art not so black as my heart,
    Nor half so brittle as her heart, thou art;
What would'st thou say? Shall both our properties
            by thee be spoke,
    Nothing more endless, nothing sooner broke?

 Marriage rings are not of this stuff;
 O, why should ought less precious, or less tough
Figure our loves? Except in thy name thou have bid it
  say,
 I'am cheap, and nought but fashion, fling me'away.

 Yet stay with me since thou art come,
 Circle this finger's top, which did'st her thumb. 10
Be justly proud, and gladly safe, that thou dost dwell
  with me,
 She that, O, broke her faith, would soon break thee.

Negative Love

 I never stooped so low, as they
 Which on an eye, cheek, lip, can prey,
  Seldom to them, which soar no higher
  Than virtue or the mind to'admire,
 For sense and understanding may
  Know what gives fuel to their fire:
 My love, though silly, is more brave,
 For may I miss whene'er I crave,
 If I know yet what I would have.

 If that be simply perfectest 10
 Which can by no way be expressed
  But negatives, my love is so.
  To all, which all love, I say no.
 If any who deciphers best
  What we know not, ourselves, can know,
 Let him teach me that nothing; this
 As yet my ease and comfort is,
 Though I speed not, I cannot miss.

The Prohibition

Take heed of loving me,
At least remember, I forbade it thee;
Not that I shall repair my'unthrifty waste
Of breath and blood, upon thy sighs and tears,
By being to thee then what to me thou wast;
But so great joy our life at once outwears.
Then, lest thy love, by my death, frustrate be,
If thou love me, take heed of loving me.

Take heed of hating me,
Or too much triumph in the victory.
Not that I shall be mine own officer,
And hate with hate again retaliate;
But thou wilt lose the style of conqueror,
If I, thy conquest, perish by thy hate.
Then, lest my being nothing lessen thee,
If thou hate me, take heed of hating me.

Yet, love and hate me too,
So these extremes shall neither's office do:
Love me, that I may die the gentler way;
Hate me, because thy love'is too great for me;
Or let these two, themselves, not me decay;
So shall I live thy stage, not triumph be.
Lest thou thy love and hate and me undo,
To let me live, O love and hate me too.

The Expiration

So, so, break off this last lamenting kiss,
    Which sucks two souls, and vapours both away;
Turn thou, ghost, that way, and let me turn this,
    And let ourselves benight our happiest day;
We asked none leave to love, nor will we owe
    Any, so cheap a death as saying, Go;

Go, and if that word have not quite killed thee,
   Ease me with death by bidding me go too.
Or, if it have, let my word work on me,
   And a just office on a murderer do,   10
Except it be too late to kill me so,
   Being double dead, going, and bidding go.

The Computation

For the first twenty years, since yesterday,
   I scarce believed thou could'st be gone away;
For forty more, I fed on favours past,
   And forty'on hopes, that thou would'st they might
      last.
Tears drowned one hundred, and sighs blew out two;
   A thousand, I did neither think, nor do,
   Or not divide, all being one thought of you;
   Or, in a thousand more, forgot that too.
Yet call not this, long life, but think that I
Am, by being dead, immortal; can ghosts die?   10

The Paradox

No lover saith, I love, nor any other
   Can judge a perfect lover;
He thinks that else none can or will agree
   That any loves but he:
I cannot say I loved, for who can say
   He was killed yesterday.
Love with excess of heat, more young than old,
   Death kills with too much cold;
We die but once, and who loved last did die,
   He that saith twice, doth lie,   10
For though he seem to move, and stir awhile,
   It doth the sense beguile.

Such life is like the light which bideth yet
    When the light's life is set,
Or like the heat, which fire in solid matter
    Leaves behind, two hours after.
Once I loved and died; and am now become
    Mine epitaph and tomb.
Here dead men speak their last, and so do I;
20   Love-slain, lo, here I lie.

Farewell to Love

    Whil'st yet to prove,
I thought there was some deity in love,
    So did I reverence, and gave
Worship, as atheists at their dying hour
Call what they cannot name an unknown power,
    As ignorantly did I crave;
        Thus when
Things not yet known are coveted by men,
    Our desires give them fashion, and so
10 As they wax lesser, fall, as they size, grow.

      But, from late fair
His Highness, sitting in a golden chair,
    Is not less cared for after three days
By children, than the thing which lovers so
Blindly admire, and with such worship woo;
    Being had, enjoying it decays,
        And thence,
What before pleased them all, takes but one sense,
    And that so lamely, as it leaves behind
20 A kind of sorrowing dullness to the mind.

Ah, cannot we,
As well as cocks and lions jocund be
  After such pleasures, unless wise
Nature decreed (since each such act, they say,
Diminisheth the length of life a day)
  This, as she would man should despise
    The sport;
Because that other curse, of being short
  And only for a minute made to be
Eager, desires to raise posterity. 30

Since so, my mind
Shall not desire what no man else can find,
  I'll no more dote and run
To pursue things which had endamaged me.
And when I come where moving beauties be,
  As men do when the summer's sun
    Grows great,
Though I admire their greatness, shun their heat;
  Each place can afford shadows. If all fail,
'Tis but applying worm-seed to the tail. 40

Lecture upon the Shadow

Stand still, and I will read to thee
A lecture, love, in love's philosophy.
    These three hours that we have spent
    Walking here, two shadows went
Along with us, which we ourselves produced;
But now the sun is just above our head,
    We do those shadows tread;
    And to brave clearness all things are reduced.
So whil'st our infant loves did grow,
Disguises did, and shadows, flow, 10
    From us, and our cares; but, now 'tis not so.

That love hath not attained the high'st degree,
Which is still diligent lest others see.

Except our loves at this noon stay,
We shall new shadows make the other way.
    As the first were made to blind
    Others; these which come behind
Will work upon ourselves, and blind our eyes.
If our loves faint, and westwardly decline;
    To me thou, falsely, thine,
    And I to thee mine actions shall disguise.
  The morning shadows wear away,
  But these grow longer all the day,
  But O, love's day is short, if love decay.

Love is a growing, or full constant light,
And his first minute, after noon, is night.

EPIGRAMS

Hero and Leander

Both robbed of air, we both lie in one ground,
Both whom one fire had burnt, one water drowned.

Pyramus and Thisbe

Two, by themselves, each other, love and fear,
Slain, cruel friends, by parting, have joined here.

Niobe

By children's birth, and death, I am become
So dry, that I am now mine own sad tomb.

A Burnt Ship

Out of a fired ship, which, by no way
But drowning, could be rescued from the flame,
Some men leaped forth, and ever as they came
Near the foes' ships, did by their shot decay;
So all were lost, which in the ship were found,
   They in the sea being burnt, they in the burnt ship
      drowned.

Fall of a Wall

Under an undermined and shot-bruised wall
A too-bold captain perished by the fall,
Whose brave misfortune happiest men envied,
That had a town for a tomb, his bones to hide.

A Lame Beggar

   I am unable, yonder beggar cries,
     To stand or move; if he say true, he lies.

A Self Accuser

Your mistress, that you follow whores, still taxeth you:
'Tis strange that she should thus confess it, though it be
   true.

A Licentious Person

Thy sins and hairs may no man equal call,
For as thy sins increase, thy hairs do fall.

Antiquary

If in his study he hath so much care
To'hang all old strange things, let his wife beware.

Disinherited

Thy father all from thee, by his last will
Gave to the poor; thou hast good title still.

Phryne

Thy flattering picture, Phryne, is like thee
Only in this, that you both painted be.

An Obscure Writer

Philo, with twelve years study, hath been grieved,
To be understood. When will he be believed?

Raderus

Why this man gelded Martial I muse,
Except himself alone his tricks would use,
As Katherine, for the Court's sake, put down stews.

Mercurius Gallo-Belgicus

Like Aesop's fellow-slaves, O Mercury,
Which could do all things, thy faith is; and I
Like Aesop's self, which nothing; I confess
I should have had more faith if thou had'st less.
Thy credit lost thy credit: 'Tis sin to do,
In this case, as thou would'st be done unto,
To believe all. Change thy name: thou art like
Mercury in stealing, but liest like a Greek.

Ralphius

Compassion in the world again is bred:
Ralphius is sick, the broker keeps his bed.

Sir John Wingefield

Beyond th'old pillars many'have travailed
Towards the sun's cradle, and his throne, and bed.
A fitter pillar our Earl did bestow
In that late island; for he well did know
Farther than Wingefield no man dares to go.

The Liar

Thou in the fields walk'st out thy supping hours,
And yet thou swear'st thou hast supped like a king;
Like Nebuchadnezzar perchance with grass and
    flowers,
A salad worse than Spanish dieting.

Cales and Guiana

If you from spoil of th'old world's farthest end
To the new world your kindled valours bend,
What brave examples then do prove it true
That one thing's end doth still begin a new.

Klockius

Klockius so deeply'hath sworn, ne'er more to come
In bawdy house, that he dares not go home.

The Juggler

Thou call'st me effeminate, for I love women's joys;
I call not thee manly, though thou follow boys.

Faustus

Faustus keeps his sister and a whore,
Faustus keeps his sister and no more.

ELEGIES

Elegy: The Anagram

Marry, and love thy Flavia, for she
Hath all things whereby others beauteous be.
For though her eyes be small, her mouth is great,
Though they be ivory, yet her teeth be *jet*,

Though they be dim, yet she is light enough,
And though her harsh hair fall, her skin is rough.
What though her cheeks be yellow, her hair's red,
Give her thine, and she hath a maidenhead.
These things are beauty's elements, where these
Meet in one, that one must as perfect please.   10
If red and white and each good quality
Be in thy wench, ne'er ask where it doth lie.
In buying things perfumed, we ask if there
Be musk and amber in it, but not where.
Though all her parts be not in th'usual place,
She'hath yet an anagram of a good face.
If we might put the letters but one way,
In the lean dearth of words, what could we say?
When by the gamut some musicians make
A perfect song, others will undertake   20
By the same gamut changed, to equal it.
Things simply good can never be unfit.
She's fair as any, if all be like her,
And if none be, then she is singular.
All love is wonder; if we justly do
Account her wonderful, why'not lovely too?
Love built on beauty, soon as beauty, dies,
Choose this face changed by no deformities.
Women are all like angels: the fair be
Like those which fell to worse, but such as she,   30
Like to good angels, nothing can impair;
'Tis less grief to be foul than to'have been fair.
For one night's revels silk and gold we choose,
But in long journeys cloth and leather use.
Beauty is barren oft; best husbands say
There is best land where there is foulest way.
O what a sovereign plaster will she be
If thy past sins have taught thee jealousy!
Here needs no spies, nor eunuchs; her commit
Safe to thy foes, yea, to a marmoset.   40
When Belgia's cities, the round countries drown,
That dirty foulness guards and arms the town;

So doth her face guard her. And so for thee,
Which forced by business, absent oft must be,
She, whose face, like clouds, turns the day to night,
Who, mightier than the sea, makes Moors seem white,
Who, though seven year, she in the stews had laid,
A nunnery durst receive and think a maid,
And though in childbirth's labour she did lie,
Midwives would swear, 'twere but a tympany,
Whom, if she'accuse herself, I credit less
Than witches which impossibles confess,
Whom dildoes, bedstaves, and her velvet glass
Would be as loath to touch as Joseph was;
One like none, and liked of none, fittest were,
For things in fashion every man will wear.

Elegy: Change

Although thy hand, and faith, and good works too,
Have sealed thy love which nothing should undo,
Yea, though thou fall back, that apostasy
Confirm thy love; yet much, much I fear thee.
Women are like the arts, forced unto none,
Open to all searchers, unprized if unknown.
If I have caught a bird and let him fly,
Another fowler using these means as I,
May catch the same bird; and as these things be,
Women are made for men, not him, nor me.
Foxes and goats, all beasts change when they please,
Shall women more hot, wily, wild than these,
Be bound to one man, and did nature then
Idly make them apter to'endure than men?
They'are our clogs, not their own; if a man be
Chained to a galley, yet the galley'is free.
Who hath a plough-land casts all his seed corn there,
And yet allows his ground more corn should bear.
Though Danuby into the sea must flow,
The sea receives the Rhine, Volga, and Po.

By nature, which gave it, this liberty
Thou lov'st, but O, canst thou love it and me?
Likeness glues love: then if so thou do
To make us like and love, must I change too?
More than thy hate, I hate'it; rather let me
Allow her change, than change as oft as she,
And so not teach, but force my'opinion
To love not anyone, nor everyone.
To live in one land is captivity,
To run all countries, a wild roguery.   30
Waters stink soon if in one place they bide,
And in the vast sea are worse putrefied;
But when they kiss one bank, and leaving this
Never look back, but the next bank do kiss,
Then are they purest. Change'is the nursery
Of music, joy, life, and eternity.

Elegy: The Perfume

Once, and but once found in thy company,
All thy supposed escapes are laid on me;
And as a thief at bar is questioned there
By all the men that have been robbed that year,
So am I (by this traitorous means surprised)
By thy hydroptic father catechized.
Though he had wont to search with glazed eyes
As though he came to kill a cockatrice,
Though he hath oft sworn that he would remove
Thy beauty's beauty and food of our love,   10
Hope of his goods, if I with thee were seen,
Yet close and secret as our souls we'have been.
Though thy immortal mother which doth lie
Still buried in her bed yet will not die,
Takes this advantage to sleep out daylight,
And watch thy entries and returns all night,
And when she takes thy hand and would seem kind,
Doth search what rings and armlets she can find,

And kissing, notes the colour of thy face,
And fearing lest thou'art swoll'n, doth thee embrace,
To try if thou long, doth name strange meats,
And notes thy paleness, blushing, sighs, and sweats;
And politicly will to thee confess
The sins of her own youth's rank lustiness;
Yet love these sorceries did remove, and move
Thee to gull thine own mother for my love.
Thy little brethren, which like fairy sprights
Oft skipped into our chamber those sweet nights,
And kissed and ingled on thy father's knee,
Were bribed next day to tell what they did see.
The grim eight-foot-high iron-bound serving-man,
That oft names God in oaths, and only then,
He, that to bar the first gate doth as wide
As the great Rhodian Colossus stride,
Which, if in hell no other pains there were,
Makes me fear hell because he must be there,
Though by thy father he were hired for this,
Could never witness any touch or kiss.
But O, too common ill, I brought with me
That which betrayed me to my enemy:
A loud perfume which at my entrance cried
Even at thy father's nose; so were we spied.
When, like a tyrant king that in his bed
Smelled gunpowder, the pale wretch shivered.
Had it been some bad smell, he would have thought
That his own feet, or breath, that smell had wrought.
But as we in our isle imprisoned
Where cattle only'and diverse dogs are bred,
The precious unicorns, strange monsters, call,
So thought he good, strange, that had none at all.
I taught my silks their whistling to forbear,
Even my oppressed shoes dumb and speechless were,
Only thou bitter sweet whom I had laid
Next me, me traitorously hast betrayed,

And unsuspected hast invisibly
At once fled unto him and stayed with me.
Base excrement of earth, which dost confound
Sense from distinguishing the sick from sound;
By thee the seely amorous sucks his death
By drawing in a leprous harlot's breath;   60
By thee, the greatest stain to man's estate
Falls on us, to be called effeminate;
Though you be much loved in the prince's hall,
There, things that seem exceed substantial.
Gods, when ye fumed on altars, were pleased well
Because you'were burnt, not that they liked your
    smell.
You'are loathsome all, being taken simply'alone,
Shall we love ill things joined and hate each one?
If you were good, your good doth soon decay;
And you are rare, that takes the good away.   70
All my perfumes I give most willingly
To'embalm thy father's corpse. What? Will he die?

Elegy: His Picture

Here take my picture, though I bid farewell;
Thine in my heart, where my soul dwells, shall dwell.
'Tis like me now, but I dead, 'twill be more
When we are shadows both, than 'twas before.
When weather-beaten I come back – my hand,
Perhaps with rude oars torn or sunbeams tanned,
My face and breast of haircloth, and my head
With care's rash sudden hoariness o'erspread,
My body'a sack of bones broken within,
And powder's blue stains scattered on my skin –   10
If rival fools tax thee to'have loved a man
So foul and coarse as, O, I may seem then,
This shall say what I was; and thou shalt say,
Do his hurts reach me? Doth my worth decay?

Or do they reach his judging mind that he
Should now love less, what he did love to see?
That which in him was fair and delicate
Was but the milk which in love's childish state
Did nurse it; who now is grown strong enough
20   To feed on that which to'disused tastes seems tough.

Elegy: O, let me not serve so

O, let me not serve so, as those men serve
Whom honour's smokes at once fatten and starve,
Poorly enriched with great men's words or looks;
Nor so write my name in thy loving books
As those idolatrous flatterers which still
Their prince's styles with many realms fulfil
Whence they no tribute have, and where no sway.
Such services I offer as shall pay
Themselves. I hate dead names; O then let me
10   Favourite in ordinary or no favourite be.
When my soul was in her own body sheathed,
Nor yet by oaths betrothed, nor kisses breathed
Into my purgatory, faithless thee,
Thy heart seemed wax and steel thy constancy.
So careless flowers strewed on the water's face,
The curled whirlpools suck, smack, and embrace,
Yet drown them; so the taper's beamy eye,
Amorously twinkling, beckons the'giddy fly,
Yet burns his wings; and such the devil is,
20   Scarce visiting them who'are entirely his.
When I behold a stream, which from the spring
Doth with doubtful melodious murmuring,
Or in a speechless slumber calmly ride
Her wedded channel's bosom, and then chide
And bend her brows, and swell if any bough
Do but stoop down or kiss her upmost brow;
Yet, if her often gnawing kisses win
The traitorous banks to gape and let her in,

She rusheth violently, and doth divorce
Her from her native and her long-kept course,   30
And roars, and braves it, and in gallant scorn,
In flattering eddies promising return,
She flouts the channel, who thenceforth is dry;
Then say I, that is she, and this am I.
Yet let not thy deep bitterness beget
Careless despair in me, for that will whet
My mind to scorn; and, O, love dulled with pain
Was ne'er so wise, nor well armed as disdain.
Then with new eyes I shall survey thee,'and spy
Death in thy cheeks, and darkness in thine eye.   40
Though hope bred faith and love, thus taught, I
      shall
As nations do from Rome, from thy love fall.
My hate shall outgrow thine, and utterly
I will renounce thy dalliance; and when I
Am the recusant, in that resolute state,
What hurts it me to be'excommunicate?

Elegy: Nature's Lay Idiot

Nature's lay idiot, I taught thee to love,
And in that sophistry, O, thou dost prove
Too subtle, fool, thou didst not understand
The mystic language of the eye nor hand,
Nor could'st thou judge the difference of the air
Of sighs, and say, This lies, this sounds despair;
Nor by th'eye's water call a malady
Desperately hot or changing feverously.
I had not taught thee then the alphabet
Of flowers, how they, devisefully being set   10
And bound up, might with speechless secrecy
Deliver errands mutely'and mutually.
Remember since all thy words used to be
To every suitor, I,'if my friends agree;

Since household charms, thy husband's name to teach,
Were all the love tricks that thy wit could reach;
And since an hour's discourse could scarce have made
One answer in thee, and that ill arrayed
In broken proverbs and torn sentences.
20 Thou art not by so many duties his,
That from the'world's common having severed thee,
Inlaid thee, neither to be seen, nor see,
As mine, who have with amorous delicacies
Refined thee'into a blissful paradise.
Thy graces and good words my creatures be;
I planted knowledge and life's tree in thee,
Which, O, shall strangers taste? Must I alas
Frame and enamel plate, and drink in glass?
Chafe wax for others' seals? Break a colt's force
30 And leave him then, being made a ready horse?

Elegy: The Comparison

As the sweet sweat of roses in a still,
As that which from chafed muskats' pores doth trill,
As the almighty balm of th'early East,
Such are the sweat drops on my mistress breast.
And on her neck her skin such lustre sets,
They seem no sweat drops but pearl carcanets.
Rank sweaty froth thy mistress's brow defiles,
Like spermatic issue'of ripe menstruous boils,
Or like the scum which, by need's lawless law
10 Enforced, Sanserra's starved men did draw
From parboiled shoes and boots, and all the rest
Which were with any sovereign fatness blest.
And like vile stones lying in saffroned tin,
Or warts, or wheals, they hang upon her skin.
Round as the world's her head on every side
Like to the fatal ball which fell on Ide,
Or that whereof God had such jealousy,
As, for the ravishing thereof we die.

Thy head is like a rough-hewn statue'of jet,
Where marks for eyes, nose, mouth, are yet scarce   20
   set;
Like the first Chaos, or flat-seeming face
Of Cynthia when th'earth's shadows her embrace.
Like Proserpina's white beauty-keeping chest,
Or Jove's best fortune's urn, is her fair breast.
Thine's like worm-eaten trunks clothed in seals' skin,
Or grave that's dust without and stink within.
And like that slender stalk, at whose end stands
The woodbine quivering, are her arms and hands.
Like rough-barked elm boughs, or the russet skin
Of men late scourged for madness or for sin,   30
Like sun-parched quarters on the city gate,
Such is thy tanned skin's lamentable state.
And like a bunch of ragged carrots stand
The short swoll'n fingers of her gouty hand.
Then like the chemic's masculine equal fire,
Which in the limbeck's warm womb doth inspire
Into th'earth's worthless dirt a soul of gold,
Such cherishing heat her best loved part doth hold.
Thine's like the dread mouth of a fired gun,
Or like hot liquid metals newly run   40
Into clay moulds, or like to that Etna
Where round about the grass is burnt away.
Are not your kissings then as filthy'and more,
As a worm sucking an envenomed sore?
Doth not thy fearful hand in feeling quake,
As one which gath'ring flowers, still fears a snake?
Is not your last act harsh and violent,
As when a plough a stony ground doth rent?
So kiss good turtles, so devoutly nice
Are priests in handling reverent sacrifice,   50
And nice in searching wounds the surgeon is
As we, when we embrace, or touch, or kiss.
Leave her, and I will leave comparing thus,
She and comparisons are odious.

Elegy: The Autumnal

No spring nor summer beauty hath such grace,
  As I have seen in one autumnal face.
Young beauties force our love, and that's a rape;
  This doth but counsel, yet you cannot 'scape.
If t'were a shame to love, here t'were no shame;
  Affections here take reverence's name.
Were her first years the Golden Age? That's true,
  But now she's gold oft tried, and ever new.
That was her torrid and inflaming time,
  This is her habitable tropic clime.
Fair eyes, who asks more heat than comes from hence,
  He in a fever wishes pestilence.
Call not these wrinkles, graves; if graves they were,
  They were Love's graves; for else he is nowhere.
Yet lies not Love dead here, but here doth sit
  Vowed to this trench like an anachorite.
And here, till hers, which must be his death, come,
  He doth not dig a grave, but build a tomb.
Here dwells he, though he sojourn ev'rywhere
  In progress, yet his standing house is here.
Here, where still evening is, not noon, nor night,
  Where no voluptuousness, yet all delight.
In all her words, unto all hearers fit,
  You may at revels, you at council, sit.
This is love's timber, youth his under-wood;
  There he, as wine in June, enrages blood,
Which then comes seasonabliest when our taste
  And appetite to other things is past.
Xerxes' strange Lydian love, the plantain tree,
  Was loved for age, none being so large as she,
Or else because, being young, Nature did bless
  Her youth with age's glory, barrenness.
If we love things long sought, age is a thing
  Which we are fifty years in compassing.

If transitory things which soon decay,
    Age must be loveliest at the latest day.
But name not winter faces, whose skin's slack,
    Lank, as an unthrift's purse, but a soul's sack.
Whose eyes seek light within, for all here's shade;
    Whose mouths are holes, rather worn out, than
        made;   40
Whose every tooth to'a several place is gone,
    To vex their souls at Resurrection;
Name not these living death's-heads unto me,
    For these not ancient, but antique be.
I hate extremes; yet I had rather stay
    With tombs than cradles to wear out a day.
Since such love's natural lation is, may still
    My love descend and journey down the hill,
Not panting after growing beauties, so
    I shall ebb on with them who homeward go.   50

Elegy: Image of her whom I love

Image of her whom I love, more than she
    Whose fair impression in my faithful heart
Makes me her medal, and makes her love me
    As kings do coins to which their stamps impart
The value: go, and take my heart from hence,
    Which now is grown too great and good for me.
Honours oppress weak spirits, and our sense
    Strong objects dull; the more, the less we see.
When you are gone, and reason gone with you,
    Then fantasy is queen, and soul, and all;   10
She can present joys meaner than you do,
    Convenient, and more proportional.
So, if I dream I have you, I have you,
    For all our joys are but fantastical.
And so I 'scape the pain, for pain is true;
    And sleep, which locks up sense, doth lock out all.

After a such fruition I shall wake,
   And, but the waking, nothing shall repent;
And shall to love more thankful sonnets make
20   Than if more honour, tears, and pains were spent.
But dearest heart, and dearer image, stay;
   Alas, true joys at best are dream enough.
Though you stay here you pass too fast away:
   For even at first life's taper is a snuff.
Filled with her love, may I be rather grown
   Mad with much heart, than idiot with none.

Elegy: The Bracelet
*Upon the loss of his mistress' chain, for which he
made satisfaction*

Not that in colour it was like thy hair,
For armlets of that thou may'st let me wear;
Nor that thy hand it oft embraced and kissed,
For so it had that good, which oft I missed;
Nor for that silly old morality
That as these links are tied, our love should be,
Mourn I that I thy sevenfold chain have lost;
Nor for the luck's sake, but the bitter cost.
O, shall twelve righteous angels, which as yet
10 No leaven of vile solder did admit;
Nor yet by any taint have strayed or gone
From the first state of their creation;
Angels, which heaven commanded to provide
All things to me, and be my faithful guide
To gain new friends, t'appease great enemies,
To comfort my soul when I lie or rise.
Shall these twelve innocents, by thy severe
Sentence, dread judge, my sin's great burden bear?
Shall they be damned and in the furnace thrown,
20 And punished for offences not their own?
They save not me, they do not ease my pains,
When in that hell they'are burnt and tied in chains.

Were they but crowns of France, I cared not,
For most of them, their natural country's rot
I think possesseth; they come here to us
So lean, so pale, so lame, so ruinous,
And howsoe'er French kings most Christian be,
Their crowns are circumcised most Jewishly;
Or were they Spanish stamps, still travelling,
That are become as Catholic as their king,   30
Those unlicked bear-whelps, unfiled pistolets
That, more than cannon shot, avails or lets;
Which negligently left unrounded look
Like many-angled figures in the book
Of some great conjurer that would enforce
Nature, as these do justice, from her course;
Which, as the soul quickens head, feet and heart,
As streams, like veins, run through th'earth's every
            part,
Visit all countries, and have slyly made
Gorgeous France, ruined, ragged and decayed,   40
Scotland, which knew no state, proud in one day,
And mangled seventeen-headed Belgia.
Or were it such gold as that, wherewithal
Almighty chemics from each mineral
Having by subtle fire a soul out-pulled,
Are dirtily and desperately gulled,
I would not spit to quench the fire they'are in,
For they are guilty of much heinous sin.
But shall my harmless angels perish? Shall
I lose my guard, my ease, my food, my all?   50
Much hope which they should nourish will be dead,
Much of my able youth and lustihead
Will vanish; if thou love, let them alone,
For thou wilt love me less when they are gone;
O be content that some loud squeaking crier,
Well-pleased with one lean threadbare groat for hire,
May like a devil roar through every street,
And gall the finder's conscience if they meet.

Or let me creep to some dread conjurer,
Which with fantastic schemes fills full much paper;
Which hath divided heaven in tenements,
And with whores, thieves, and murderers stuffed his
    rents
So full, that though he pass them all in sin,
He leaves himself no room to enter in.
    And if, when all his art and time is spent,
He say 'twill ne'er be found; O be content.
Receive from him that doom ungrudgingly,
Because he is the mouth of destiny.
    Thou say'st, alas, the gold doth still remain,
Though it be changed, and put into a chain;
So in the first fallen angels resteth still
Wisdom and knowledge, but 'tis turned to ill,
As these should do good works and should provide
Necessities, but now must nurse thy pride.
And they are still bad angels; mine are none,
For form gives being, and their form is gone.
Pity these angels yet; their dignities
Pass Virtues, Powers, and Principalities.
    But thou art resolute; thy will be done;
Yet with such anguish, as her only son
The mother in the hungry grave doth lay,
Unto the fire these martyrs I betray.
Good souls, for you give life to everything,
Good angels, for good messages you bring,
Destined you might have been to such an one
As would have loved and worshipped you alone,
One that would suffer hunger, nakedness,
Yea, death, ere he would make your number less.
But I am guilty of your sad decay;
May your few fellows longer with me stay.
    But O thou wretched finder whom I hate
So that I almost pity thy estate;
Gold being the heaviest metal amongst all,
May my most heavy curse upon thee fall.

Here fettered, manacled, and hanged in chains
First may'st thou be; then chained to hellish pains;
Or be with foreign gold bribed to betray
Thy country,'and fail both of that and thy pay.
May the next thing thou stoop'st to reach contain
Poison, whose nimble fume rot thy moist brain,   100
Or libels, or some interdicted thing,
Which negligently kept, thy ruin bring.
Lust-bred diseases rot thee'and dwell with thee
Itching desire, and no ability.
May all the evils that gold ever wrought,
All mischief which all devils ever thought,
Want after plenty, poor and gouty age,
The plagues of travellers, love, marriage
Afflict thee, and at thy life's last moment,
May thy swoll'n sins themselves to thee present.   110
    But I forgive; repent thee honest man:
Gold is restorative, restore it then:
Or if with it thou be'st loath to'depart,
Because 'tis cordial, would 'twere at thy heart.

Elegy: His Parting from Her

Since she must go and I must mourn, come night,
Environ me with darkness whil'st I write:
Shadow that hell unto me which alone
I am to suffer when my love is gone;
Alas, the darkest magic cannot do'it,
Thou and great hell to boot are shadows to'it.
Should Cynthia quit thee, Venus, and each star,
It would not form one thought dark as mine are.
I could lend thee obscureness now, and say,
Out of myself, there should be no more day.   10
Such is already my felt want of sight
Did not the fire within me force a light.
O Love, that fire and darkness should be mixed,
Or to thy triumphs such strange torments fixed.

Is't because thou thyself art blind that we,
Thy martyrs, must no more each other see?
Or tak'st thou pride to break us on thy wheel,
And view old Chaos in the pains we feel?
Or have left undone some mutual rite
20 That thus with parting thou seek'st us to spite?
No, no. The fault is mine, impute'it to me,
Or rather to conspiring destiny,
Which (since I loved) for me before decreed
That I should suffer when I loved indeed;
And therefore, now, sooner than I can say
I saw the golden fruit, 'tis rapt away,
Or as I'had watched one drop in the vast stream,
And I left wealthy only in a dream.
Yet Love, thou'rt blinder than thyself in this
30 To vex my dove-like friend for my amiss:
And where one sad truth may expiate
Thy wrath, to make her fortune run my fate.
So blinded Justice doth, when favourites fall,
Strike them, their house, their friends, their followers
    all.
Was't not enough that thou did'st dart thy fires
Into our bloods, informing our desires,
And made'st us sigh, and glow, and pant, and burn,
And then thyself into our flames did'st turn?
Was't not enough that thou didst hazard us
40 To paths in love so dark and dangerous,
And those so ambushed round with household spies,
And over all the towered husbands eyes
That flamed with oily sweat of jealousy,
Yet went we not still on with constancy?
Have we for this kept our guards, like spy on spy,
Had correspondence whil'st the foe stood by?
Stol'n (more to sweeten them) our many blisses
Of meetings, conference, embracements, kisses,
Shadowed with negligence our best respects,
50 Varied our language through all dialects

Of becks, winks, looks, and often under-boards
Spoke dialogues with our feet, far from our words?
Have we proved all these secrets of our art,
Yea, thy pale colours inward as thy heart?
And, after all this passed purgatory,
Must sad divorce make us the vulgar story?
First let our eyes be riveted quite through
Our turning brains, and both our lips grow to.
Let our arms clasp like ivy, and our fear
Freeze us together, that we may stick here   60
Till fortune, that would rive us with the deed,
Strain her eyes open; and it make them bleed.
For Love it cannot be, whom hitherto
I have accused, should such a mischief do.
O fortune, thou'rt not worth my least exclaim,
And plague enough thou hast in thy own shame.
Do thy great worst; my friend and I have arms,
Though not against thy strokes, against thy harms.
Rend us asunder; thou canst not divide
Our bodies so, but that our souls are tied;   70
And we can love by letters still, and gifts,
And thoughts, and dreams; love never wanteth shifts.
I will not look upon the quick'ning sun,
But straight her beauty to my sense shall run.
The air shall note her soft, the fire, most pure,
Waters suggest her clear, and the earth, sure.
Time shall not loose our passages, the spring,
How fresh our love was in the beginning,
The summer, how it enripened the year,
And autumn, what our golden harvests were.   80
The winter I'll not think on to spite thee,
But count it a lost season, so shall she.
And, dearest friend, since we must part, drown night
With hope of day; burdens well borne are light.
The cold and darkness longer hang somewhere,
Yet Phoebus equally lights all the sphere.
And what we cannot in like portion pay,
The world enjoys in mass, and so we may.

Be then ever yourself, and let no woe
90   Win on your health, your youth, your beauty; so
Declare yourself base fortune's enemy;
No less be your contempt than her inconstancy,
That I may grow enamoured on your mind
When my own thoughts I here neglected find.
And this to th'comfort of my dear I vow,
My deeds shall still be what my words are now.
The poles shall move to teach me ere I start,
And when I change my love, I'll change my heart.
Nay, if I wax but cold in my desire,
100 Think heaven hath motion lost, and the world, fire.
Much more I could, but many words have made
That oft suspected which men most persuade.
Take therefore all in this: I love so true
As I will never look for less in you.

Elegy: The Expostulation

To make the doubt clear that no woman's true,
    Was it my fate to prove it strong in you?
Thought I but one had breathed purest air,
    And must she needs be false because she's fair?
Is it your beauty's mark, or of your youth,
    Or your perfection, not to study truth?
Or think you heaven is deaf, or hath no eyes?
    Or those it hath smile at your perjuries?
Are vows so cheap with women, or the matter
10   Whereof they'are made, that they are writ in
            water,
And blown away with wind? Or doth their breath
    (Both hot and cold) at once make life and death?
Who could have thought so many accents sweet
    Formed into words, so many sighs should meet
As from our hearts, so many oaths and tears
    Sprinkled among (all sweeter by our fears

And the divine impression of stol'n kisses,
    That sealed the rest), should now prove empty
        blisses?
Did you draw bonds, to forfeit? Sign, to break?
    Or must we read you quite from what you speak,   20
And find the truth out the wrong way? Or must
    He first desire you false, would wish you just?
O, I profane, though most of women be
    This kind of beast, my thought shall except thee;
My dearest love, though froward jealousy
    With circumstance might urge thy'inconstancy,
Sooner I'll think the sun will cease to cheer
    The teeming earth, and that forget to bear,
Sooner that rivers will run back, or Thames
    With ribs of ice in June would bind his streams,   30
Or Nature, by whose strength the world endures,
    Would change her course, before you alter yours;
But, O, that treacherous breast to whom weak you
    Did trust our counsels, and we both may rue,
Having his falsehood found too late, 'twas he
    That made me cast you guilty, and you me,
Whil'st he, black wretch, betrayed each simple word
    We spake unto the cunning of a third.
Curst may he be that so our love hath slain,
    And wander on the earth, wretched as Cain,   40
Wretched as he, and not deserve least pity;
    In plaguing him, let misery be witty,
Let all eyes shun him, and he shun each eye,
    Till he be noisome as his infamy.
May he without remorse deny God thrice,
    And not be trusted more on his soul's price;
And after all self-torment, when he dies,
    May wolves tear out his heart, vultures his eyes,
Swine eat his bowels, and his falser tongue,
    That uttered all, be to some raven flung,   50
And let his carrion corpse be'a longer feast
    To the king's dogs than any other beast.

Now have I cursed, let us our love revive;
   In me the flame was never more alive.
I could begin again to court and praise,
   And in that pleasure lengthen the short days
Of my life's lease, like painters that do take
   Delight, not in made work, but whiles they make.
I could renew those times when first I saw
60   Love in your eyes, that gave my tongue the law
To like what you liked; and at masks and plays
   Commend the self-same actors, the same ways;
Ask how you did, and often with intent
   Of being officious, be impertinent.
All which were such soft pastimes as in these
   Love was subtly catched, as a disease;
But being got, it is a treasure sweet
   Which to defend is harder than to get;
And ought not be profaned on either part,
70   For though 'tis got by chance, 'tis kept by art.

Elegy: To His Mistress Going to Bed

Come, madam, come, all rest my powers defy;
Until I labour, I in labour lie.
The foe oft-times having the foe in sight,
Is tired with standing though he never fight.
Off with that girdle, like heaven's zones glistering,
But a far fairer world encompassing.
Unpin that spangled breastplate which you wear
That th'eyes of busy fools may be stopped there.
Unlace yourself, for that harmonious chime
10   Tells me from you that now 'tis your bedtime.
Off with that happy busk, which I envy,
That still can be, and still can stand so nigh.
Your gown going off, such beauteous state reveals
As when from flow'ry meads th'hill's shadow steals.
Off with that wiry coronet and show
The hairy diadem which on you doth grow.

Now off with those shoes, and then safely tread
In this love's hallowed temple, this soft bed.
In such white robes, heaven's angels used to be
Received by men; thou, angel, bring'st with thee   20
A heaven like Mahomet's paradise; and though
Ill spirits walk in white, we easily know
By this these angels from an evil sprite,
Those set our hairs, but these our flesh upright.
　　License my roving hands, and let them go
Behind, before, above, between, below.
O my America, my new-found-land,
My kingdom, safeliest when with one man manned,
My mine of precious stones, my empery,
How blest am I in this discovering thee!   30
To enter in these bonds is to be free;
Then where my hand is set, my seal shall be.
　　Full nakedness, all joys are due to thee,
As souls unbodied, bodies unclothed must be
To taste whole joys. Gems which you women use
Are like Atlanta's balls, cast in men's views,
That when a fool's eye lighteth on a gem,
His earthly soul may covet theirs, not them.
Like pictures or like books' gay coverings made
For lay-men, are all women thus arrayed.   40
Themselves are mystic books, which only we
(Whom their imputed grace will dignify)
Must see revealed. Then, since that I may know,
As liberally as to a midwife show
Thyself. Cast all, yea, this white linen hence,
There is no penance, much less to innocence.
　　To teach thee, I am naked first; why then,
What need'st thou have more covering than a man?

Elegy: Love's Progress

Whoever loves, if he do not propose
The right true end of love, he's one that goes
To sea for nothing but to make him sick.
Love is a bear-whelp born; if we o'er lick
Our love, and force it new strange shapes to take,
We err, and of a lump a monster make.
Were not a calf a monster that were grown
Faced like a man, though better than his own?
Perfection is in unity: prefer
One woman first, and then one thing in her.
I, when I value gold, may think upon
The ductileness, the application,
The wholesomeness, the ingenuity,
From rust, from soil, from fire ever free.
But if I love it, 'tis because 'tis made
By our new nature (use) the soul of trade.
  All these in women we might think upon
(If women had them), and yet love but one.
Can men more injure women than to say
They love them for that by which they're not they?
Makes virtue woman? Must I cool my blood
Till I both be, and find one, wise and good?
May barren angels love so? But if we
Make love to woman, virtue is not she,
As beauty'is not, nor wealth; he that strays thus
From her to hers is more adulterous
Than if he took her maid. Search every sphere
And firmament, our Cupid is not there;
He's an infernal god, and underground
With Pluto dwells where gold and fire abound;
Men to such gods their sacrificing coals
Did not on altars lay, but pits and holes.
Although we see celestial bodies move
Above the earth, the earth we till and love;

10

20

30

So we her airs contemplate, words, and heart,
And virtues, but we love the centric part.
    Nor is the soul more worthy or more fit
For love than this, as infinite as it.
But in attaining this desired place
How much they err that set out at the face.   40
The hair a forest is of ambushes,
Of springes, snares, fetters and manacles.
The brow becalms us when 'tis smooth and plain,
And when 'tis wrinkled, shipwrecks us again;
Smooth, 'tis a paradise, where we would have
Immortal stay, but wrinkled 'tis a grave.
The nose (like to the first meridian) runs
Not 'twixt an East and West, but 'twixt two suns;
It leaves a cheek, a rosy hemisphere
On either side, and then directs us, where   50
Upon the islands fortunate we fall
(Not faint Canaries, but ambrosial),
Unto her swelling lips when we are come,
We anchor there, and think ourselves at home,
For they seem all; there Sirens' songs, and there
Wise Delphic oracles do fill the ear.
There in a creek, where chosen pearls do swell
The remora, her cleaving tongue doth dwell.
These and (the glorious promontory)'her chin
O'er past, and the strait Hellespont between   60
The Sestos and Abydos of her breasts,
Not of two lovers, but two loves, the nests,
Succeeds a boundless sea; but yet thine eye
Some island moles may scattered there descry;
And sailing towards her India, in that way
Shall at her fair Atlantic navel stay.
Though thence the current be thy pilot made,
Yet ere thou be, where thou would'st be embayed,
Thou shalt upon another forest set
Where some do shipwreck, and no further get.   70
When thou art there, consider what this chase
Misspent by thy beginning at the face.

Rather set out below; practise my art,
Some symmetry the foot hath with that part
Which thou dost seek, and is thy map for that
Lovely enough to stop, but not stay at.
Least subject to disguise and change it is;
Men say the Devil never can change his.
It is the emblem that hath figured
80 Firmness; 'tis the first part that comes to bed.
Civility, we see, refined the kiss
Which at the face began, transplanted is
Since to the hand, since to the'imperial knee,
Now at the papal foot delights to be.
If kings think that the nearer way, and do
Rise from the foot, lovers may do so too.
For as free spheres move faster far than can
Birds, whom the air resists, so may that man
Which goes this empty and ethereal way,
90 Than if at beauty's elements he stay.
Rich nature hath in women wisely made
Two purses, and their mouths aversely laid:
They then which to the lower tribute owe,
That way, which that exchequer looks, must go;
He which doth not, his error is as great
As who by clyster gave the stomach meat.

Elegy: On His Mistress

By our first strange and fatal interview,
By all desires which thereof did ensue,
By our long starving hopes, by that remorse
Which my words' masculine persuasive force
Begot in thee, and by the memory
Of hurts which spies and rivals threatened me,
I calmly beg. But by thy father's wrath,
By all pains which want and divorcement hath,
I conjure thee; and all the oaths which I
10 And thou have sworn to seal joint constancy

Here I unswear, and overswear them thus,
Thou shalt not love by ways so dangerous.
Temper, O fair love, love's impetuous rage,
Be my true mistress still, not my feigned page.
I'll go, and by thy kind leave, leave behind
Thee, only worthy to nurse in my mind
Thirst to come back; O, if thou die before,
My soul from other lands to thee shall soar.
Thy (else almighty) beauty cannot move
Rage from the seas, nor thy love teach them love,   20
Nor tame wild Boreas's harshness; thou hast read
How roughly he in pieces shivered
Fair Orithea whom he swore he loved.
Fall ill or good, 'tis madness to have proved
Dangers unurged; feed on this flattery,
That absent lovers one in th'other be.
Dissemble nothing, not a boy, nor change
Thy body's habit, nor mind's; be not strange
To thyself only.'All will spy in thy face
A blushing, womanly, discovering grace;   30
Richly clothed apes are called apes, and as soon
Eclipsed as bright, we call the moon the moon.
Men of France, changeable chameleons,
Spitals'of diseases, shops of fashions,
Love's fuellers, and the rightest company
Of players which upon the world's stage be,
Will quickly know thee, and no less, alas,
Th'indifferent Italian, as we pass
His warm land, well content to think thee page,
Will hunt thee with such lust and hideous rage   40
As Lot's fair guests were vexed. But none of these
Nor spongy'hydroptic Dutch shall thee displease
If thou stay here. O stay here, for, for thee
England is only'a worthy gallery
To walk in expectation, till from thence
Our greatest King call thee to His presence.
When I am gone, dream me some happiness,
Nor let thy looks our long hid love confess,

Nor praise, nor dispraise me, nor bless nor curse
Openly love's force, nor in bed fright thy nurse
With midnight's startings, crying out, O, O,
Nurse, O my love is slain, I saw him go
O'er the white Alps alone; I saw him, I,
Assailed, fight, taken, stabbed, bleed, fall, and die.
Augur me better chance, except dread Jove
Think it enough for me to'have had thy love.

THE EPITHALAMIONS OR
MARRIAGE SONGS

An Epithalamion, or Marriage Song, on the
Lady Elizabeth and Count Palatine Being Married on
St Valentine's Day

I

Hail Bishop Valentine whose day this is;
    All the air is thy diocese,
    And all the chirping choristers
And other birds are thy parishioners.
    Thou marriest every year
The lyric lark and the grave whispering dove,
The sparrow that neglects his life for love,
The household bird with the red stomacher.
    Thou mak'st the blackbird speed as soon
As doth the goldfinch or the halcyon;
The husband cock looks out and straight is sped,
And meets his wife which brings her featherbed.
This day more cheerfully than ever shine,
This day which might inflame thyself, Old Valentine.

II

Till now, thou warmed'st with multiplying loves
    Two larks, two sparrows, or two doves;
    All that is nothing unto this,
For thou this day couplest two phoenixes;
      Thou mak'st a taper see
What the sun never saw, and what the ark   20
(Which was of fowls and beasts, the cage and park)
Did not contain, one bed contains through thee,
    Two phoenixes whose joined breasts
Are unto one another mutual nests,
Where motion kindles such fires as shall give
Young phoenixes, and yet the old shall live,
Whose love and courage never shall decline,
But make the whole year through, thy day, O
      Valentine.

III

Up then fair phoenix-bride, frustrate the sun.
    Thyself from thine affection   30
    Tak'st warmth enough, and from thine eye
All lesser birds will take their jollity.
      Up, up, fair bride, and call,
Thy stars from out their several boxes, take
Thy rubies, pearls, and diamonds forth, and make
Thyself a constellation of them all,
    And by their blazing signify
That a great princess falls but doth not die.
Be thou a new star that to us portends
Ends of much wonder, and be thou those ends.   40
Since thou dost this day in new glory shine,
May all men date records from this, thy Valentine.

IV

Come forth, come forth, and as one glorious flame
    Meeting another grows the same,
    So meet thy Frederick, and so
To an inseparable union grow.
       Since separation
Falls not on such things as are infinite,
Nor things which are but one can disunite,
50   You'are twice inseparable, great, and one.
      Go then to where the bishop stays
To make you one his way, which diverse ways
Must be effected; and when all is past,
And that you'are one by hearts and hands made fast,
You two have one way left yourselves to'entwine,
Besides this Bishop's knot of Bishop Valentine.

V

But oh, what ails the sun that here he stays
    Longer today than other days?
    Stays he new light from these to get,
60   And, finding here such stars, is loath to set?
      And why do you two walk
So slowly paced in this procession?
Is all your care but to be looked upon,
And be to others spectacle and talk?
    The feast with gluttonous delays
Is eaten, and too long their meat they praise;
The maskers come too late, and,'I think, will stay
Like fairies till the cock crow them away.
    Alas, did not antiquity assign
70   A night as well as day to thee, O Valentine?

VI

They did, and night is come; and yet we see
    Formalities retarding thee.
    What mean these ladies which (as though
They were to take a clock in pieces) go

So nicely'about the bride?
A bride, before a good night could be said,
Should vanish from her clothes into her bed,
As souls from bodies steal, and are not spied.
But now she'is laid; what though she be?
Yet there are more delays, for where is he? 80
He comes, and passes through sphere after sphere,
First her sheets, then her arms, then anywhere.
Let not this day then, but this night be thine,
Thy day was but the eve to this, O Valentine.

VII

Here lies a she Sun, and a he Moon here;
She gives the best light to his sphere,
Or each is both, and all, and so
They unto one another nothing owe.
And yet they do, but are
So just and rich in that coin which they pay 90
That neither would, nor needs forbear nor stay;
Neither desires to be spared, nor to spare.
They quickly pay their debt, and then
Take no acquittances but pay again;
They pay, they give, they lend, and so let fall
No such occasion to be liberal.
More truth, more courage in these two do shine,
Than all thy turtles have, and sparrows, Valentine.

VIII

And by this act of these two phoenixes
Nature again restorèd is, 100
For since these two are two no more,
There's but one phoenix still as was before.
Rest now at last, and we,
As satyrs watch the sun's uprise, will stay
Waiting when your eyes opened let out day,
Only desired because your face we see.
Others, near you, shall whispering speak,
And wagers lay at which side day will break,

And win by'observing then whose hand it is
110   That opens first a curtain, hers or his.
This will be tried tomorrow after nine,
Till which hour we thy day enlarge, O Valentine.

Epithalamion Made at Lincoln's Inn

The sunbeams in the east are spread,
Leave, leave, fair bride, your solitary bed,
   No more shall you return to it alone.
It nurseth sadness and your body's print,
Like to a grave, the yielding down doth dint.
      You and your other, you meet there anon.
      Put forth, put forth that warm, balm-breathing
            thigh,
Which when next time you in these sheets will
            smother,
      There it must meet another
10   Which never was, but must be oft, more nigh;
Come glad from thence, go gladder than you came,
Today put on perfection and a woman's name.

Daughters of London, you which be
Our golden mines and furnished treasury,
   You which are angels, yet still bring with you
Thousands of angels on your marriage days,
Help with your presence, and devise to praise
      These rites which also unto you grow due.
      Conceitedly dress her, and be assigned
20   By you fit place for every flower and jewel;
      Make her for love fit fuel,
         As gay as Flora and as rich as Ind;
So may she fair, rich, glad, and in nothing lame,
Today put on perfection and a woman's name.

And you frolic patricians,
Sons of these senators, wealth's deep oceans,
   Ye painted courtiers, barrels of others' wits,
Ye country men who but your beasts love none,
Ye of those fellowships whereof he's one,
   Of study'and play made strange hermaphrodites,   30
   Here shine; this bridegroom to the temple bring.
Lo, in yon path which store of strewed flowers graceth,
   The sober virgin paceth;
      Except my sight fail, 'tis no other thing.
Weep not, nor blush, here is no grief nor shame,
Today put on perfection and a woman's name.

Thy two-leaved gates, fair temple,'unfold,
And these two in thy sacred bosom hold,
   Till mystically joined, but one they be;
Then may thy lean and hunger-starvèd womb   40
Long time expect their bodies and their tomb,
   Long after their own parents fatten thee.
   All elder claims and all cold barrenness,
All yielding to new loves, be far for ever,
   Which might these two dissever.
      Always, all th'other may each one possess;
For the best bride, best worthy'of praise and fame,
Today puts on perfection and a woman's name.

O winter days bring much delight,
Not for themselves, but for they soon bring night;   50
   Other sweets wait thee than these diverse meats,
Other disports than dancing jollities,
Other love-tricks than glancing with the eyes,
   But that the sun still in our half-sphere sweats;
   He flies in winter, but he now stands still.
Yet shadows turn; noon point he hath attained,
   His steeds will be restrained,
      But gallop lively down the western hill;
Thou shalt, when he hath run the world's half frame,
Tonight put on perfection and a woman's name.   60

The amorous evening star is rose,
Why then should not our amorous star enclose
   Herself in her wished bed? Release your strings
Musicians, and dancers take some truce
With these, your pleasing labours; for great use
    As much weariness as perfection brings.
    You, and not only you, but all toiled beasts
Rest duly;'at night all their toils are dispensed,
    But in their beds commenced
70   Are other labours and more dainty feasts.
She goes a maid, who, lest she turn the same,
Tonight puts on perfection and a woman's name.

Thy virgin's girdle now untie,
And in thy nuptial bed (love's altar) lie
   A pleasing sacrifice; now dispossess
Thee of these chains and robes which were put on
T'adorn the day, not thee; for thou alone,
    Like virtue'and truth, art best in nakedness;
    This bed is only to virginity
80 A grave, but to a better state, a cradle;
    Till now thou wast but able
      To be what now thou art; then, that by thee
No more be said, *I may be*, but, *I am*,
Tonight put on perfection and a woman's name.

Even like a faithful man content
That this life for a better should be spent,
   So she a mother's rich style doth prefer,
And at the bridegroom's wished approach doth lie
Like an appointed lamb when tenderly
90   The priest comes on his knees t'embowel her;
      Now sleep or watch with more joy; and, O light
Of heaven, tomorrow rise thou hot and early;
    This sun will love so dearly
      Her rest, that long, long we shall want her sight;
Wonders are wrought, for she, which had no maim,
Tonight puts on perfection and a woman's name.

Eclogue
1613. December 26.

Allophanes finding Idios in the country in Christmas-time,
reprehends his absence from court, at the marriage of the Earl
of Somerset; Idios gives an account of his purpose therein, and
of his absence thence.

ALLOPHANES
Unseasonable man, statue of ice,
    What could to country's solitude entice
Thee, in this year's cold and decrepit time?
    Nature's instinct draws to the warmer clime
Even small birds, who by that courage dare
    In numerous fleets sail through their sea, the air.
What delicacy can in fields appear
    Whil'st Flora'herself doth a frieze jerkin wear?
Whil'st winds do all the trees and hedges strip
    Of leaves, to furnish rods enough to whip   10
Thy madness from thee; and all springs by frost
    Have taken cold, and their sweet murmur lost;
If thou thy faults or fortunes would'st lament
    With just solemnity, do it in Lent.
At court the spring already advanced is,
    The sun stays longer up; and yet not his
The glory is, far other, other fires.
    First, zeal to prince and state; then love's desires
Burn in one breast, and like heaven's two great
        lights,
    The first doth govern days, the other nights.   20
And then that early light, which did appear
    Before the sun and moon created were,
The prince's favour is diffused o'er all,
    From which all fortunes, names, and natures fall;
Then from those wombs of stars, the bride's bright
        eyes,
    At every glance, a constellation flies,

And sows the court with stars, and doth prevent
   In light and power, the all-eyed firmament.
First her eyes kindle other ladies' eyes,
30   Then from their beams, their jewels' lustres rise,
And from their jewels, torches do take fire,
   And all is warmth, and light, and good desire;
Most other courts, alas, are like to hell,
   Where in dark plots, fire without light doth dwell;
Or but like stoves, for lust and envy get
   Continual but artificial heat;
Here zeal and love grown one, all clouds digest,
   And make our court an everlasting east.
And can'st thou be from thence?

IDIOS
                      No, I am there.
40 As heaven, to men disposed, is everywhere,
So are those courts whose princes animate
   Not only all their house, but all their state.
Let no man think, because he'is full, he'hath all;
Kings (as their pattern, God) are liberal
Not only'in fullness, but capacity,
   Enlarging narrow men to feel and see,
And comprehend the blessings they bestow.
   So reclused hermits oftentimes do know
50 More of heaven's glory than a worldling can.
   As man is of the world, the heart of man
Is an epitome of God's great book
   Of creatures, and man need no farther look;
So is the country'of courts, where sweet peace doth,
   As their one common soul, give life to both;
I am not then from court.

ALLOPHANES
                  Dreamer, thou art.
Think'st thou, fantastic, that thou hast a part
In the East Indian fleet because thou hast
60   A little spice or amber in thy taste?

Because thou art not frozen, art thou warm?
  See'st thou all good because thou see'st no harm?
The earth doth in her inward bowels hold
  Stuff well-disposed, and which would fain be gold,
But never shall, except it chance to lie
  So upward that heaven gild it with his eye;
As for divine things, faith comes from above,
  So, for best civil use, all tinctures move
From higher powers; from God religion springs,
  Wisdom and honour from the use of kings.   70
Then unbeguile thyself, and know with me
  That angels, though on earth employed they be,
Are still in heav'n; so is he still at home
  That doth abroad to honest actions come.
Chide thyself then, O fool, which yesterday
  Might'st have read more than all thy books bewray.
Hast thou a history which doth present
  A court, where all affections do assent
Unto the king's, and that the king's are just?
  And where it is no levity to trust?   80
Where there is no ambition but to'obey,
  Where men need whisper nothing, and yet may;
Where the king's favours are so placed that all
  Find that the king therein is liberal
To them in him, because his favours bend
  To virtue unto which they all pretend?
Thou hast no such; yet here was this, and more,
  An earnest lover, wise then and before.
Our little Cupid hath sued livery,
  And is no more in his minority;   90
He is admitted now into that breast
  Where the king's counsels and his secrets rest.
What hast thou lost, O ignorant man?

IDIOS
                        I knew
All this, and only therefore I withdrew.

To know and feel all this, and not to have
    Words to express it, makes a man a grave
Of his own thoughts; I would not therefore stay
    At a great feast, having no grace to say.
And yet I 'scaped not here; for being come
    Full of the common joy, I uttered some.
Read then this nuptial song, which was not made
    Either the court or men's hearts to invade,
But since I'm dead and buried, I could frame
    No epitaph which might advance my fame
So much as this poor song, which testifies
    I did unto that day some sacrifice.

Epithalamion

I
The Time of the Marriage

Thou art reprieved, old year, thou shalt not die,
    Though thou upon thy death-bed lie,
      And should'st within five days expire,
Yet thou art rescued by a mightier fire
    Than thy old soul, the sun,
When he doth in his largest circle run.
The passage of the west or east would thaw,
And open wide their easy liquid jaw
To all our ships, could a Promethean art
Either unto the Northern Pole impart
The fire of these inflaming eyes, or of this loving
      heart.

II
Equality of Persons

But undiscerning Muse, which heart, which eyes,
    In this new couple dost thou prize,

When his eye as inflaming is
As hers, and her heart loves as well as his?
    Be tried by beauty,'and then
The bridegroom is a maid, and not a man.
If by that manly courage they be tried
Which scorns unjust opinion, then the bride
Becomes a man. Should chance or envy's art
Divide these two, whom nature scarce did part,
Since both have th'inflaming eyes, and both the
        loving heart?

III
Raising of the Bridegroom

Though it be some divorce to think of you   130
    Singly, so much one are you two,
    Yet let me here contemplate thee
First, cheerful Bridegroom, and first let me see
    How thou prevent'st the sun,
And his red foaming horses dost outrun,
How, having laid down in thy sovereign's breast
All businesses, from thence to reinvest
Them when these triumphs cease, thou forward art
To show to her, who doth the like impart,
The fire of thy inflaming eyes, and of thy loving   140
    heart.

IV
Raising of the Bride

But now, to thee, fair bride, it is some wrong
    To think thou wert in bed so long.
    Since soon thou liest down first, 'tis fit
Thou in first rising should'st allow for it.
    Powder thy radiant hair,
Which if without such ashes thou would'st wear,
Thou, which to all which come to look upon,
Art meant for Phoebus, would'st be Phaëton.

For our ease give thine eyes th'unusual part
150   Of joy, a tear; so quenched, thou may'st impart
       To us that come, thy'inflaming eyes, to him thy
           loving heart.

V
Her Apparelling

Thus thou descend'st to our infirmity
      Who can the sun in water see.
      So dost thou, when in silk and gold
Thou clad'st thyself; since we, which do behold,
      Are dust and worms, 'tis just
Our objects be the fruits of worms and dust;
Let every jewel be a glorious star,
Yet stars are not so pure as their spheres are.
160   And though thou stoop to'appear to us in part,
Still in that picture thou entirely art,
Which thy inflaming eyes have made within his
           loving heart.

VI
Going to the Chapel

Now from your easts you issue forth, and we,
      As men which through a cypress see
      The rising sun, do think it two,
So as you go to church, do think of you.
      But that veil being gone,
By the church rites you are from thenceforth one.
The Church Triumphant made this match before,
170   And now the Militant doth strive no more.
Then, reverend priest, who God's recorder art,
Do, from His dictates to these two impart
All blessings which are seen, or thought, by angel's
          eye or heart.

VII
The Benediction

Blest pair of swans, O may you interbring
    Daily new joys, and never sing;
    Live till all grounds of wishes fail,
Till honour, yea till wisdom grow so stale
    That new great heights to try,
It must serve your ambition to die;
Raise heirs, and may here to the world's end live   180
Heirs from this king to take thanks, yours to give,
Nature and grace do all, and nothing art.
May never age or error overthwart
With any west these radiant eyes, with any north
      this heart.

VIII
Feasts and Revels

But you are over-blest. Plenty this day
    Injures; it causeth time to stay.
    The tables groan, as though this feast
Would, as the flood, destroy all fowl and beast.
    And were the doctrine new
That the earth moved, this day would make it true;   190
For every part to dance and revel goes.
They tread the air, and fall not where they rose.
Though six hours since, the sun to bed did part,
The masks and banquets will not yet impart
A sunset to these weary eyes, a centre to this heart.

IX
The Bride's Going to Bed

What mean'st thou, bride, this company to keep,
    To sit up till thou fain would'st sleep?
    Thou may'st not, when thou'art laid, do so.
Thyself must to him a new banquet grow,
    And you must entertain
And do all this day's dances o'er again.
Know that if sun and moon together do
Rise in one point, they do not set so too.
Therefore thou may'st, fair bride, to bed depart;
Thou art not gone being gone; where'er thou art
Thou leav'st in him thy watchful eyes, in him thy
      loving heart.

X
The Bridegroom's Coming

As he that sees a star fall, runs apace,
    And finds a jelly in the place,
    So doth the bridegroom haste as much,
Being told this star is fallen, and finds her such.
    And as friends may look strange
By a new fashion, or apparel's change,
Their souls, though long acquainted they had been,
These clothes, the bodies, never yet had seen.
Therefore at first she modestly might start,
But must forthwith surrender every part,
As freely as each to'each before gave either eye or
      heart.

XI
The Good-Night

Now, as in Tullia's tomb, one lamp burnt clear,
    Unchanged for fifteen hundred year,
        May these love-lamps we here enshrine,   220
In warmth, light, lasting, equal the divine.
        Fire ever doth aspire,
And makes all like itself, turns all to fire,
But ends in ashes, which these cannot do,
For none of these is fuel, but fire too.
This is joy's bonfire, then, where love's strong arts
Make of so noble individual parts
One fire of four inflaming eyes, and of two loving
            hearts.

IDIOS
As I have brought this song that I may do
    A perfect sacrifice, I'll burn it too.   230

ALLOPHANES
No, sir, this paper I have justly got,
    For in burnt incense, the perfume is not
His only that presents it, but of all.
    What ever celebrates this festival
Is common, since the joy thereof is so.
    Nor may yourself be priest; but let me go
Back to the court, and I will lay it upon
    Such altars as prize your devotion.

SATIRES

Satire I

Away thou fondling motley humorist,
Leave me, and in this standing wooden chest,
Consorted with these few books, let me lie
In prison,'and here be coffined when I die;
Here are God's conduits, grave divines; and here
Nature's secretary, the philosopher;
And jolly statesmen, which teach how to tie
The sinews of a city's mystic body;
Here gathering chroniclers, and by them stand
Giddy fantastic poets of each land.
Shall I leave all this constant company,
And follow headlong, wild uncertain thee?
First swear by thy best love in earnest
(If thou which lov'st all, canst love any best)
Thou wilt not leave me in the middle street,
Though some more spruce companion thou dost meet,
Not though a captain do come in thy way,
Bright parcel, gilt with forty dead men's pay,
Not though a brisk, perfumed, pert courtier
Deign with a nod thy courtesy to answer,
Nor come a velvet justice with a long
Great train of blue coats, twelve or fourteen strong,
Wilt thou grin or fawn on him, or prepare
A speech to court his beauteous son and heir?
For better or worse take me, or leave me;
To take and leave me is adultery.
O monstrous, superstitious puritan,
Of refined manners, yet ceremonial man,
That when thou meet'st one, with enquiring eyes
Dost search, and like a needy broker prize
The silk and gold he wears, and to that rate
So high or low, dost raise thy formal hat,

That wilt consort none, until thou have known
What lands he hath in hope, or of his own,
As though all thy companions should make thee
Jointures, and marry thy dear company.
Why should'st thou (that dost not only approve,
But in rank itchy lust, desire and love
The nakedness and bareness to enjoy,
Of thy plump muddy whore, or prostitute boy)   40
Hate virtue, though she be naked and bare?
At birth, and death, our bodies naked are;
And till our souls be unapparelled
Of bodies, they from bliss are banished.
Man's first blest state was naked; when by sin
He lost that, yet he was clothed but in beasts' skin,
And in this coarse attire, which I now wear,
With God and with the muses I confer.
But since thou like a contrite penitent,
Charitably warned of thy sins, dost repent   50
These vanities and giddinesses, lo
I shut my chamber door, and come; let's go.
But sooner may a cheap whore, who hath been
Worn by as many several men in sin
As are black feathers or musk-colour hose,
Name her child's right true father 'mongst all those;
Sooner may one guess who shall bear away
Th'Infanta'of London, heir to'an India;
And sooner may a gulling weather-spy
By drawing forth heaven's scheme tell certainly   60
What fashioned hats, or ruffles, or suits next year
Our subtle-witted, antic youths will wear;
Than thou, when thou depart'st from me, canst
            show
Whither, why, when, or with whom thou
            would'st go.
But how shall I be pardoned my offence
That thus have sinned against my conscience?
Now we are in the street; he first of all
Improvidently proud, creeps to the wall,

And so imprisoned and hemmed in by me
70   Sells for a little state his liberty;
Yet though he cannot skip forth now to greet
Every fine silken painted fool we meet,
He them to him with amorous smiles allures,
And grins, smacks, shrugs, and such an itch endures,
As prentices or schoolboys which do know
Of some gay sport abroad, yet dare not go.
And as fiddlers stop lowest, at highest sound,
So to the most brave, stoops he nigh'st the ground.
But to a grave man, he doth move no more
80   Than the wise politic horse would heretofore,
Or thou, O elephant or ape, wilt do,
When any names the King of Spain to you.
Now leaps he upright, jogs me, and cries, Do'you see
Yonder well favoured youth? Which? O, 'tis he
That dances so divinely; O, said I,
Stand still, must you dance here for company?
He drooped, we went, till one (which did excel
Th'Indians in drinking his tobacco well)
Met us; they talked; I whispered, Let us go,
90   'T may be you smell him not, truly I do.
He hears not me, but, on the other side
A many-coloured peacock having spied,
Leaves him and me; I for my lost sheep stay;
He follows, overtakes, goes on the way,
Saying, him whom I last left, all repute
For his device in handsoming a suit,
To judge of lace, pink, panes, print, cut, and plight,
Of all the court, to have the best conceit.
Our dull comedians want him, let him go;
100   But O, God strengthen thee, why stop'st thou so?
Why? He hath travailed; long? No, but to me
(Which understand none) he doth seem to be
Perfect French, and Italian. I replied,
So is the pox. He answered not, but spied
More men of sort, of parts, and qualities;
At last his love he in a window spies,

And like light dew exhaled, he flings from me,
Violently ravished to his lechery.
Many were there, he could command no more;
He quarreled, fought, bled; and turned out of door,   110
  Directly came to me hanging the head,
  And constantly awhile must keep his bed.

Satire II

Sir, though (I thank God for it) I do hate
Perfectly all this town; yet there's one state
In all ill things so excellently best,
That hate, towards them, breeds pity towards the rest.
Though poetry indeed be such a sin
As I think that brings dearths, and Spaniards in,
Though like the pestilence and old fashioned love,
Riddlingly it catch men, and doth remove
Never, till it be starved out; yet their state
Is poor, disarmed, like papists, not worth hate.   10
One (like a wretch, which at bar judged as dead,
Yet prompts him which stands next, and cannot read,
And saves his life) gives idiot actors means
(Starving himself) to live by'his laboured scenes;
As in some organ, puppets dance above
And bellows pant below, which them do move.
One would move love by rhythms, but witchcraft's
    charms
Bring not now their old fears, nor their old harms;
Rams and slings now are seely battery,
Pistolets are the best artillery.   20
And they who write to lords, rewards to get,
Are they not like singers at doors for meat?
And they who write, because all write, have still
That excuse for writing, and for writing ill.
But he is worst who (beggarly) doth chaw
Others' wits' fruits, and in his ravenous maw

Rankly digested, doth those things out-spew
As his own things; and they're his own, 'tis true,
For if one eat my meat, though it be known
30 The meat was mine, th'excrement is his own.
But these do me no harm, nor they which use
To outdo dildoes, and out-usure Jews;
To'out-drink the sea, to'out-swear the Litany;
Who with sins of'all kinds as familiar be
As confessors; and for whose sinful sake,
Schoolmen new tenements in hell must make;
Whose strange sins, canonists could hardly tell
In which commandment's large receipt they dwell.
But these punish themselves; the insolence
40 Of Coscus only breeds my just offence,
Whom time (which rots all, and makes botches pox,
And plodding on, must make a calf an ox)
Hath made a lawyer, which was (alas) of late
But scarce a poet, jollier of this state
Than are new beneficed ministers, he throws
Like nets, or lime-twigs, wheresoe'er he goes,
His title'of barrister, on every wench,
And woos in language of the pleas and bench:
A motion, Lady; speak Coscus; I have been
50 In love ever since tricesimo of'the Queen,
Continual claims I'have made, injunctions got
To stay my rival's suit, that he should not
Proceed. Spare me. In Hilary term I went;
You said, if I return next size in Lent,
I should be in remitter of your grace;
In th'interim my letters should take place
Of affidavits; words, words, which would tear
The tender labyrinth of a soft maid's ear
More, more, than ten Sclavonians' scolding, more
60 Than when winds in our ruined abbeys roar;
When sick with poetry, and possessed with muse
Thou wast, and mad, I hoped; but men which choose
Law practice for mere gain, bold soul, repute
Worse than embrothelled strumpet's prostitute.

Now like an owl-like watchman, he must walk
His hand still at a bill; now he must talk
Idly, like prisoners, which whole months will swear
That only suretyship hath brought them there,
And to'every suitor lie in every thing,
Like a king's favorite, yea like a king;   70
Like a wedge in a block, wring to the bar,
Bearing like asses; and more shameless far
Than carted whores lie to the grave judge; for
Bastardy'abounds not in kings' titles, nor
Simony'and sodomy in churchmen's lives,
As these things do in him; by these he thrives.
Shortly'(as the sea) he'll compass all our land,
From Scots to Wight, from Mount to Dover
          strand.
And spying heirs melting with luxury,
Satan will not joy at their sins, as he.   80
For as a thrifty wench scrapes kitchen stuff,
And barreling the droppings and the snuff
Of wasting candles, which in thirty year
(Relic-like kept) perchance buys wedding gear;
Piecemeal he gets lands, and spends as much time
Wringing each acre, as men pulling prime.
In parchments then, large as his fields, he draws
Assurances, big as glossed civil laws,
So huge that men (in our time's forwardness)
Are Fathers of the Church for writing less.   90
These he writes not; nor for these written pays,
Therefore spares no length; as in those first days
When Luther was professed, he did desire
Short Pater nosters, saying as a friar
Each day his beads, but having left those laws,
Adds to Christ's prayer the power and glory clause.
But when he sells or changes land, he'impairs
His writings, and (unwatched) leaves out, *ses heires*,
As slyly'as any commenter goes by
Hard words, or sense; or in divinity   100

As controverters, in vouched texts, leave out
Shrewd words, which might against them clear the
    doubt.
Where are those spread woods which clothed heretofore
Those bought lands? Not built, nor burnt within door.
Where's th'old landlord's troops, and alms? In great halls
Carthusian fasts, and fulsome bacchanals
Equally'I hate; means bless; in rich men's homes
I bid kill some beasts, but no hecatombs,
None starve, none surfeit so; but (O) we'allow
110 Good works as good, but out of fashion now,
Like old rich wardrobes; but my words none draws
Within the vast reach of th'huge statute laws.

Satire III

Kind pity chokes my spleen; brave scorn forbids
Those tears to issue which swell my eyelids;
I must not laugh, nor weep sins, and be wise;
Can railing then cure these worn maladies?
Is not our mistress, fair Religion,
As worthy'of all our soul's devotion
As virtue was to the first blinded age?
Are not heaven's joys as valiant to assuage
Lusts as earth's honour was to them? Alas,
10 As we do them in means, shall they surpass
Us in the end, and shall thy father's spirit
Meet blind philosophers in heaven, whose merit
Of strict life may be'imputed faith, and hear
Thee, whom he taught so easy ways and near
To follow, damned? O, if thou dar'st, fear this;
This fear great courage and high valour is.
Dar'st thou aid mutinous Dutch, and dar'st thou lay
Thee in ships, wooden sepulchres, a prey
To leaders' rage, to storms, to shot, to dearth?
20 Dar'st thou dive seas and dungeons of the earth?

Hast thou courageous fire to thaw the ice
Of frozen North discoveries? And thrice
Colder than salamanders, like divine
Children in th'oven, fires of Spain, and the line,
Whose countries limbecks to our bodies be,
Canst thou for gain bear? And must every he
Which cries not, Goddess, to thy mistress, draw,
Or eat thy poisonous words? Courage of straw!
O desperate coward, wilt thou seem bold, and
To thy foes and His (Who made thee to stand   30
Sentinel in His world's garrison) thus yield,
And for forbidden wars, leave th'appointed field?
Know thy foe, the foul Devil he'is, whom thou
Strivest to please, for hate, not love, would allow
Thee fain, His whole realm to be quit; and as
The world's all parts wither away and pass,
So the world's self, thy other loved foe, is
In her decrepit wane, and thou, loving this,
Dost love a withered and worn strumpet; last,
Flesh (itself's death) and joys which flesh can taste,   40
Thou lov'st; and thy fair goodly soul, which doth
Give this flesh power to taste joy, thou dost loathe.
Seek true religion. O where? Mirreus
Thinking her unhoused here, and fled from us,
Seeks her at Rome; there, because he doth know
That she was there a thousand years ago,
He loves her rags so, as we here obey
The statecloth where the Prince sat yesterday.
Crants to such brave loves will not be enthralled,
But loves her only, who'at Geneva'is called   50
Religion, plain, simple, sullen, young,
Contemptuous, yet unhandsome, as among
Lecherous humours, there is one that judges
No wenches wholesome, but coarse country drudges.
Graius stays still at home here, and because
Some preachers, vile ambitious bawds, and laws,
Still new like fashions, bid him think that she
Which dwells with us is only perfect, he

Embraceth her whom his godfathers will
60   Tender to him, being tender, as wards still
Take such wives as their guardians offer, or
Pay values. Careless Phrygius doth abhor
All because all cannot be good, as one
Knowing some women whores, dares marry none.
Gracchus loves all as one, and thinks that so
As women do in diverse countries go
In diverse habits, yet are still one kind,
So doth, so is Religion; and this blind-
ness too much light breeds; but unmoved thou
70   Of force must one, and forced but one allow;
And the right; ask thy father which is she,
Let him ask his; though truth and falsehood be
Near twins, yet truth a little elder is;
Be busy to seek her; believe me this,
He's not of none, nor worst, that seeks the best.
To'adore, or scorn an image, or protest,
May all be bad; doubt wisely; in strange way
To stand inquiring right is not to stray;
To sleep, or run wrong, is. On a huge hill,
80   Cragged and steep, Truth stands, and he that will
Reach her, about must, and about must go;
And what the'hill's suddenness resists, win so;
Yet strive so, that before age, death's twilight,
Thy soul rest, for none can work in that night.
To will implies delay; therefore now do;
Hard deeds, the body's pains; hard knowledge too
The mind's endeavours reach, and mysteries
Are like the sun, dazzling, yet plain to'all eyes.
Keep the'truth which thou hast found; men do not
       stand
90   In so ill case, that God hath with His hand
Signed kings' blank charters to kill whom they hate,
Nor are they vicars, but hangmen to fate.
Fool and wretch, wilt thou let thy soul be tied
To man's laws, by which she shall not be tried

At the last day? Will it then boot thee
To say a Philip or a Gregory,
A Harry or a Martin taught thee this?
Is not this excuse for mere contraries
Equally strong? Cannot both sides say so?
That thou mayest rightly'obey power, her bounds   100
    know;
Those passed, her nature,'and name is changed; to be
Then humble to her is idolatry.
As streams are, power is; those blest flowers that
    dwell
At the rough stream's calm head thrive and do well,
But having left their roots, and themselves given
To the stream's tyrannous rage, alas, are driven
Through mills, and rocks, and woods, and at last,
    almost
Consumed in going, in the sea are lost:
So perish souls, which more choose men's unjust
Power from God claimed, than God Himself to   110
    trust.

Satire V

Thou shalt not laugh in this leaf, Muse, nor they
Whom any pity warms; he which did lay
Rules to make courtiers (he, being understood,
May make good courtiers, but who courtiers good?)
Frees from the sting of jests all who'in extreme
Are wretched or wicked: of these two a theme
Charity and liberty give me. What is he
Who officers' rage and suitors' misery
Can write, and jest? If all things be in all,
As I think, since all which were, are, and shall   10
Be, be made of the same elements,
Each thing, each thing implies or represents.
Then man is a world in which officers
Are the vast ravishing seas; and suitors,

Springs, now full, now shallow, now dry, which to
That which drowns them, run; these self reasons do
Prove the world a man, in which officers
Are the devouring stomach, and suitors
The excrements which they void. All men are dust;
How much worse are suitors, who to men's lust
Are made preys. O worse than dust, or worm's meat,
For they do eat you now, whose selves worms shall eat.
They are the mills which grind you, yet you are
The wind which drives them; and a wasteful war
Is fought against you, and you fight it; they
Adulterate law, and you prepare their way
Like wittols; th'issue your own ruin is.
Greatest and fairest Empress, know you this?
Alas, no more than Thames' calm head doth know
Whose meads her arms drown, or whose corn o'erflow;
You, sir, whose righteousness she loves, whom I,
By having leave to serve, am most richly
For service paid, authorized, now begin
To know and weed out this enormous sin.
O age of rusty iron! Some better wit
Call it some worse name if ought equal it,
The Iron Age that was when justice was sold, now
Injustice is sold dearer far. Allow
All demands, fees, and duties; gamesters, anon
The money which you sweat, and swear for, is gone
Into other hands, so controverted lands
'Scape, like Angelica, the strivers' hands.
If law be in the judge's heart, and he
Have no heart to resist letter or fee,
Where wilt thou'appeal? Power of the courts below
Flow from the first main head, and these can throw
Thee, if they suck thee in, to misery,
To fetters, halters; but if th'injury
Steel thee to dare complain, alas, thou goest
Against the stream, when upwards, when thou'art most
Heavy'and most faint; and in these labours they,
'Gainst whom thou should'st complain, will in the way

20

30

40

50

Become great seas, o'er which, when thou shalt be
Forced to make golden bridges, thou shalt see
That all thy gold was drowned in them before;
All things follow their like, only who have may have
 more.
Judges are gods; he, who made and said them so,
Meant not that men should be'forced to them to go
By means of angels; when supplications
We send to God, to Dominations,   60
Powers, Cherubim, and all heaven's courts, if we
Should pay fees as here, daily bread would be
Scarce to kings; so 'tis. Would it not anger
A stoic, a coward, yea a martyr,
To see a pursuivant come in, and call
All his clothes, copes; books, primers; and all
His plate, chalices; and mistake them away,
And ask a fee for coming? O, ne'er may
Fair law's white reverend name be strumpeted
To warrant thefts; she is established   70
Recorder to Destiny on earth, and she
Speaks Fate's words, and but tells us who must be
Rich, who poor, who in chairs, who in jails;
She is all fair, but yet hath foul long nails
With which she scratcheth suitors; in bodies
Of men, so'in law, nails are th'extremities,
So'officers stretch to more than law can do,
As our nails reach what no else part comes to.
Why barest thou to yon officer? Fool, hath he
Got those goods, for which erst men bared to thee? 80
Fool, twice, thrice, thou hast bought wrong, and now
 hungrily
Beg'st right; but that dole comes not till these die.
Thou had'st much, and law's Urim and Thummim try
Thou would'st for more; and for all hast paper
Enough to clothe all the great carrack's pepper.
Sell that, and by that thou much more shalt lease
Than Haman when he sold his antiquities.

O wretch that thy fortunes should moralize
Aesop's fables, and make tales, prophecies.
90 Thou'art the swimming dog whom shadows cozened,
And divest, near drowning, for what vanished.

LETTERS

The Storm
To Mr Christopher Brooke

Thou which art I ('tis nothing to be so),
Thou which art still thyself, by these shalt know
Part of our passage; and a hand or eye
By Hilliard drawn is worth a history
By a worse painter made; and (without pride)
When by thy judgement they are dignified,
My lines are such. 'Tis the pre-eminence
Of friendship only to'impute excellence.
England, to whom we'owe what we be and have,
10 Sad that her sons did seek a foreign grave
(For Fate's or Fortune's drifts none can soothsay;
Honour and misery have one face and way.)
From out her pregnant entrails sighed a wind
Which at th'air's middle marble room did find
Such strong resistance that itself it threw
Downward again; and so when it did view
How in the port our fleet dear time did lose,
Withering like prisoners which lie but for fees,
Mildly it kissed our sails, and fresh and sweet,
20 As to a stomach starved, whose insides meet,
Meat comes, it came; and swelled our sails, when we
So joyed, as Sara'her swelling joyed to see.

But 'twas but so kind as our countrymen,
Which bring friends one day's way, and leave them
    then.
Then like two mighty kings, which dwelling far
Asunder, meet against a third to war,
The south and west winds joined, and as they blew,
Waves like a rolling trench before them threw.
Sooner than you read this line, did the gale,
Like shot not feared till felt, our sails assail;   30
And what at first was called a gust, the same
Hath now a storm's, anon a tempest's name.
Jonah, I pity thee, and curse those men
Who, when the storm raged most, did wake thee then;
Sleep is pain's easiest salve, and doth fulfil
All offices of death, except to kill.
But when I waked, I saw that I saw not.
I and the sun which should teach me'had forgot
East, west, day, night, and I could only say,
If'the world had lasted, now it had been day.   40
Thousands our noises were, yet we'mongst all
Could none by his right name, but thunder call;
Lightning was all our light, and it rained more
Than if the sun had drunk the sea before;
Some coffined in their cabins lie,'equally
Grieved that they are not dead, and yet must die.
And as sin-burdened souls from graves will creep
At the last day, some forth their cabins peep,
And tremblingly'ask what news, and do hear so,
As jealous husbands, what they would not know.   50
Some sitting on the hatches would seem there,
With hideous gazing, to fear away fear.
Then note they the ship's sicknesses, the mast
Shaked with this ague, and the hold and waist
With a salt dropsy clogged, and all our tacklings
Snapping, like too-high-stretched treble strings.
And from our tattered sails, rags drop down so,
As from one hanged in chains a year ago.

Even our ordnance, placed for our defence,
60   Strive to break loose, and 'scape away from thence.
Pumping hath tired our men, and what's the gain?
Seas into seas thrown, we suck in again;
Hearing hath deaf'd our sailors; and if they
Knew how to hear, there's none knows what to say.
Compared to these storms, death is but a qualm,
Hell somewhat lightsome, the'Bermudas calm.
Darkness, light's elder brother, his birthright
Claims o'er this world, and to heaven hath chased light.
All things are one, and that one none can be,
70   Since all forms uniform deformity
Doth cover, so that we, except God say
Another Fiat, shall have no more day.
So violent, yet long, these furies be,
That though thine absence starve me,'I wish not thee.

The Calm

Our storm is past, and that storm's tyrannous rage,
A stupid calm, but nothing it doth 'suage.
The fable is inverted, and far more
A block afflicts now than a stork before.
Storms chafe, and soon wear out themselves, or us;
In calms heaven laughs to see us languish thus.
As steady'as I can wish that my thoughts were,
Smooth as thy mistress glass or what shines there,
The sea is now. And as the isles which we
10   Seek when we can move, our ships rooted be.
As water did in storms, now pitch runs out,
As lead when a fired church becomes one spout.
And all our beauty and our trim decays,
Like courts removing or like ended plays.
The fighting place now seamen's rags supply;
And all the tackling is a frippery.
No use of lanterns; and in one place lay
Feathers and dust, today and yesterday.

Earth's hollownesses, which the world's lungs are,
Have no more wind than the'upper vault of air.   20
We can nor lost friends nor sought foes recover,
But meteor-like, save that we move not, hover.
Only the calenture together draws
Dear friends which meet dead in great fishes' jaws;
And on the hatches, as on altars, lies
Each one, his own priest and own sacrifice.
Who live, that miracle do multiply
Where walkers in hot ovens do not die.
If in despite of these we swim, that hath
No more refreshing than our brimstone bath;   30
But from the sea into the ship we turn,
Like parboiled wretches on the coals to burn.
Like Bajazet encaged, the shepherds scoff,
Or like slack-sinewed Sampson, his hair off,
Languish our ships. Now as a myriad
Of ants durst th'Emperor's loved snake invade,
The crawling galleys, sea-gaols, finny chips,
Might brave our pinnaces, now bed-rid ships.
Whether a rotten state and hope of gain,
Or, to disuse me from the queasy pain   40
Of being beloved and loving, or the thirst
Of honour or fair death, out pushed me first,
I lose my end: for here as well as I
A desperate may live and a coward die.
Stag, dog, and all which from or towards flies,
Is paid with life, or pray, or doing dies.
Fate grudges us all, and doth subtly lay
A scourge,'gainst which we all forget to pray;
He that at sea prays for more wind, as well
Under the poles may beg cold, heat in hell.   50
What are we then? How little more, alas,
Is man now than before he was? He was
Nothing; for us, we are for nothing fit;
Chance or ourselves still disproportion it.
We have no power, no will, no sense; I lie,
I should not then thus feel this misery.

To Mr Henry Wotton

Here's no more news than virtue; I may as well
Tell you Calis or St Michael's tale for news, as tell
That vice doth here habitually dwell.

Yet, as to'get stomachs, we walk up and down,
And toil, to sweeten rest, so may God frown,
If but to loathe both, I haunt court or town.

For here no one is from the'extremity
Of vice by any other reason free,
But that the next to'him still is worse than he.

10   In this world's warfare they whom rugged Fate
(God's commissary) doth so thoroughly hate
As in'the court's squadron to marshal their state,

If they stand armed with seely honesty,
With wishing prayers and neat integrity,
Like Indians'gainst Spanish hosts they be.

Suspicious boldness to this place belongs,
And to'have as many ears as all have tongues,
Tender to know, tough to acknowledge wrongs.

Believe me, sir, in my youth's giddiest days,
20   When to be like the court was a play's praise,
Plays were not so like courts, as courts'are like plays.

Then let us at these mimic antics jest,
Whose deepest projects and egregious gests
Are but dull morals of a game at chess.

But now 'tis incongruity to smile;
Therefore I end, and bid farewell a while,
At Court, though *From Court* were the better style.

To Mr Henry Wotton

Sir, more than kisses, letters mingle souls,
For thus friends absent speak. This ease controls
The tediousness of my life; but for these
I could ideate nothing which could please,
But I should wither in one day, and pass
To'a bottle'of hay, that am a lock of grass.
Life is a voyage, and in our life's ways
Countries, courts, towns are rocks or remoras;
They break or stop all ships, yet our state's such
That, though than pitch they stain worse, we must   10
    touch.
If in the furnace of the even line,
Or under th'adverse icy poles thou pine,
Thou know'st two temperate regions girded in
Dwell there, but O, what refuge canst thou win,
Parched in the court and in the country frozen?
Shall cities built of both extremes be chosen?
Can dung or garlic be'a perfume? Or can
A scorpion or torpedo cure a man?
Cities are worst of all three; of all three
(O knotty riddle)'each is worst equally.   20
Cities are sepulchres; they who dwell there
Are carcasses, as if no such there were,
And courts are theatres where some men play
Princes, some slaves, all to one end and of one clay.
The country is a desert where no good,
Gained as habits, not born, is understood.
There men become beasts and prone to more evils;
In cities, blocks, and in a lewd court, devils.
As in the first Chaos confusedly
Each element's qualities were in th'other three,   30
So pride, lust, covetise, being several
To these three places, yet all are in all,
And mingled thus, their issue'incestuous.
Falsehood is denizened. Virtue'is barbarous.

Let no man say there, Virtue's flinty wall
Shall lock vice in me, I'll do none, but know'all.
Men are sponges which to pour out, receive;
Who know false play, rather then lose, deceive.
For in best understandings, sin began;
40 Angels sinned first, then devils, and then man.
Only perchance beasts sin not; wretched we
Are beasts in all but white integrity.
I think if men, which in these places live,
Durst look for themselves and themselves retrieve,
They would like strangers greet themselves, seeing then
Utopian youth grown old Italian.
   Be thou thine own home, and in thy self dwell;
Inn anywhere, continuance maketh hell.
And seeing the snail, which everywhere doth roam
50 Carrying his own house still, still is at home,
Follow (for he is easy paced) this snail,
Be thine own palace, or the world's thy jail.
And in the world's sea do not like cork sleep
Upon the water's face, nor in the deep
Sink like a lead without a line, but as
Fishes glide, leaving no print where they pass
Nor making sound, so closely thy course go;
Let men dispute whether thou breathe or no.
Only'in this one thing, be no Galenist. To make
60 Court's hot ambitions wholesome, do not take
A dram of country's dullness; do not add
Correctives, but as chemics, purge the bad.
But, sir, I'advise not you; I rather do
Say o'er those lessons which I learned of you,
Whom, free from German schisms, and lightness
Of France, and fair Italy's faithlessness,
Having from these sucked all they had of worth,
And brought home that faith which you carried forth,
I thoroughly love. But if myself I'have won
To know my rules, I have, and you have,

70 DONNE.

To Mr Rowland Woodward

Like one who'in her third widowhood doth profess
Herself a nun, tied to retiredness,
So'affects my muse now a chaste fallowness,

Since she to few, yet to too many,'hath shown
How love-song weeds and satiric thorns are grown
Where seeds of better arts were early sown.

Though to use and love poetry, to me,
Betrothed to no'one art, be no'adultery,
Omissions of good, ill as ill deeds be.

For though to us it seem'and be light and thin,   10
Yet in those faithful scales, where God throws in
Men's works, vanity weighs as much as sin.

If our souls have stained their first white, yet we
May clothe them with faith and dear honesty
Which God imputes as native purity.

There is no virtue but religion:
Wise, valiant, sober, just are names which none
Want, which want not vice-covering discretion.

Seek we then ourselves in ourselves; for as
Men force the sun with much more force to pass   20
By gathering his beams with a crystal glass,

So we, if we into ourselves will turn,
Blowing our sparks of virtue may out-burn
The straw which doth about our hearts sojourn.

You know, physicians, when they would infuse
Into any'oil the souls of simples, use
Places where they may lie still warm to choose.

So works retiredness in us; to roam
Giddily and be everywhere but at home,
Such freedom doth a banishment become.

We are but termers of ourselves, yet may,
If we can stock ourselves and thrive, uplay
Much, much dear treasure, for the great rent day.

Manure thyself then, to thyself be'approved,
And with vain outward things be no more moved,
But to know that I love thee'and would be loved.

To Mr T. W.

All hail sweet poet, more full of more strong fire
    Than hath or shall enkindle any spirit,
    I loved what nature gave thee, but this merit
Of wit and art I love not but admire;
Who have before or shall write after thee,
Their works, though toughly laboured, will be
    Like infancy or age to man's firm stay,
    Or early and late twilights to mid-day.

Men say, and truly, that they better be
    Which be envied than pitied; therefore I,
    Because I wish thee best, do thee envy;
O would'st thou, by like reason, pity me,
But care not for me; I, that ever was
In nature's, and in fortune's gifts, alas
    (Before thy grace got in the Muses' school),
    A monster and a beggar, am a fool.

O how I grieve, that late borne modesty
    Hath got such root in easy waxen hearts,
    That men may not themselves, their own good parts
Extol, without suspect of surquedry,

For, but thyself, no subject can be found
Worthy thy quill, nor any quill resound
  Thy worth but thine: how good it were to see
  A poem in thy praise, and writ by thee.

Now if this song be too'harsh for rhyme, yet, as
  The painter's bad god made a good devil,
  'Twill be good prose, although the verse be evil,
If thou forget the rhyme as thou dost pass.
Then write, that I may follow, and so be
Thy debtor, thy'echo, thy foil, thy zany.   30
  I shall be thought, if mine like thine I shape,
  All the world's Lyon, though I be thy ape.

To Mr T. W.

Haste thee harsh verse as fast as thy lame measure
  Will give thee leave, to him, my pain and pleasure.
I have given thee, and yet thou art too weak,
  Feet and a reasoning soul and tongue to speak.
Plead for me, and so by thine and my labour,
  I am thy Creator, thou my Saviour.
Tell him, all questions, which men have defended
  Both of the place and pains of hell, are ended;
And 'tis decreed our hell is but privation
  Of him, at least in this earth's habitation: 10
And 'tis where I am, where in every street
  Infections follow, overtake, and meet.
Live I or die, by you my love is sent,
  And you'are my pawns, or else my testament.

To Mr T. W.

Pregnant again with th'old twins, Hope and Fear,
Oft have I asked for thee, both how and where
Thou wert, and what my hopes of letters were,

As in our streets sly beggars narrowly
Watch motions of the giver's hand and eye,
And evermore conceive some hope thereby.

And now thy alms is given, thy letter'is read,
The body risen again, the which was dead,
And thy poor starveling bountifully fed.

10 After this banquet my soul doth say grace,
And praise thee for'it, and zealously embrace
Thy love, though I think thy love in this case
  To be as gluttons, which say'midst their meat,
    They love that best of which they most do eat.

To Mr T. W.

At once, from hence, my lines and I depart,
I to my soft still walks, they to my heart,
I to the nurse, they to the child of art;

Yet as a firm house, though the carpenter
Perish, doth stand, as an ambassador
Lies safe, how e'er his king be in danger,

So, though I languish, pressed with melancholy,
My verse, the strict map of my misery,
Shall live to see that for whose want I die.

Therefore I envy them, and do repent   10
That from unhappy me, things happy'are sent;
Yet as a picture, or bare sacrament,
  Accept these lines, and if in them there be
  Merit of love, bestow that love on me.

To Mr R. W.

Zealously my muse doth salute all thee,
Enquiring of that mystic trinity
Whereof thou'and all to whom heavens do infuse
Like fire, are made: thy body, mind, and muse.
Dost thou recover sickness, or prevent?
Or is thy mind travailed with discontent?
Or art thou parted from the world and me
In a good scorn of the world's vanity?
Or is thy devout muse retired to sing
Upon her tender elegiac string?   10
Our minds part not, join then thy muse with mine,
For mine is barren thus divorced from thine.

To Mr R. W.

Muse not that by thy mind thy body'is led,
For by thy mind, my mind's distempered.
So thy care lives long, for I bearing part,
It eats not only thine, but my swoll'n heart.
And when it gives us intermission,
We take new hearts for it to feed upon.
But as a lay man's genius doth control
Body and mind, the muse being the soul's soul
Of poets, that methinks should ease our anguish,
Although our bodies wither and minds languish.   10
Wright then, that my griefs, which thine got, may be
Cured by thy charming sovereign melody.

To Mr C. B.

Thy friend, whom thy deserts to thee enchain,
   Urged by this inexcusable'occasion,
   Thee and the saint of his affection
Leaving behind, doth of both wants complain;
And let the love I bear to both sustain
   No blot nor maim by this division.
   Strong is this love which ties our hearts in one,
And strong that love pursued with amorous pain;
But though besides thyself I leave behind
   Heaven's liberal and earth's thrice-fair sun,
   Going to where stern winter aye doth won,
Yet, love's hot fires, which martyr my sad mind,
   Do send forth scalding sighs, which have the art
   To melt all ice, but that which walls her heart.

To Mr R. W.

If, as mine is, thy life a slumber be,
   Seem, when thou read'st these lines, to dream of me;
Never did Morpheus nor his brother wear
   Shapes so like those shapes, whom they would appear,
As this my letter is like me, for it
   Hath my name, words, hand, feet, heart, mind and
      wit;
It is my deed of gift of me to thee,
   It is my will, my self the legacy.
So thy retirings I love, yea envy,
   Bred in thee by a wise melancholy,
That I rejoice, that unto where thou art,
   Though I stay here, I can thus send my heart,
As kindly'as any'enamoured patient
   His picture to his absent love hath sent.

All news I think sooner reach thee than me;
 Havens are heavens, and ships, winged angels be,
The which both gospel and stern threat'nings bring;
 Guiana's harvest is nipped in the spring
I fear; and with us (me thinks) Fate deals so
 As with the Jew's guide God did; he did show   20
Him the rich land, but barred his entry in.
 O, slowness is our punishment and sin;
Perchance, these Spanish business being done,
 Which as earth between the moon and sun
Eclipse the light which Guiana would give,
 Our discontinued hopes we shall retrieve;
But if (as all th'All must) hopes smoke away,
 Is not almighty virtue'an India?

If men be worlds, there is in every one
 Some thing to answer in some proportion   30
All the world's riches; and in good men, this
 Virtue our form's form and our soul's soul is.

To Mr R. W.

Kindly'I envy thy song's perfection,
 Built of all th'elements as our bodies are.
 That little'of earth that'is in it is a fair
Delicious garden where all sweets are sown.
In it is cherishing fire which dries in me
 Grief which did drown me, and half quenched by it
 Are satiric fires which urged me to have writ
In scorn of all, for now I admire thee.
 And as air doth fulfill the hollowness
 Of rotten walls, so it mine emptiness,   10
Where tossed and moved it did beget this sound
Which as a lame echo'of thine doth rebound.
 O, I was dead, but since thy song new life did give,
 I recreated even by thy creature live.

H. W. in Hiber. Belligeranti

Went you to conquer? and have so much lost
Yourself that what in you was best and most
Respective friendship should so quickly die?
In public gain my share'is not such that I
Would lose your love for Ireland; better cheap
I pardon death (who though he do not reap,
Yet gleans he many of our friends away)
Than that your waking mind should be a prey
To lethargies. Let shots, and bogs, and skeins
With bodies deal, as fate bids or restrains;
Ere sicknesses attack, young death is best,
Who pays before his death doth 'scape arrest.
Let not your soul (at first with graces filled,
And since and through crooked limbecks, stilled
In many schools and courts which quicken it)
Itself unto the Irish negligence submit.
I ask not laboured letters which should wear
Long papers out, nor letters which should fear
Dishonest carriage or seers' art,
Nor such as from the brain come, but the heart.

To Sir H. W. at His Going Ambassador to Venice

After those reverend papers, whose soul is
    Our good and great King's loved hand and feared
        name,
By which to you he derives much of his,
    And (how he may) makes you almost the same,

A taper of his torch, a copy writ
    From his original, and a fair beam
Of the same warm and dazzling sun, though it
    Must in another sphere his virtue stream,

After those learned papers which your hand
   Hath stored with notes of use and pleasures too,   10
From which rich treasury you may command
   Fit matter whether you will write or do,

After those loving papers, where friends send
   With glad grief, to your seaward steps, farewell,
Which thicken on you now, as prayers ascend
   To heaven in troops at'a good man's passing bell,

Admit this honest paper, and allow
   It such an audience as you yourself would ask;
What you must say at Venice this means now,
   And hath for nature, what you have for task: 20

To swear much love, not to be changed before
   Honour alone will to your fortune fit;
Nor shall I then honour your fortune more
   Than I have done your honour wanting it.

But 'tis an easier load (though both oppress)
   To want, than govern, greatness, for we are
In that our own and only business,
   In this, we must for others' vices care;

'Tis therefore well your spirits now are placed
   In their last furnace, in activity,   30
Which fits them (schools and courts and wars o'erpast)
   To touch and test in any best degree.

For me (if there be such a thing as I)
   Fortune (if there be such a thing as she)
Spies that I bear so well her tyranny
   That she thinks nothing else so fit for me;

But though she part us, to hear my oft prayers
   For your increase, God is as near me here;
And to send you what I shall beg, His stairs
40   In length and ease are alike everywhere.

To Sir Henry Goodyere

Who makes the past a pattern for next year
   Turns no new leaf, but still the same things reads;
Seen things he sees again, heard things doth hear,
   And makes his life but like a pair of beads.

A palace, when 'tis that, which it should be,
   Leaves growing and stands such, or else decays;
But he which dwells there is not so, for he
   Strives to urge upward, and his fortune raise;

So had your body'her morning, hath her noon,
10   And shall not better; her next change is night;
But her fair larger guest, to'whom sun and moon
   Are sparks and short lived, claims another right.

The noble soul by age grows lustier,
   Her appetite and her digestion mend;
We must not starve, nor hope to pamper her
   With women's milk and pap unto the end.

Provide you manlier diet; you have seen
   All libraries, which are schools, camps, and courts;
But ask your garners if you have not been
20   In harvests too indulgent to your sports.

Would you redeem it? Then yourself transplant
   A while from hence. Perchance outlandish ground
Bears no more wit than ours, but yet more scant
   Are those diversions there which here abound.

To be a stranger hath that benefit,
  We can beginnings, but not habits choke.
Go, whither? Hence, you get, if you forget;
  New faults, till they prescribe in us, are smoke.

Our soul, whose country'is heaven, and God her
    father,
  Into this world, corruption's sink, is sent;   30
Yet so much in her travail she doth gather
  That she returns home wiser than she went.

It pays you well, if it teach you to spare,
  And make you'ashamed, to make your hawk's
    praise, yours,
Which when herself she lessens in the air,
  You then first say that high enough she towers.

Howsoever, keep the lively taste you hold
  Of God; love him as now, but fear him more,
And in your afternoons think what you told
  And promised him at morning prayer before.   40

Let falsehood like a discord anger you,
  Else be not froward. But why do I touch
Things of which none is in your practice new,
  And tables or fruit-trenchers teach as much;

But thus I make you keep your promise, sir;
  Riding I had you, though you still stayed there,
And in these thoughts, although you never stir,
  You came with me to Mitcham, and are here.

To the Countess of Huntingdon

That unripe side of earth, that heavy clime
That gives us man up now, like Adam's time
Before he ate; man's shape, that would yet be
(Knew they not it, and feared beasts' company)
So naked at this day, as though man there
From paradise so great a distance were,
As yet the news could not arrived be
Of Adam's tasting the forbidden tree,
Deprived of that free state which they were in,
And wanting the reward, yet bear the sin;
    But, as from extreme heights who downward looks,
Sees men at children's shapes, rivers at brooks,
And loseth younger forms, so to your eye
These (Madame), that without your distance lie,
Must either mist or nothing seem to be,
Who are at home but wit's mere atomi.
But I, who can behold them move and stay,
Have found myself to you just their midway,
And now must pity them; for as they do
Seem sick to me, just so must I to you,
Yet neither will I vex your eyes to see
A sighing ode, nor cross-armed elegy.
I come not to call pity from your heart,
Like some white-livered dotard that would part
Else from his slippery soul with a faint groan,
And faithfully (without you smiled) were gone.
I cannot feel the tempest of a frown,
I may be raised by love, but not thrown down.
Though I can pity those sigh twice a day,
I hate that thing whispers itself away.
Yet since all love is fever, who to trees
Doth talk, doth yet in love's cold ague freeze.
'Tis love, but with such fatal weakness made
That it destroys itself with its own shade.

Who first looked sad, grieved, pined, and showed his
    pain,
Was he that first taught women to disdain.
  As all things were one nothing, dull and weak,
Until this raw disordered heap did break,
And several desires led parts away –
Water declined with earth, the air did stay,   40
Fire rose, and each from other but untied,
Themselves unprisoned were and purified –
So was love first in vast confusion hid,
An unripe willingness which nothing did,
A thirst, an appetite which had no ease,
That found a want but knew not what would please.
What pretty innocence in those days moved?
Man ignorantly walked by her he loved;
Both sighed and interchanged a speaking eye,
Both trembled and were sick, both knew not why.   50
That natural fearfulness that struck man dumb,
Might well (those times considered) man become.
As all discoverers whose first assay
Finds but the place, after, the nearest way,
So passion is to woman's love, about,
Nay farther off, than when we first set out.
It is not love that sueth or doth contend;
Love either conquers, or but meets a friend.
Man's better part consists of purer fire,
And finds itself allowed ere it desire.   60
Love is wise here, keeps home, gives reason sway,
And journeys not till it find summer-way.
A weather-beaten lover but once known
Is sport for every girl to practise on.
Who strives through woman's scorns, women to
    know,
Is lost, and seeks his shadow to outgo;
It must be sickness after one disdain,
Though he be called aloud to look again.
Let others sigh and grieve; one cunning slight
Shall freeze my love to crystal in a night.   70

I can love first, and (if I win) love still,
And cannot be removed unless she will.
It is her fault if I unsure remain,
She only can untie, and bind again.
The honesties of love with ease I do,
But am no porter for a tedious woe.

   But (Madame) I now think on you, and here
Where we are at our heights, you but appear;
We are but clouds, you rise from our noon-ray
80   But a foul shadow, not your break of day.
You are at first hand all that's fair and right,
And others' good reflects but back your light.
You are a perfectness, so curious hit
That youngest flatteries do scandal it.
For what is more doth what you are restrain,
And though beyond, is down the hill again.
We'have no next way to you, we cross to it:
You are the straight line, thing praised, attribute,
Each good in you's a light; so many'a shade
90   You make, and in them are your motions made.
These are your pictures to the life. From far
We see you move, and here your zanies are,
So that no fountain good there is doth grow
In you, but our dim actions faintly show.

   Then find I, if man's noblest part be love,
Your purest lustre must that shadow move.
The soul with body is a heaven combined
With earth, and for man's ease, but nearer joined.
Where thoughts the stars of soul we understand,
100   We guess not their large natures but command.
And love in you that bounty is of light
That gives to all, and yet hath infinite.
Whose heat doth force us thither to intend,
But soul we find too earthly to ascend,
Till slow access hath made it wholly pure,
Able immortal clearness to endure.
Who dares aspire this journey with a stain
Hath weight will force him headlong back again.

No more can impure man retain and move
In that pure region of a worthy love   110
Than earthly substance can unforced aspire,
And leave his nature to converse with fire;
   Such may have eye and hand, may sigh, may speak,
But like swoll'n bubbles, when they'are high'st they
      break.
Though far-removed northern fleets scarce find
The sun's comfort, others think him too kind.
There is an equal distance from her eye;
Men perish too far off, and burn too nigh.
But as air takes the sunbeam's equal bright
From the first rays to his last opposite,   120
So able men, blest with a virtuous love,
Remote or near, or howsoe'er they move,
Their virtue breaks all clouds that might annoy;
There is no emptiness, but all is joy.
He much profanes whom violent heats do move
To still his wandering rage of passion, love.
Love that imparts in everything delight,
Is feigned which only tempts man's appetite.
Why love among the virtues is not known
Is that love is them all contract in one.   130

To Mrs M. H.

Mad paper stay, and grudge not here to burn
   With all those suns whom my brain did create;
At least lie hid with me till thou return
   To rags again, which is thy native state.

What though thou have enough unworthiness
   To come unto great place as others do,
That's much (emboldens, pulls, thrusts I confess),
   But 'tis not all; thou should'st be wicked too.

And that thou canst not learn, or not of me;
10   Yet thou wilt go. Go, since thou goest to her
Who lacks but faults to be a prince, for she,
      Truth, whom they dare not pardon, dares prefer.

But when thou com'st to that perplexing eye
      Which equally claims love and reverence,
Thou wilt not long dispute it, thou wilt die;
      And, having little now, have then no sense.

Yet when her warm redeeming hand, which is
      A miracle, and made such to work more,
Doth touch thee (saple's leaf), thou grow'st by this
20   Her creature, glorified more than before.

Then, as a mother which delights to hear
      Her early child misspeak half uttered words,
Or because majesty doth never fear
      Ill or bold speech, she audience affords.

And then, cold speechless wretch, thou diest again,
      And wisely; what discourse is left for thee?
For speech of ill, and her, thou must abstain,
      And is there any good which is not she?

Yet may'st thou praise her servants, though not her,
30   And wit, and virtue,'and honour her attend;
And since they'are but her clothes, thou shalt not err
      If thou her shape and beauty'and grace commend.

Who knows thy destiny? When thou hast done,
      Perchance her cabinet may harbour thee,
Whither all noble,'ambitious wits do run,
      A nest almost as full of good as she.

When thou art there, if any whom we know
   Were saved before, and did that heaven partake,
When she revolves his papers, mark what show
   Of favour, she, alone, to them doth make.   40

Mark, if to get them, she o'er skip the rest;
   Mark, if she read them twice, or kiss the name;
Mark, if she do the same that they protest;
   Mark, if she mark whether her woman came.

Mark, if slight things be'objected, and o'er blown;
   Mark, if her oaths against him be not still
Reserved, and that she grieves she's not her own,
   And chides the doctrine that denies freewill.

I bid thee not do this to be my spy,
   Nor to make myself her familiar;   50
But so much do I love her choice that I
   Would fain love him that shall be loved of her.

To the Countess of Bedford

Madame,
Reason is our soul's left hand, faith her right,
By these we reach divinity, that's you;
Their loves, who have the blessings of your light,
Grew from their reason, mine from fair faith grew.

But as, although a squint left-handedness
Be'ungracious, yet we cannot want that hand,
So would I, not to increase but to'express
My faith, as I believe, so understand.

Therefore I study you first in your saints,
Those friends whom your election glorifies,   10
Then in your deeds, accesses, and restraints,
And what you read, and what yourself devise.

But soon the reasons why you'are loved by all
Grow infinite, and so pass reason's reach,
Then back again to'implicit faith I fall,
And rest on what the catholic voice doth teach:

That you are good, and not one heretic
Denies it; if he did, yet you are so.
For rocks, which high-topped and deep-rooted stick,
20   Waves wash, not undermine, nor overthrow.

In every thing there naturally grows
A balsamum to keep it fresh and new,
If'twere not injured by extrinsic blows;
Your birth and beauty are this balm in you.

But you of learning, and religion,
And virtue,'and such ingredients have made
A mithridate whose operation
Keeps off or cures what can be done or said.

Yet this is not your physic, but your food,
30   A diet fit for you; for you are here
The first good angel, since the world's frame stood,
That ever did in woman's shape appear.

Since you are then God's masterpiece, and so
His factor for our loves, do as you do,
Make your return home gracious, and bestow
This life on that; so make one life of two.
      For so God help me,'I would not miss you there
      For all the good which you can do me here.

To the Countess of Bedford

Honour is so sublime perfection,
And so refined, that when God was alone
And creatureless at first, himself had none;

But as of the'elements, these which we tread
Produce all things with which we'are joyed or fed,
And those are barren both above our head;

So from low persons doth all honour flow;
Kings, whom they would have honoured, to us show,
And but direct our honour, not bestow.

For when from herbs the pure part must be won   10
From gross, by stilling, this is better done
By despised dung, than by the fire or sun.

Care not then, Madame,'how low your praisers lie;
In labourers' ballads oft more piety
God finds than in Te Deums' melody.

And ordnance raised on towers so many mile
Send not their voice, nor last so long a while
As fires from th'earth's low vaults in Sicil Isle.

Should I say I lived darker than were true,
Your radiation can all clouds subdue,   20
But one,'tis best light to contemplate you –

You, for whose body God made better clay,
Or took soul's stuff such as shall late decay,
Or such as needs small change at the last day.

This, as an amber drop enwraps a bee,
Covering discovers your quick soul, that we
May in your through-shine front your heart's thoughts
        see.

You teach (though we learn not) a thing unknown
To our late times, the use of specular stone,
30   Through which all things within without were shown.

Of such were temples; so'and of such you are;
Being and seeming is your equal care,
And virtue's whole sum is but know and dare.

But as our souls of growth and souls of sense
Have birthright of our reason's soul, yet hence
They fly not from that, nor seek precedence.

Nature's first lesson, so, discretion,
Must not grudge zeal a place, nor yet keep none,
Not banish itself, nor religion.

40   Discretion is a wiseman's soul, and so
Religion is a Christian's, and you know
How these are one; her yea is not her no.

Nor may we hope to solder still and knit
These two, and dare to break them, nor must wit
Be colleague to religion, but be it.

In those poor types of God (round circles) so
Religion tips, the pieceless centres flow,
And are in all the lines which all ways go.

If either ever wrought in you alone
50   Or principally, then religion
Wrought your ends, and your ways, discretion.

Go thither still, go the same way you went,
Who so would change, do covet or repent;
Neither can reach you, great and innocent.

To the Countess of Bedford

Madame,
You have refined me, and to worthiest things
Virtue, art, beauty, fortune, now I see
Rareness or use, not nature, value brings;
And such, as they are circumstanced, they be.
    Two ills can ne'er perplex us, sin to'excuse;
    But of two good things, we may leave and choose.

Therefore at court, which is not virtue's clime,
Where a transcendent height (as lowness me)
Makes her not be, or not show, all my rhyme
Your virtues challenge which there rarest be;   10
    For as dark texts need notes, there some must be
    To usher virtue, and say, This is she.

So in the country'is beauty; to this place
You are the season (Madame), you the day,
'Tis but a grave of spices till your face
Exhale them, and a thick close bud display.
    Widowed and reclused else, her sweets
        she'enshrines
    As China when the sun at Brazil dines.

Out from your chariot morning breaks at night,
And falsifies both computations so;   20
Since a new world doth rise here from your light,
We your new creatures, by new reck'nings go.
    This shows that you from nature loathly stray,
    That suffer not an artificial day.

In this you'have made the court the'antipodes,
And willed your delegate, the vulgar sun,
To do profane autumnal offices,
Whil'st here to you, we sacrificers run;
   And whether priests or organs, you we'obey,
30   We sound your influence, and your dictates say.

Yet to that deity which dwells in you,
Your virtuous soul, I now not sacrifice;
These are petitions and not hymns; they sue
But that I may survey the edifice.
   In all religions as much care hath been
   Of temples' frames and beauty,'as rites within.

As all which go to Rome do not thereby
Esteem religions, and hold fast the best,
But serve discourse and curiosity,
40   With that which doth religion but invest,
    And shun th'entangling labyrinths of schools,
    And make it wit to think the wiser fools;

So in this pilgrimage I would behold
You as you'are, virtue's temple, not as she,
What walls of tender crystal her enfold,
What eyes, hands, bosom, her pure altars be;
   And after this survey, oppose to all
   Babblers of chapels, you th'Escuriall.

Yet not as consecrate, but merely'as fair;
50 On these I cast a lay and country eye.
Of past and future stories which are rare,
I find you all record, all prophecy.
   Purge but the book of fate that it admit
   No sad nor guilty legends, you are it.

If good and lovely were not one, of both
You were the transcript and original,
The elements, the parent, and the growth,
And every piece of you is both their all,
    So'entire are all your deeds and you that you
    Must do the same thing still; you cannot two.   60

But these (as nice thin school divinity
Serves heresy to further or repress)
Taste of poetic rage, or flattery,
And need not, where all hearts one truth profess;
    Oft from new proofs and new phrase, new doubts
        grow,
    As strange attire aliens the men we know.

Leaving then the busy praise and all appeal
To higher courts, sense's decree is true,
The mine, the magazine, the commonweal,
The story'of beauty'in Twicknam is, and you.   70
    Who hath seen one, would both, as who had been
    In paradise would seek the Cherubim.

To the Countess of Bedford

T'have written then, when you writ, seemed to me
    Worst of spiritual vices, simony,
And not t'have written then seems little less
    Than worst of civil vices, thanklessness.
In this, my debt, I seemed loath to confess,
    In that I seemed to shun beholdingness.
But 'tis not so; nothings, as I am, may
    Pay all they have, and yet have all to pay.
Such borrow in their payments, and owe more,
    By having leave to write so, than before.   10
Yet since rich mines in barren grounds are shown,
    May not I yield (not gold) but coal or stone?

Temples were not demolished though profane:
   Here Peter Jove's, there Paul hath Dian's fane.
So whether my hymns you admit or choose,
   In me you'have hallowed a pagan muse,
And denizened a stranger who, mistaught
   By blamers of the times they marred, hath sought
Virtues in corners, which now bravely do
20   Shine in the world's best part, or all it, you.
I have been told that virtue'in courtiers' hearts
   Suffers an ostracism and departs.
Profit, ease, fitness, plenty, bid it go,
   But whither, only, knowing you, I know;
Your (or you) virtue two vast uses serves,
   It ransoms one sex, and one court preserves;
There's nothing but your worth, which being true,
   Is known to any other, not to you.
And you can never know it; to admit
30   No knowledge of your worth is some of it.
But since to you, your praises discords be,
   Stoop, others' ills to meditate with me.
O! to confess we know not what we should
   Is half excuse; we know not what we would.
Lightness depresseth us, emptiness fills,
   We sweat and faint, yet still go down the hills;
As new philosophy arrests the sun,
   And bids the passive earth about it run,
So we have dulled our mind, it hath no ends;
40   Only the body's busy and pretends;
As dead, low earth eclipses and controls
   The quick, high moon, so doth the body, souls.
In none but us are such mixed engines found
   As hands of double office: for the ground
We till with them, and them to heaven we raise;
   Who prayer-less labours, or, without this, prays,
Doth but one half, that's none; he which said, *Plough*
   And look not back, to look up doth allow.
Good seed degenerates, and oft obeys
50   The soil's disease and into cockle strays.

Let the mind's thoughts be but transplanted so
 Into the body,'and bastardly they grow.
What hate can hurt our bodies like our love?
 We, but no foreign tyrants, could remove
These not engraved but inborn dignities,
 Caskets of souls, temples, and palaces,
For bodies shall from death redeemed be,
 Souls but preserved, not naturally free;
As men to'our prisons, new souls to'us are sent,
 Which learn vice there and come in innocent. 60
First seeds of every creature are in us,
 What ere the world hath bad or precious
Man's body can produce; hence it hath been
 That stones, worms, frogs, and snakes in man are
   seen;
But who e'er saw, though nature can work so,
 That pearl, or gold, or corn in man did grow?
We'have added to the world Virginia,'and sent
 Two new stars lately to the firmament;
Why grudge we us (not heaven) the dignity
 T'increase with ours, those fair souls' company! 70
But I must end this letter, though it do
 Stand on two truths, neither is true to you.
Virtue hath some perverseness, for she will
 Neither believe her good, nor others ill.
Even in you, virtue's best paradise,
 Virtue hath some, but wise degrees of vice.
Too many virtues or too much of one
 Begets in you unjust suspicion.
And ignorance of vice makes virtue less,
 Quenching compassion of our wretchedness. 80
But these are riddles; some aspersion
 Of vice becomes well some complexion.
Statesmen purge vice with vice, and may corrode
 The bad with bad, a spider with a toad,
For so ill thralls not them, but they tame ill
 And make her do much good against her will;

But in your commonwealth, or world in you,
   Vice hath no office or good work to do.
Take then no vicious purge, but be content
90   With cordial virtue, your known nourishment.

To the Countess of Bedford, on New Year's Day

This twilight of two years, not past nor next,
   Some emblem is of me, or I of this,
Who meteor-like, of stuff and form perplexed,
   Whose what and where in disputation is,
   If I should call me anything, should miss.

I sum the years and me, and find me not
   Debtor to th'old nor creditor to th'new,
That cannot say, My thanks I have forgot,
   Nor trust I this with hopes, and yet scarce true,
10   This bravery is since these times showed me you.

In recompense I would show future times
   What you were, and teach them to'urge towards such.
Verse embalms virtue;'and tombs, or thrones of rhymes,
   Preserve frail transitory fame as much
   As spice doth bodies from corrupt air's touch.

Mine are short-lived; the tincture of your name
   Creates in them, but dissipates as fast
New spirits, for strong agents with the same
   Force that doth warm and cherish us do waste;
20   Kept hot with strong extracts, no bodies last.

So my verse, built of your just praise, might want
   Reason and likelihood, the firmest base,
And made of miracle, now faith is scant,
   Will vanish soon, and so possess no place,
   And you, and it, too much grace might disgrace.

When all (as truth commands assent) confess
  All truth of you, yet they will doubt how I,
One corn of one low anthill's dust, and less,
    Should name, know, or express a thing so high,
    And not an inch, measure infinity.   30

I cannot tell them, nor myself, nor you,
  But leave, lest truth be'endangered by my praise,
And turn to God, who knows I think this true,
    And useth oft, when such a heart mis-says,
    To make it good, for such a praiser prays.

He will best teach you, how you should lay out
  His stock of beauty, learning, favour, blood;
He will perplex security with doubt,
    And clear those doubts; hide from you,'and show
      you good,
    And so increase your appetite and food;   40

He will teach you that good and bad have not
  One latitude in cloisters and in court;
Indifference there the greatest space hath got;
    Some pity'is not good there, some vain disport,
    On this side, sin with that place may comport.

Yet he, as he bounds seas, will fix your hours,
  Which pleasure and delight may not ingress,
And though what none else lost, be truliest yours,
    He will make you, what you did not, possess,
    By using others, not vice, but weakness.   50

He will make you speak truths, and credibly,
  And make you doubt that others do not so;
He will provide you keys and locks to spy
    And 'scape spies, to good ends, and he will show
    What you may not acknowledge, what not know.

For your own conscience, he gives innocence,
    But for your fame, a discreet wariness,
And though to 'scape than to revenge offence
    Be better, he shows both, and to repress
60   Joy, when your state swells, sadness when 'tis less.

From need of tears he will defend your soul,
    Or make a rebaptizing of one tear;
He cannot (that's, he will not) dis-enrol
    Your name; and when with active joy we hear
    This private gospel, then 'tis our New Year.

To Sir Edward Herbert, at Juliers

Man is a lump where all beasts kneaded be,
    Wisdom makes him an ark where all agree;
The fool, in whom these beasts do live at jar,
    Is sport to others and a theatre,
Nor 'scapes he so, but is himself their prey;
    All which was man in him is eat away,
And now his beasts on one another feed,
    Yet couple'in anger, and new monsters breed;
How happy'is he which hath due place assigned
10   To'his beasts, and disaforested his mind!
Impaled himself to keep them out, not in;
    Can sow, and dares trust corn, where they have
      been;
Can use his horse, goat, wolf, and every beast,
    And is not ass himself to all the rest.
Else man not only is the herd of swine,
    But he's those devils too which did incline
Them to a headlong rage, and made them worse,
    For man can add weight to heaven's heaviest curse.
As souls (they say) by our first touch take in
20   The poisonous tincture of original sin,
So to the punishments which God doth fling,
    Our apprehension contributes the sting.

To us, as to His chickens, He doth cast
    Hemlock, and we as men, His hemlock taste.
We do infuse to what He meant for meat,
    Corrosiveness, or intense cold or heat.
For, God no such specific poison hath
    As kills we know not how; His fiercest wrath
Hath no antipathy, but may be good
    At least for physic, if not for our food.   30
Thus man, that might be'his pleasure, is his rod,
    And is his devil, that might be his God.
Since then, our business is to rectify
    Nature to what she was; we'are led awry
By them who man to us in little show;
    Greater than due, no form we can bestow
On him; for man into himself can draw
    All; all his faith can swallow,'or reason chew.
All that is filled, and all that which doth fill,
    All the round world to man is but a pill,   40
In all it works not, but it is in all
    Poisonous, or purgative, or cordial,
For knowledge kindles calentures in some,
    And is to others icy opium.
As brave as true is that profession then
    Which you do use to make, that you know man.
This makes it credible: you have dwelt upon
    All worthy books, and now are such an one.
Actions are authors, and of those in you
    Your friends find every day a mart of new.   50

To the Countess of Huntingdon

Madame,
Man to God's image, Eve to man's, was made,
    Nor find we that God breathed a soul in her;
Canons will not church functions you invade,
    Nor laws to civil office you prefer.

Who vagrant transitory comets sees,
   Wonders, because they'are rare; but a new star,
Whose motion with the firmament agrees,
   Is miracle, for there no new things are;

In woman so perchance mild innocence
   A seldom comet is, but active good
A miracle, which reason 'scapes and sense;
   For art and nature this in them withstood.

As such a star the Magi led to view
   The manger-cradled infant, God below,
By virtue's beams, by fame derived from you,
   May apt souls – and the worst may – virtue know.

If the world's age and death be argued well
   By the sun's fall, which now towards earth doth
      bend,
Then we might fear that virtue, since she fell
   So low as woman, should be near her end.

But she's not stooped, but raised; exiled by men
   She fled to heaven, that's heavenly things, that's
     you;
She was in all men thinly scattered then,
   But now amassed, contracted in a few.

She gilded us, but you are gold, and she;
   Us she informed, but transubstantiates you;
Soft dispositions which ductile be,
   Elixir-like, she makes not clean, but new.

Though you a wife's and mother's name retain,
   'Tis not as woman, for all are not so,
But virtue, having made you virtue,'is fain
   T'adhere in these names, her and you to show,

10

20

30

Else, being alike pure, we should neither see,
   As water being into air rarefied,
Neither appear, till in one cloud they be,
   So, for our sakes you do low names abide;

Taught by great constellations, which being framed
   Of the most stars, take low names, Crab and Bull,
When single planets by the gods are named,
   You covet not great names, of great things full.   40

So you, as woman, one doth comprehend,
   And in the veil of kindred others see;
To some ye are revealed as in a friend,
   And as a virtuous prince far off, to me.

To whom, because from you all virtues flow,
   And 'tis not none to dare contemplate you,
I, which do so, as your true subject owe
   Some tribute for that, so these lines are due.

If you can think these flatteries, they are,
   For then your judgement is below my praise,   50
If they were so, oft flatteries work as far
   As counsels, and as far th'endeavour raise.

So my ill reaching you might there grow good,
   But I remain a poisoned fountain still;
But not your beauty, virtue, knowledge, blood
   Are more above all flattery, than my will.

And if I flatter any, 'tis not you
   But my own judgement, who did long ago
Pronounce that all these praises should be true,
   And virtue should your beauty,'and birth   60
      outgrow.

Now that my prophecies are all fulfilled,
   Rather than God should not be honoured too,
And all these gifts confessed, which he instilled,
   Yourself were bound to say that which I do.

So I but your recorder am in this,
   Or mouth, and speaker of the universe,
A ministerial notary, for 'tis
   Not I, but you and fame, that makes this verse;

I was your prophet in your younger days,
70   And now your chaplain, God in you to praise.

A Letter to the Lady Carey, and Mistress Essex Rich, from Amiens

Madame,
Here, where by all, all saints invoked are
   T'were too much schism to be singular,
And 'gainst a practice general to war;

Yet, turning to saints, should my humility
   To other saint, than you, directed be,
That were to make my schism heresy.

Nor would I be a convertite so cold
   As not to tell it; if this be too bold,
Pardons are in this market cheaply sold.

10   Where, because faith is in too low degree,
   I thought it some apostleship in me,
To speak things which by faith alone I see:

That is, of you; who are a firmament
   Of virtues, where no one is grown, nor spent;
They'are your materials, not your ornament.

Others, whom we call virtuous, are not so
In their whole substance, but their virtues grow
But in their humours, and at seasons show.

For when through tasteless flat humility,
In dough-baked men, some harmlessness we see,   20
'Tis but his phlegm that's virtuous, and not he.

So is the blood sometimes; who ever ran
To danger unimportuned, he was then
No better than a sanguine virtuous man.

So cloistral men who in pretence of fear,
All contributions to this life forbear,
Have virtue in melancholy, and only there.

Spiritual choleric critics, which in all
Religions, find faults, and forgive no fall,
Have, through this zeal, virtue, but in their gall.   30

We'are thus but parcel-gilt; to gold we'are
        grown,
When virtue is our soul's complexion;
Who knows his virtue's name, or place, hath none.

Virtue is but aguish, when 'tis several;
By'occasion waked, and circumstantial;
True virtue is soul, always in all deeds all.

This virtue, thinking to give dignity
To your soul, found there no infirmity;
For your soul was as good virtue as she.

She therefore wrought upon that part of you,   40
Which is scarce less than soul, as she could do,
And so hath made your beauty virtue too;

Hence comes it, that your beauty wounds not hearts
As others, with profane and sensual darts,
But, as an influence, virtuous thoughts imparts.

But if such friends, by the'honour of your sight
Grow capable of this so great a light,
As to partake your virtues, and their might,

What must I think that influence must do,
Where it finds sympathy, and matter too,
Virtue, and beauty, of the same stuff, as you:

Which is, your noble worthy sister; she,
Of whom, if what in this my ecstasy
And revelation of you both, I see,

I should write here, as in short galleries
The master at the end large glasses ties,
So to present the room twice to our eyes,

So I should give this letter length, and say
That which I said of you, there is no way
From either, but by th'other, not to stray.

May therefore this be'enough to testify
My true devotion, free from flattery.
He that believes himself, doth never lie.

To the Honourable lady
   the lady Carew.

Sappho to Philænis

Where is that holy fire, which verse is said
  To have? Is that enchanting force decayed?
Verse that draws Nature's works from Nature's law,
  Thee, her best work, to her work cannot draw.

Have my tears quenched my old poetic fire?
   Why quenched they not as well that of desire?
Thoughts, my mind's creatures, often are with thee,
   But I, their maker, want their liberty.
Only thine image in my heart doth sit,
   But that is wax, and fires environ it.   10
My fires have driven, thine have drawn it hence;
   And I am robbed of picture, heart, and sense.
Dwells with me still mine irksome memory,
   Which both to keep and lose grieves equally.
That tells me'how fair thou art: thou art so fair
   As gods, when gods to thee I do compare,
Are graced thereby; and to make blind men see
   What things gods are, I say they'are like to thee.
For if we justly call each silly man
   A little world, what shall we call thee then?   20
Thou art not soft, and clear, and straight, and fair
   As down, as stars, cedars, and lilies are,
But thy right hand, and cheek, and eye only
   Are like thy other hand, and cheek, and eye.
Such was my Phao awhile, but shall be never,
   As thou wast, art, and, O, may'st be ever.
Here lovers swear in their idolatry,
   That I am such, but grief discolours me.
And yet I grieve the less, lest grief remove
   My beauty, and make me unworthy of thy love.   30
Plays some soft boy with thee, O, there wants yet
   A mutual feeling which should sweeten it.
His chin, a thorny hairy'unevenness
   Doth threaten, and some daily change possess.
Thy body is a natural paradise
   In whose self, unmanured, all pleasure lies,
Nor needs perfection; why should'st thou then
   Admit the tillage of a harsh, rough man?
Men leave behind them that which their sin shows,
   And are as thieves traced, which rob when it   40
      snows.

But of our dalliance no more signs there are
    Than fishes leave in streams, or birds in air.
And between us all sweetness may be had,
    All, all that Nature yields, or art can add.
My two lips, eyes, thighs, differ from thy two,
    But so as thine from one another do;
And, O, no more; the likeness being such,
    Why should they not alike in all parts touch?
Hand to strange hand, lip to lip none denies;
50   Why should they breast to breast, or thighs to
        thighs?
Likeness begets such strange self-flattery
    That touching myself, all seems done to thee.
Myself I'embrace, and mine own hands I kiss,
    And amorously thank myself for this.
Me in my glass, I call thee; but alas,
    When I would kiss, tears dim mine eyes and glass.
O cure this loving madness, and restore
    Me to me; thee, my half, my all, my more.
So may thy cheeks' red outwear scarlet dye,
60   And their white, whiteness of the galaxy,
So may thy mighty'amazing beauty move
    Envy'in all women, and in all men, love,
And so be change and sickness far from thee,
    As thou by coming near, keep'st them from me.

FUNERAL ELEGIES

The First Anniversary. An Anatomy of the World

When that rich soul which to her heaven is gone,   *The entry*
Whom all they celebrate, who know they have one   *into the*
(For who is sure he hath a soul, unless   *work*
It see, and judge, and follow worthiness,

And by deeds praise it? He who doth not this,
May lodge an inmate soul, but 'tis not his),
When that queen ended here her progress time,
And, as to'her standing house, to heaven did climb,
Where, loath to make the saints attend her long,
She's now a part both of the choir and song,   10
This world in that great earthquake languished;
For in a common bath of tears it bled,
Which drew the strongest vital spirits out;
But succoured then with a perplexed doubt,
Whether the world did lose or gain in this
(Because since now no other way there is,
But goodness to see her, whom all would see,
All must endeavour to be good as she),
This great consumption to a fever turned,
And so the world had fits; it joyed, it mourned.   20
And as men think that agues physic are,
And th'ague being spent, give over care,
So thou, sick world, mistak'st thyself to be
Well, when alas, thou'rt in a lethargy.
Her death did wound and tame thee then, and then
Thou might'st have better spared the sun or man;
That wound was deep, but 'tis more misery,
That thou hast lost thy sense and memory.
T'was heavy then to hear thy voice of moan,
But this is worse, that thou art speechless grown.   30
Thou hast forgot thy name thou hadst; thou wast
Nothing but she, and her thou hast o'erpast.
For as a child kept from the font until
A prince, expected long, come to fulfil
The cer'monies, thou unnamed hadst laid,
Had not her coming, thee her palace made;
Her name defined thee, gave thee form and frame,
And thou forget'st to celebrate thy name.
Some months she hath been dead (but being dead,
Measures of times are all determined),   40
But long she'hath been away, long, long, yet none
Offers to tell us who it is that's gone.

But as in states doubtful of future heirs,
When sickness without remedy impairs
The present prince, they're loath it should be said,
The prince doth languish, or the prince is dead;
So mankind feeling now a general thaw,
A strong example gone equal to law,
The cement which did faithfully compact
50   And glue all virtues, now resolved, and slacked,
Thought it some blasphemy to say she'was dead,
Or that our weakness was discovered
In that confession; therefore, spoke no more
Than tongues, the soul being gone, the loss deplore.
But though it be too late to succour thee,
Sick world, yea dead, yea putrified, since she,
Thy'intrinsic balm and thy preservative,
Can never be renewed, thou never live,
I (since no man can make thee live) will try
60   What we may gain by thy anatomy.
Her death hath taught us dearly that thou art
Corrupt and mortal in thy purest part.
Let no man say, the world itself being dead,
'Tis labour lost to have discovered
The world's infirmities, since there is none
Alive to study this dissection;
For there's a kind of world remaining still,   *What life*
Though she which did inanimate and fill   *the world*
The world be gone, yet in this last long   *hath still*
          night
70   Her ghost doth walk: that is, a glimmering light,
A faint weak love of virtue and of good
Reflects from her on them which understood
Her worth. And though she have shut in all day,
The twilight of her memory doth stay,
Which, from the carcass of the old world free,
Creates a new world, and new creatures be
Produced. The matter and the stuff of this,
Her virtue, and the form, our practice is.

And though to be thus elemented, arm
These creatures from home-born intrinsic harm   80
(For all assumed unto this dignity,
So many weedless paradises be,
Which of themselves produce no venomous sin,
Except some foreign serpent bring it in),
Yet, because outward storms the strongest break,
And strength itself by confidence grows weak,
This new world may be safer being told
The dangers and diseases of the old;   *The sicknesses*
For with due temper men do then forgo,   *of the world*
Or covet things, when they their true   90
   worth know.
There is no health: physicians say   *Impossibility*
   that we,   *of health*
At best, enjoy but a neutrality.
And can there be worse sickness than to know
That we are never well, nor can be so?
We are born ruinous: poor mothers cry
That children come not right, nor orderly,
Except they headlong come, and fall upon
An ominous precipitation.
How witty's ruin? How importunate
Upon mankind? It laboured to frustrate   100
Even God's purpose, and made woman, sent
For man's relief, cause of his languishment.
They were to good ends, and they are so still,
But accessory, and principal in ill.
For that first marriage was our funeral:
One woman at one blow then killed us all,
And singly, one by one, they kill us now.
We do delightfully ourselves allow
To that consumption; and profusely blind,
We kill ourselves to propagate our kind.   110
And yet we do not that, we are not men:
There is not now that mankind which was then

When as the sun and man did seem to strive
(Joint tenants of the world) who should   *Shortness*
   survive   *of life*
When stag, and raven, and the long-lived tree,
Compared with man, died in minority;
When, if a slow-paced star had stol'n away
From the observer's marking, he might stay
Two or three hundred years to see'it again,
And then make up his observation plain;
When, as the age was long, the size was great:
Man's growth confessed, and recompensed the meat,
So spacious and large, that every soul
Did a fair kingdom and large realm control;
And when the very stature thus erect,
Did that soul a good way towards heaven direct.
Where is this mankind now? Who lives to age,
Fit to be made Methusalem his page?
Alas, we scarce live long enough to try
Whether a new made clock run right or lie.
Old grandsires talk of yesterday with sorrow,
And for our children we reserve tomorrow.
So short is life that every peasant strives
In a torn house, or field, to have three lives.
And as in lasting, so in length is man
Contracted to an inch, who was a span.   *Smallness*
For had a man at first in forests strayed,   *of stature*
Or shipwrecked in the sea, one would have laid
A wager that an elephant or whale
That met him would not hastily assail
A thing so equal to him; now, alas,
The fairies and the pigmies well may pass
As credible; mankind decays so soon,
We're scarce our fathers' shadows cast at noon.
Only death adds to'our length, nor are we grown
In stature to be men, till we are none.
But this were light, did our less volume hold
All the old text; or had we changed to gold

120

130

140

Their silver; or disposed into less glass,
Spirits of virtue, which then scattered was.   150
But 'tis not so: we're not retired, but damped;
And as our bodies, so our minds are cramped:
'Tis shrinking, not close-weaving, that hath thus
In mind and body both be-dwarfed us.
We seem ambitious, God's whole work to'undo;
Of nothing He made us, and we strive too
To bring ourselves to nothing back; and we
Do what we can to do'it so soon as He.
With new diseases on ourselves we war,
And with new physic, a worse engine far.   160
Thus man, this world's vice-emperor, in whom
All faculties, all graces are at home,
And if in other creatures they appear,
They're but man's ministers, and legates there,
To work on their rebellions, and reduce
Them to civility, and to man's use.
This man, whom God did woo, and loath to'attend
Till man came up, did down to man descend,
This man, so great, that all that is, is His,
O what a trifle and poor thing he is!   170
If man were anything, he's nothing now;
Help, or at least some time to waste, allow
T'his other wants, yet when he did depart
With her whom we lament, he lost his heart.
She, of whom th'ancients seemed to prophesy
When they called virtues by the name of she;
She in whom virtue was so much refined
That for alloy unto so pure a mind
She took the weaker sex; she that could drive
The poisonous tincture, and the stain of Eve,   180
Out of her thoughts and deeds, and purify
All by a true religious alchemy;
She, she is dead, she's dead; when thou knowest this,
Thou know'st how poor a trifling thing man is.
And learn'st thus much by our anatomy:
The heart being perished, no part can be free.

And that except thou feed (not banquet) on
The supernatural food, religion,
Thy better growth grows withered and scant;
190   Be more than man, or thou'rt less than an ant.
Then, as mankind, so is the world's whole frame
Quite out of joint, almost created lame;
For, before God had made up all the rest,
Corruption entered and depraved the best;
It seized the angels, and then first of all
The world did in her cradle take a fall,
And turned her brains, and took a general maim,
Wronging each joint of th'universal frame.
The noblest part, man, felt it first; and then
200   Both beasts and plants, cursed in the curse
        of man.
So did the world from the first hour decay,   *Decay of*
The evening was beginning of the day,   *nature in*
And now the springs and summers which   *other parts*
        we see,
Like sons of women after fifty be.
And new philosophy calls all in doubt,
The element of fire is quite put out;
The sun is lost, and th'earth, and no man's wit
Can well direct him where to look for it.
And freely men confess that this world's spent,
210   When in the planets and the firmament
They seek so many new; they see that this
Is crumbled out again to his atomies.
'Tis all in pieces, all coherence gone;
All just supply and all relation,
Prince, subject, father, son, are things forgot,
For every man alone thinks he hath got
To be a phoenix, and that there can be
None of that kind, of which he is, but he.
This is the world's condition now, and now
220   She that should all parts to reunion bow,
She that had all magnetic force alone,
To draw and fasten sundered parts in one;

She whom wise nature had invented then
When she observed that every sort of men
Did in their voyage in this world's sea stray,
And needed a new compass for their way;
She that was best, and first original
Of all fair copies, and the general
Steward to fate; she whose rich eyes and breast
Gilt the West Indies and perfumed the East;   230
Whose having breathed in this world did bestow
Spice on those isles, and bade them still smell so,
And that rich Indie which doth gold inter
Is but as single money, coined from her;
She to whom this world must itself refer,
As suburbs, or the microcosm of her,
She, she is dead, she's dead; when thou know'st
          this,
Thou know'st how lame a cripple this world is.
And learn'st thus much by our anatomy,
That this world's general sickness doth not lie   240
In any humour, or one certain part;
But, as thou saw'st it rotten at the heart,
Thou see'st a hectic fever hath got hold
Of the whole substance, not to be controlled;
And that thou hast but one way not to'admit
The world's infection, to be none of it.
For the world's subtlest immaterial parts
Feel this consuming wound and age's darts.
For the world's beauty is decayed, or gone,   249
Beauty, that's colour, and proportion.   *Disformity*
We think the heavens enjoy their spherical,   *of parts*
Their round proportion embracing all.
But yet their various and perplexed course,
Observed in diverse ages, doth enforce
Men to find out so many'eccentric parts,
Such diverse downright lines, such overthwarts,
As disproportion that pure form. It tears
The firmament in eight and forty shares,

And in those constellations there arise
New stars, and old do vanish from our eyes,
As though heav'n suffered earthquakes, peace or
    war,
When new towns rise, and old demolished are.
They have impaled within a zodiac
The free-born sun, and keep twelve signs awake
To watch his steps; the Goat and Crab control,
And fright him back, who else to either pole
(Did not these tropics fetter him) might run,
For his course is not round; nor can the sun
Perfect a circle, or maintain his way
One inch direct; but where he rose today
He comes no more, but with a cozening line,
Steals by that point, and so is serpentine;
And seeming weary with his reeling thus,
He means to sleep, being now fallen nearer us.
So, of the stars which boast that they do run
In circle still, none ends where he begun.
All their proportion's lame, it sinks, it swells.
For of meridians and parallels,
Man hath weaved out a net, and this net thrown
Upon the heavens, and now they are his own.
Loath to go up the hill, or labour thus
To go to heaven, we make heaven come to us.
We spur, we rain the stars, and in their race
They're diversely content to'obey our pace.
But keeps the earth her round proportion still?
Doth not a Tenerife, or higher hill,
Rise so high like a rock, that one might think
The floating moon would shipwreck there and sink?
Seas are so deep that whales, being struck today,
Perchance tomorrow, scarce at middle way
Of their wished journey's end, the bottom, die.
And men, to sound depths, so much line untie,
As one might justly think that there would rise
At end thereof one of the'antipodes;

If under all, a vault infernal be
(Which sure is spacious, except that we
Invent another torment, that there must
Millions into a strait hot room be thrust),
Then solidness and roundness have no place.
Are these but warts and pockholes in the face   300
Of th'earth? Think so, but yet confess, in this
The world's proportion disfigured is,
That those two legs whereon it doth rely,   *Disorder in*
Reward and punishment, are bent awry.   *the world*
And, O, it can no more be questioned
That beauty's best, proportion, is dead,
Since even grief itself, which now alone
Is left us, is without proportion.
She by whose lines proportion should be
Examined, measure of all symmetry,   310
Whom had that ancient seen, who thought souls
      made
Of harmony, he would at next have said
That harmony was she, and thence infer
That souls were but resultances from her,
And did from her into our bodies go,
As to our eyes the forms from objects flow;
She, who if those great doctors truly said
That th'ark to man's proportions was made,
Had been a type for that, as that might be
A type of her in this, that contrary   320
Both elements and passions lived at peace
In her, who caused all civil war to cease;
She, after whom, what form soe'er we see,
Is discord and rude incongruity;
She, she is dead, she's dead; when thou know'st this,
Thou know'st how ugly a monster this world is;
And learn'st thus much by our anatomy,
That here is nothing to enamour thee,
And that, not only faults in inward parts,
Corruptions in our brains, or in our hearts,   330

Poisoning the fountains, whence our actions spring,
Endanger us: but that if everything
Be not done fitly'and in proportion,
To satisfy wise and good lookers-on
(Since most men be such as most think they be),
They're loathsome too, by this deformity.
For good, and well, must in our actions meet:
Wicked is not much worse than indiscreet.
But beauty's other second element,
340   Colour and lustre now is as near spent.
And had the world his just proportion,
Were it a ring still, yet the stone is gone.
As a compassionate turquoise which doth tell
By looking pale, the wearer is not well,
As gold falls sick being stung with mercury,
All the world's parts of such complexion be.
When nature was most busy, the first week,
Swaddling the newborn earth, God seemed to like
That she should sport herself sometimes and play,
350   To mingle and vary colours every day.
And then, as though she could not make enough,
Himself His various rainbow did allow.
Sight is the noblest sense of any one,
Yet sight hath only colour to feed on,
And colour is decayed: summer's robe grows
Dusky, and like an oft dyed garment shows.
Our blushing red, which used in cheeks to spread,
Is inward sunk, and only our souls are red.
Perchance the world might have recovered,
360   If she whom we lament had not been dead;
But she, in whom all white, and red, and blue
(Beauty's ingredients) voluntary grew
As in an unvexed paradise; from whom
Did all things verdure, and their lustre come;
Whose composition was miraculous,
Being all colour, all diaphanous
(For air, and fire but thick, gross bodies were,
And liveliest stones but drowsy and pale to her),

She, she is dead, she's dead; when thou knowest
    this,
Thou know'st how wan a ghost this our world is;   370
And learn'st thus much by our anatomy,
That it should more affright than pleasure thee.
And that, since all fair colour then did sink,
'Tis now but wicked vanity to think
To colour vicious deeds with good   *Weakness*
    pretence,   *in the want of*
Or with bought colours to elude men's   *correspondence*
    sense.   *of heaven and*
Nor in ought more this world's decay   *earth*
    appears,
Than that her influence the heav'n forbears,
Or that the elements do not feel this,
The father or the mother barren is.   380
The clouds conceive not rain, or do not pour
In the due birthtime down the balmy shower.
Th'air doth not motherly sit on the earth,
To hatch her seasons, and give all things birth.
Spring-times were common cradles, but are tombs;
And false conceptions fill the general wombs.
Th'air shows such meteors as none can see,
Not only what they mean, but what they be;
Earth such new worms, as would have troubled
    much
Th'Egyptian mages to have made more such.   390
What artist now dares boast that he can bring
Heaven hither, or constellate anything,
So as the influence of those stars may be
Imprisoned in an herb, or charm, or tree,
And do by touch all which those stars could do?
The art is lost, and correspondence too.
For heav'n gives little, and the earth takes less,
And man least knows their trade and purposes.
If this commerce 'twixt heaven and earth were not
Embarred, and all this traffic quite forgot,   400

She, for whose loss we have lamented thus,
Would work more fully'and pow'rfully on us.
Since herbs and roots by dying lose not all,
But they, yea ashes too, are medicinal,
Death could not quench her virtue so, but that
It would be (if not followed) wondered at,
And all the world would be one dying swan,
To sing her funeral praise, and vanish then.
But as some serpents poison hurteth not,
410   Except it be from the live serpent shot,
So doth her virtue need her here to fit
That unto us, she working more than it.
But she, in whom to such maturity,
Virtue was grown, past growth, that it must die;
She from whose influence all impressions came,
But, by receivers' impotencies, lame;
Who, though she could not transubstantiate
All states to gold, yet gilded every state,
So that some princes have some temperance,
420   Some counsellors some purpose to advance
The common profit, and some people have
Some stay, no more than kings should give, to crave,
Some women have some taciturnity,
Some nunneries, some grains of chastity;
She that did thus much, and much more could do,
But that our age was iron, and rusty too,
She, she is dead, she's dead; when thou knowest this,
Thou know'st how dry a cinder this world is.
And learn'st thus much by our anatomy,
430   That 'tis in vain to dew or mollify
It with thy tears, or sweat, or blood: nothing
Is worth our travail, grief, or perishing,
But those rich joys which did possess her heart,
Of which she's now partaker, and a part.
But as in cutting up a man that's dead,   *Conclusion*
The body will not last out to have read
On every part, and therefore men direct
Their speech to parts that are of most effect,

So the world's carcass would not last if I
Were punctual in this anatomy.   440
Nor smells it well to hearers if one tell
Them their disease, who fain would think they're well.
Here therefore be the end: And, blessed maid,
Of whom is meant what ever hath been said,
Or shall be spoken well by any tongue,
Whose name refines coarse lines, and makes prose
      song,
Accept this tribute and his first year's rent,
Who till his dark short taper's end be spent,
As oft as thy feast sees this widowed earth,
Will yearly celebrate thy second birth,   450
That is, thy death. For though the soul of man
Be got when man is made, 'tis born but then
When man doth die. Our body's as the womb,
And as a midwife, death directs it home.
And you her creatures, whom she works upon
And have your last and best concoction
From her example and her virtue, if you
In reverence to her, do think it due
That no one should her praises thus rehearse,
As matter fit for chronicle, not verse,   460
Vouchsafe to call to mind that God did make
A last and lasting'st piece, a song. He spake
To Moses to deliver unto all,
That song, because He knew they would let fall,
The law, the prophets, and the history,
But keep the song still in their memory.
Such an opinion (in due measure) made
Me this great office boldly to invade.
Nor could incomprehensibleness deter
Me from thus trying to imprison her,   470
Which when I saw that a strict grave could do,
I saw not why verse might not do so too.
Verse hath a middle nature: heaven keeps souls,
The grave keeps bodies, verse the fame enrols.

Epitaph on Himself. To the Countess of Bedford

Madame,
That I might make your cabinet my tomb,
   And for my fame, which I love next my soul,
Next to my soul provide the happiest room,
   Admit to that place this last funeral scroll.
      Others by wills give legacies, but I,
      Dying, of you do beg a legacy.

My fortune and my choice this custom break,
When we are speechless grown, to make stones
    speak,
Though no stone tell thee what I was, yet thou
In my grave's inside see'st what thou art now:
Yet thou'art not yet so good; till death us lay
To ripe and mellow here, we'are stubborn clay.
Parents make us earth, and souls dignify
Us to be glass; here to grow gold we lie;
Whil'st in our souls, sin bred and pampered is,
Our souls become worm-eaten carcasses,
So we ourselves miraculously destroy.
Here bodies with less miracle enjoy
Such privileges, enabled here to scale
Heaven, when the trumpet's air shall them exhale.
Hear this, and mend thyself, and thou mend'st me,
By making me being dead, do good to thee,
   And think me well composed, that I could now
   A last-sick hour to syllables allow.

Epitaph on Anne Donne

ANNÆ
Georgii More de Filiæ
Roberti Lothesley Soror:
Willemi Equit: Nept:
Christophori Aurat: Pronept:
Fæminæ Lectissimæ, dilectissimæque;
Coniugi charissimæ, castissimæque;
Matri Piissimæ, Indulgentissimæque;
Xv annis in coniugio transactis,
Vii post xii^m Partum (quorum vii superstant) dies
Immani febre correptæ   10
(Quod hoc saxum farj iussit
Ipse, præ dolore Infans)
Maritus (miserrimum dictu) olim charæ charus
Cineribus cineres spondet suos
Nouo matrimonio (annuat Deus) hoc loco sociandos
Iohannes Donne
Sacr: Theolog: Profess:
Secessit
A° xxxiii° Ætat: suæ et sui Iesu
CIƆDC xvii   20
Aug: xv.

ANNE
Daughter of [Sir] George More, of Loseley, Gilt/
Golden Knight,
Sister of [Sir] Robert More,
Grand-daughter of [Sir] William More,

Great-grand-daughter of [Sir] Christopher More;

A woman most choice/select/read, most beloved/loving/
well-read,

A spouse most dear, most chaste,

A mother most loving/merciful/pious/dutiful, most self-
sacrificing/indulgent;

Fifteen years in union/covenant completed,

Seven days after the twelfth parturition (of whom seven
survive)

10 By a savage/immense/ravishing fever hurriedly-carried-
off/seized

(Wherefore this stone to speak he commanded

Himself, by/beyond grief [made] speechless [Infant/infant])

Her husband (most miserable/wretched to say/designation/
assertion) once dear to the dear

His own ashes to these ashes pledges [weds]

[in a] New marriage (may God assent) in this place
joining together,

John Donne

Doctor of Theology.

She withdrew

In the 33rd year of age, hers and Jesus's

20 1617th

August 15.

DIVINE POEMS

To the Lady Magdalen Herbert, of St Mary Magdalen

Her of your name, whose fair inheritance
    Bethina was, and jointure Magdalo:
An active faith so highly did advance
    That she once knew more than the Church
        did know,
The Resurrection; so much good there is
    Delivered of her that some Fathers be
Loath to believe one woman could do this,
    But think these Magdalens were two or three.
Increase their number, Lady, and their fame:
    To their devotion, add your innocence;   10
Take so much of th'example'as of the name,
    The latter half; and in some recompense
That they did harbour Christ himself, a guest,
    Harbour these hymns, to his dear name
        addressed.

La Corona

I

Deign at my hands this crown of prayer and praise,
Weaved in my low devout melancholy,
Thou which of good hast, yea art, treasury,
All changing, unchanged, Ancient of Days,
But do not with a vile crown of frail bays
Reward my muse's white sincerity,
But what Thy thorny crown gained, that give me,

A crown of glory which doth flower always;
The ends crown our works, but Thou crown'st our
    ends,
For at our end begins our endless rest;
The first, last end, now zealously possessed,
With a strong sober thirst my soul attends.
'Tis time that heart and voice be lifted high,
Salvation to all that will is nigh.

2
Annunciation

Salvation to all that will is nigh;
That all, which always is all everywhere,
Which cannot sin and yet all sins must bear,
Which cannot die, yet cannot choose but die,
Lo, faithful Virgin, yields Himself to lie
In prison in thy womb; and though He there
Can take no sin, nor thou give, yet He'will wear,
Taken from thence, flesh, which death's force may
    try.
Ere by the spheres time was created, thou
Wast in His mind, who is thy son and brother,
Whom thou conceiv'st, conceived; yea, thou art now
Thy Maker's maker and thy Father's mother,
Thou'hast light in dark; and shut'st in little room,
Immensity cloistered in thy dear womb.

3
Nativity

Immensity cloistered in thy dear womb,
Now leaves His well-beloved imprisonment;
There He hath made Himself to His intent
Weak enough now into our world to come;

But O, for thee, for Him, hath th'inn no room?
Yet lay him in this stall, and from the'Orient,
Stars and wisemen will travel to prevent
Th'effect of Herod's jealous general doom;
See'st thou, my soul, with thy faith's eyes, how He
Which fills all place, yet none holds Him, doth lie?
Was not His pity towards thee wondrous high,
That would have need to be pitied by thee?   40
Kiss Him, and with Him into Egypt go,
With His kind mother who partakes thy woe.

4
Temple

With His kind mother who partakes thy woe,
Joseph, turn back; see where your child doth sit,
Blowing, yea blowing out those sparks of wit,
Which Himself on the doctors did bestow;
The Word but lately could not speak, and lo
It suddenly speaks wonders, whence comes it,
That all which was and all which should be writ,
A shallow seeming child should deeply know?   50
His Godhead was not soul to His manhood,
Nor had time mellowed Him to this ripeness,
But as for one which hath a long task, 'tis good
With the sun to begin His business,
He in His age's morning thus began
By miracles exceeding power of man.

5
Crucifying

By miracles exceeding power of man,
He faith in some, envy in some begat,
For, what weak spirits admire, ambitious, hate;
In both affections many to Him ran,   60

But O! the worst are most, they will and can,
Alas, and do, unto the'Immaculate,
Whose creature fate is, now prescribe a fate,
Measuring self-life's infinity to'a span,
Nay to an inch. Lo, where condemned He
Bears His own cross with pain, yet by and by
When it bears Him, He must bear more and die;
Now Thou art lifted up, draw me to Thee,
And at Thy death giving such liberal dole,
70   *Moist with one drop of Thy blood my dry soul.*

6
Resurrection

Moist with one drop of Thy blood, my dry soul
Shall (though she now be in extreme degree
Too stony hard, and yet too fleshly) be
Freed by that drop, from being starved, hard, or foul,
And life, by this death abled, shall control
Death whom Thy death slew; nor shall to me
Fear of first or last death bring misery,
If in thy little book my name thou'enrol,
Flesh in that long sleep is not putrefied,
80   But made that there, of which, and for which, 'twas;
Nor can by other means be glorified.
May then sin's sleep, and death's soon from me pass,
That waked from both I again risen may
Salute the last and everlasting day.

7
Ascension

Salute the last and everlasting day,
Joy at the'uprising of this sun, and Son,
Ye, whose just tears or tribulation
Have purely washed or burnt your drossy clay;

Behold the Highest, parting hence away,
Lightens the dark clouds which He treads upon, 90
Nor doth He by ascending, show alone,
But first He, and He first, enters the way.
O strong Ram, which hast battered heaven for me,
Mild Lamb, which with Thy blood hast marked the
    path,
Bright Torch, which shin'st that I the way may see,
O, with Thy own blood quench Thy own just wrath,
And if Thy Holy Spirit my muse did raise,
Deign at my hands this crown of prayer and praise.

Holy Sonnet I

Thou hast made me, and shall Thy work decay?
Repair me now, for now mine end doth haste;
I run to death, and death meets me as fast,
And all my pleasures are like yesterday;
I dare not move my dim eyes any way,
Despair behind and death before doth cast
Such terror, and my feebled flesh doth waste
By sin in it, which it towards hell doth weigh;
Only Thou art above, and when towards Thee
By Thy leave I can look, I rise again, 10
But our old subtle foe so tempteth me,
That not one hour I can myself sustain;
Thy grace may wing me to prevent his art,
And Thou like adamant draw mine iron heart.

Holy Sonnet II

As due by many titles I resign
Myself to Thee, O God; first I was made
By Thee, and for Thee, and when I was decayed
Thy blood bought that, the which before was thine;

I am Thy son, made with Thyself to shine,
Thy servant, whose pains Thou hast still repaid,
Thy sheep, Thine image, and, till I betrayed
Myself, a temple of Thy Spirit divine;
Why doth the Devil then usurp on me?
Why doth he steal, nay ravish, that's Thy right?
Except Thou rise and for Thine own work fight,
O, I shall soon despair when I do see
That Thou lov'st mankind well, yet wilt'not choose
      me,
And Satan hates me, yet is loath to lose me.

Holy Sonnet III

O might those sighs and tears return again
Into my breast and eyes, which I have spent,
That I might in this holy discontent
Mourn with some fruit, as I have mourned in vain;
In mine idolatry what showers of rain
Mine eyes did waste? What griefs my heart did rent?
That sufferance was my sin I now repent;
Because I did suffer, I must suffer pain.
Th'hydroptic drunkard and night-scouting thief,
The itchy lecher and self-tickling proud
Have the remembrance of past joys for relief
Of coming ills. To (poor) me is allowed
No ease; for long yet vehement grief hath been
Th'effect and cause, the punishment and sin.

Holy Sonnet IV

O my black soul! Now thou art summoned
By sickness, death's herald, and champion;
Thou art like a pilgrim which abroad hath done
Treason, and durst not turn to whence he's fled,

Or like a thief, which till death's doom be read,
Wisheth himself delivered from prison,
But damned and haled to execution,
Wisheth that still he might be'imprisoned.
Yet grace, if thou repent, thou canst not lack;
But who shall give thee that grace to begin?   10
O make thyself with holy mourning black,
And red with blushing, as thou art with sin;
Or wash thee in Christ's blood, which hath this
    might,
That being red, it dyes red souls to white.

Holy Sonnet V

I am a little world made cunningly
Of elements and an angelic sprite,
But black sin hath betrayed to endless night
My world's both parts, and (O) both parts must die.
You which beyond that heaven which was most high
Have found new spheres, and of new lands can write,
Pour new seas in mine eyes, that so I might
Drown my world with my weeping earnestly,
Or wash it, if it must be drowned no more;
But, O, it must be burnt. Alas, the fire   10
Of lust and envy burnt it heretofore,
And made it fouler; let their flames retire,
And burn me, O Lord, with a fiery zeal
Of Thee'and Thy house, which doth in eating heal.

Holy Sonnet VI

This is my play's last scene, here heavens appoint
My pilgrimage's last mile; and my race
Idly, yet quickly run, hath this last pace,
My span's last inch, my minute's latest point,

And gluttonous death will instantly unjoint
My body'and soul, and I shall sleep a space,
But my'ever-waking part shall see that face
Whose fear already shakes my every joint;
Then, as my soul to'heaven, her first seat, takes flight,
And earth-born body in the earth shall dwell;
So fall my sins, that all may have their right,
To where they'are bred, and would press me, to hell.
Impute me righteous, thus purged of evil,
For thus I leave the world, the flesh, the Devil.

Holy Sonnet VII

At the round earth's imagined corners, blow
Your trumpets, angels, and arise, arise
From death, you numberless infinities
Of souls, and to your scattered bodies go,
All whom the flood did, and fire shall o'erthrow,
All whom war, dearth, age, agues, tyrannies,
Despair, law, chance, hath slain, and you whose eyes
Shall behold God and never taste death's woe.
But let them sleep, Lord, and me mourn a space,
For if above all these my sins abound,
'Tis late to ask abundance of Thy grace
When we are there; here on this lowly ground,
Teach me how to repent; for that's as good
As if Thou'hadst sealed my pardon with Thy blood.

Holy Sonnet VIII

If faithful souls be alike glorified
As angels, then my father's soul doth see,
And adds this even to full felicity,
That valiantly I hell's wide mouth o'erstride.

But if our minds to these souls be descried
By circumstances and by signs that be
Apparent in us not immediately,
How shall my mind's white truth by them be tried?
They see idolatrous lovers weep and mourn,
And vile blasphemous conjurers to call   10
On Jesus' name, and pharisaical
Dissemblers feign devotion. Then turn,
O pensive soul, to God, for He knows best
Thy grief, for He put it'into my breast.

Holy Sonnet IX

If poisonous minerals, and if that tree,
Whose fruit threw death on else immortal us,
If lecherous goats, if serpents envious
Cannot be damned, alas, why should I be?
Why should intent or reason, born in me,
Make sins, else equal, in me more heinous?
And mercy being easy and glorious
To God, in His stern wrath why threatens He?
But who am I that dare dispute with Thee?
O God, O, of Thine only worthy blood   10
And my tears make a heavenly Lethean flood,
And drown in it my sin's black memory.
That Thou remember them, some claim as debt;
I think it mercy, if Thou wilt forget.

Holy Sonnet X

Death be not proud, though some have called thee
Mighty and dreadful, for thou art not so;
For those whom thou think'st thou dost overthrow
Die not, poor Death, nor yet canst thou kill me.

From rest and sleep, which but thy pictures be,
Much pleasure; then from thee much more must flow,
And soonest our best men with thee do go,
Rest of their bones and soul's delivery.
Thou'art slave to fate, chance, kings, and desperate
    men,
10 And doth with poison, war, and sickness dwell;
And poppy'or charms can make us sleep as well,
And better than thy stroke; why swell'st thou then?
One short sleep past, we wake eternally,
And death shall be no more; Death, thou shalt die.

Holy Sonnet XI

Spit in my face, you Jews, and pierce my side,
Buffet and scoff, scourge and crucify me,
For I have sinned, and sinned, and only He,
Who could do no iniquity, hath died:
But by my death cannot be satisfied
My sins, which pass the Jews' impiety;
They killed once an inglorious man, but I
Crucify Him daily, being now glorified.
O let me then His strange love still admire:
10 Kings pardon, but He bore our punishment.
And Jacob came clothed in vile harsh attire
But to supplant, and with gainful intent;
God clothed himself in vile man's flesh that so
He might be weak enough to suffer woe.

Holy Sonnet XII

Why are we by all creatures waited on?
Why do the prodigal elements supply
Life and food to me, being more pure than I,
Simple and further from corruption?

Why brook'st thou, ignorant horse, subjection?
Who dost thou, bull and boar, so sillily
Dissemble weakness, and by'one man's stroke die,
Whose whole kind you might swallow'and feed
    upon?
Weaker I am, woe'is me, and worse than you;
You have not sinned, nor need be timorous.   10
But wonder at a greater wonder, for to us
Created nature doth these things subdue,
But their Creator, whom sin nor nature tied,
For us, His creatures and His foes, hath died.

Holy Sonnet XIII

What if this present were the world's last night?
Mark in my heart, O soul, where thou dost dwell,
The picture of Christ crucified, and tell
Whether His countenance can thee affright,
Tears in His eyes quench the amazing light,
Blood fills His frowns, which from His pierced head
    fell.
And can that tongue adjudge thee unto hell,
Which prayed forgiveness for His foes' fierce spite?
No, no; but as in my idolatry
I said to all my profane mistresses,   10
Beauty, of pity, foulness only is
A sign of rigour; so I say to thee,
To wicked spirits are horrid shapes assigned,
This beauteous form assures a piteous mind.

Holy Sonnet XIV

Batter my heart, three-personed God; for You
As yet but knock, breathe, shine, and seek to mend;
That I may rise and stand, o'erthrow me,'and bend
Your force, to break, blow, burn, and make me new.

I, like an usurped town to'another due,
Labour to'admit You, but O, to no end.
Reason, Your viceroy in me, me should defend,
But is captived, and proves weak or untrue.
Yet dearly'I love You,'and would be loved fain,
10   But am betrothed unto Your enemy;
Divorce me,'untie or break that knot again,
Take me to You, imprison me, for I,
Except You'enthral me, never shall be free,
Nor ever chaste, except You ravish me.

Holy Sonnet XV

Wilt thou love God, as He thee! Then digest,
My soul, this wholesome meditation,
How God the Spirit, by angels waited on
In heaven, doth make His temple in thy breast.
The Father, having begot a Son most blest,
And still begetting (for He ne'er begun),
Hath deigned to choose thee by adoption,
Coheir to'His glory'and sabbath's endless rest.
And as a robbed man which by search doth find
10   His stol'n stuff sold, must lose or buy'it again,
The Son of Glory came down, and was slain,
Us whom He'd made, and Satan stol'n, to'unbind.
'Twas much that man was made like God before,
But that God should be made like man, much more.

Holy Sonnet XVI

Father, part of His double interest
Unto Thy kingdom, Thy Son gives to me;
His jointure in the knotty Trinity
He keeps, and gives to me His death's conquest.

This Lamb, whose death with life the world hath blest,
Was from the world's beginning slain, and He
Hath made two wills, which with the legacy
Of His and Thy kingdom do Thy sons invest.
Yet such are these laws that men argue yet
Whether a man those statutes can fulfil;   10
None doth; but Thy all-healing grace and Spirit
Revive again what law and letter kill.
Thy law's abridgement and Thy last command
Is all but love; O let this last will stand!

Holy Sonnet XVII

Since she whom I loved hath paid her last debt
To nature, and to hers, and my good is dead,
And her soul early into heaven ravished,
Wholly in heavenly things my mind is set.
Here the admiring her my mind did whet
To seek Thee, God; so streams do show the head;
But though I have found Thee, and Thou my thirst
    hast fed,
A holy thirsty dropsy melts me yet.
But why should I beg more love, when as Thou
Dost woo my soul, for hers off'ring all Thine: 10
And dost not only fear lest I allow
My love to saints and angels, things divine,
But in Thy tender jealousy dost doubt
Lest the world, flesh, yea devil put Thee out.

Holy Sonnet XVIII

Show me, dear Christ, Thy spouse, so bright and clear.
What, is it she, which on the other shore
Goes richly painted? Or which robbed and tore
Laments and mourns in Germany and here?

Sleeps she a thousand, then peeps up one year?
Is she self-truth and errs? Now new, now'outwore?
Doth she,'and did she, and shall she evermore
On one, on seven, or on no hill appear?
Dwells she with us, or like adventuring knights
First travail we to seek and then make love?
Betray, kind husband, Thy spouse to our sights,
And let mine amorous soul court Thy mild dove,
Who is most true and pleasing to Thee then
When she'is embraced and open to most men.

Holy Sonnet XIX

O, to vex me, contraries meet in one;
Inconstancy unnaturally hath begot
A constant habit, that when I would not
I change in vows and in devotion.
As humorous is my contrition
As my profane love, and as soon forgot;
As riddlingly distempered, cold and hot,
As praying, as mute, as infinite, as none.
I durst not view heaven yesterday, and today
In prayers and flattering speeches I court God;
Tomorrow'I quake with true fear of His rod.
So my devout fits come and go away
Like a fantastic ague, save that here
Those are my best days when I shake with fear.

The Cross

Since Christ embraced the cross itself, dare I
His image, th'image of His cross deny?
Would I have profit by the sacrifice,
And dare the chosen altar to despise?
It bore all other sins, but is it fit
That it should bear the sin of scorning it?

Who from the picture would avert his eye,
How would he fly His pains, who there did die?
From me, no pulpit, nor misgrounded law,
Nor scandal taken, shall this cross withdraw;   10
It shall not, for it cannot, for the loss
Of this cross were to me another cross.
Better were worse, for no affliction,
No cross, is so extreme as to have none;
Who can blot out the cross, which th'instrument
Of God dew'd on me in the Sacrament?
Who can deny me power and liberty
To stretch mine arms and mine own cross to be?
Swim, and at every stroke thou art thy cross;
The mast and yard make one, where seas do toss.   20
Look down, thou spiest out crosses in small things;
Look up, thou see'st birds raised on crossed wings;
All the globe's frame, and spheres, is nothing else
But the meridians crossing parallels.
Material crosses then good physic be,
But yet spiritual have chief dignity.
These for extracted chemic medicine serve,
And cure much better, and as well preserve;
Then are you your own physic, or need none
When stilled or purged by tribulation.   30
For when that cross ungrudged unto you sticks,
Then are you to yourself a crucifix.
As, perchance, carvers do not faces make,
But that away, which hid them there, do take.
Let crosses, so, take what hid Christ in thee,
And be His image, or not His, but He.
But as oft alchemists do coiners prove,
So may a self-despising get self-love.
And then as worst surfeits of best meats be,
So is pride issued from humility,   40
For 'tis no child, but monster; therefore, cross
Your joy in crosses, else 'tis double loss,
And cross thy senses, else, both they and thou
Must perish soon and to destruction bow.

For if the'eye seek good objects, and will take
No cross from bad, we cannot 'scape a snake.
So with harsh, hard, sour, stinking, cross the rest,
Make them indifferent; call nothing best.
But most the eye needs crossing that can roam
50   And move; to th'others th'objects must come home.
And cross thy heart, for that in man alone
Points downwards and hath palpitation.
Cross those dejections when it downward tends,
And when it to forbidden heights pretends.
And as the brain through bony walls doth vent
By sutures, which a cross's form present,
So when thy brain works, ere thou utter it,
Cross and correct concupiscence of wit.
Be covetous of crosses, let none fall.
60   Cross no man else, but cross thyself in all.
Then doth the cross of Christ work faithfully
Within our hearts, when we love harmlessly
That cross's pictures much, and with more care
That cross's children, which our crosses are.

The Annunciation and Passion

Tamely frail body,'abstain today; today
My soul eats twice, Christ hither and away.
She sees Him man, so like God made in this
That of them both a circle emblem is,
Whose first and last concur; this doubtful day
Of feast or fast, Christ came, and went away;
She sees Him nothing twice at once, who'is all;
She sees a cedar plant itself and fall,
Her Maker put to making, and the head
10   Of life, at once, not yet alive, yet dead;
She sees at once the Virgin Mother stay
Reclused at home, public at Golgotha.

Sad and rejoiced she's seen at once, and seen
At almost fifty, and at scarce fifteen.
At once a son is promised her and gone,
Gabriel gives Christ to her, He her to John;
Not fully'a mother, she's in orbity,
At once receiver and the legacy;
All this, and all between, this day hath shown,
Th'abridgement of Christ's story, which makes one   20
(As in plain maps, the farthest west is east)
Of the'angel's *Ave*'and *Consummatum est*.
How well the Church, God's court of faculties,
Deals in some times and seldom joining these;
As by the self-fixed pole we never do
Direct our course, but the next star thereto,
Which shows where the'other is, and which we say
(Because it strays not far) doth never stray;
So God by his Church, nearest to Him, we know,
And stand firm, if we by her motion go;   30
His spirit, as His fiery pillar doth
Lead, and his Church, as cloud, to one end both:
This Church, by letting those days join, hath shown
Death and conception in mankind is one.
Or 'twas in Him the same humility,
That He would be a man and leave to be:
Or as creation He hath made, as God,
With the Last Judgement but one period,
His imitating spouse would join in one
Manhood's extremes: He shall come, He is gone;   40
Or as though one blood drop, which thence did fall,
Accepted, would have served, He yet shed all;
So though the least of His pains, deeds, or words,
Would busy'a life, she all this day affords;
This treasure then, in gross, my soul uplay,
And in my life retail it every day.

Goodfriday, 1613. *Riding Westward*

Let man's soul be a sphere, and then, in this,
The'intelligence that moves, devotion is,
And as the other spheres, by being grown
Subject to foreign motions, lose their own,
And being by others hurried every day,
Scarce in a year their natural form obey,
Pleasure or business, so, our souls admit
For their first mover, and are whirled by it.
Hence is't that I am carried towards the West
10   This day, when my soul's form bends towards the
                East.
There I should see a sun, by rising, set,
And by that setting endless day beget;
But that Christ on this cross did rise and fall,
Sin had eternally benighted all.
Yet dare I'almost be glad I do not see
That spectacle of too much weight for me.
Who sees God's face, that is self-life, must die;
What a death were it then to see God die?
It made His own lieutenant, Nature, shrink,
20   It made His footstool crack, and the sun wink.
Could I behold those hands which span the poles,
And turn all spheres at once, pierced with those holes?
Could I behold that endless height which is
Zenith to us, and our antipodes,
Humbled below us? or that blood which is
The seat of all our souls, if not of His,
Made dirt of dust, or that flesh which was worn
By God for His apparel, ragged and torn?
If on these things I durst not look, durst I
30   Upon His miserable mother cast mine eye,
Who was God's partner here, and furnished thus
Half of that sacrifice which ransomed us?
Though these things, as I ride, be from mine eye,
They're present yet unto my memory,

For that looks towards them; and Thou look'st
    towards me,
O Saviour, as Thou hang'st upon the tree;
I turn my back to Thee but to receive
Corrections, till Thy mercies bid Thee leave.
O think me worth Thine anger, punish me,
Burn off my rusts and my deformity,   40
Restore Thine image, so much, by Thy grace,
That Thou may'st know me, and I'll turn my face.

Upon the Translation of the Psalms by Sir Philip Sidney and the Countess of Pembroke, His Sister

Eternal God (for whom whoever dare
Seek new expressions, do the circle square,
And thrust into straight corners of poor wit
Thee, who art cornerless and infinite),
I would but bless Thy name, not name Thee now;
(And Thy gifts are as infinite as Thou)
Fix we our praises therefore on this one,
That as Thy blessèd spirit fell upon
These Psalms' first author in a cloven tongue
(For 'twas a double power by which he sung   10
The highest matter in the noblest form),
So Thou hast cleft that spirit to perform
That work again, and shed it here upon
Two, by their bloods and by Thy spirit one;
A brother and a sister, made by Thee
The organ where Thou art the harmony.
Two that make one John Baptist's holy voice,
And who that Psalm, now let the isles rejoice,
Have both translated and applied it too,
Both told us what and taught us how to do.   20
They show us islanders our joy, our King;
They tell us why, and teach us how to sing;

Make all this all, three choirs, heaven, earth, and
    spheres;
The first, heaven, hath a song, but no man hears;
The spheres have music, but they have no tongue,
Their harmony is rather danced than sung;
But our third choir, to which the first gives ear
(For angels learn by what the Church does here),
This choir hath all. The organist is he
30   Who hath tuned God and man, the organ we;
The songs are these, which heaven's high holy muse
Whispered to David, David to the Jews;
And David's successors in holy zeal,
In forms of joy and art do re-reveal
To us so sweetly and sincerely too
That I must not rejoice as I would do
When I behold that these Psalms are become
So well attired abroad, so ill at home,
So well in chambers, in Thy Church so ill
40   As I can scarce call that reformed until
This be reformed; would a whole state present
A lesser gift than some one man hath sent?
And shall our Church, unto our spouse and King
More hoarse, more harsh than any other, sing?
For that we pray, we praise Thy name for this,
Which, by this Moses and this Miriam, is
Already done; and as those Psalms we call
(Though some have other authors) David's all,
So though some have, some may some Psalms
    translate,
50   We Thy Sidneyan Psalms shall celebrate,
And, till we come the extemporal song to sing
(Learned the first hour that we see the King,
Who hath translated these translators) may
These, their sweet learnèd labours, all the way
Be as our tuning, that when hence we part,
We may fall in with them and sing our part.

To Mr Tilman after He Had Taken Orders

Thou, whose diviner soul hath caused thee now
To put thy hand unto the holy plough,
Making lay-scornings of the ministry
Not an impediment, but victory,
What bringst thou home with thee? How is thy mind
Affected since the vintage? Dost thou find
New thoughts and stirrings in thee? And as steel
Touched with a lodestone, dost new motions feel?
Or, as a ship after much pain and care,
For iron and cloth brings home rich Indian ware, 10
Hast thou thus traffic'd, but with far more gain
Of noble goods and with less time and pain?
Thou art the same materials as before,
Only the stamp is changed, but no more.
And as new crowned kings alter the face
But not the money's substance, so hath grace
Changed only God's old image by creation
To Christ's new stamp, at this thy coronation;
Or, as we paint angels with wings because
They bear God's message and proclaim His laws, 20
Since thou must do the like and so must move,
Art thou new feathered with celestial love?
Dear, tell me where thy purchase lies, and show
What thy advantage is above, below.
But if thy gainings do surmount expression,
Why doth the foolish world scorn that profession
Whose joys pass speech? Why do they think unfit
That gentry should join families with it,
As if their day were only to be spent
In dressing, mistressing and compliment? 30
Alas, poor joys, but poorer men, whose trust
Seems richly placed in sublimed dust
(For, such are clothes and beauties, which though gay,
Are, at the best, but of sublimèd clay),

Let then the world thy calling disrespect,
But go thou on and pity their neglect.
What function is so noble as to be
Ambassador to God and destiny,
To open life, to give kingdoms to more
40   Than kings give dignities, to keep heaven's door?
Mary's prerogative was to bear Christ, so
'Tis preachers' to convey Him, for they do
As angels out of clouds, from pulpits speak
And bless the poor beneath, the lame, the weak.
If then th'astronomers, whereas they spy
A new-found star, their optics magnify,
How brave are those who with their engines, can
Bring man to heaven, and heaven again to man?
These are thy titles and pre-eminences,
50   In whom must meet God's graces, men's offences,
And so the heavens, which beget all things here,
And the'earth our mother, which these things doth
      bear,
Both these in thee are in thy calling knit,
And make thee now a blest hermaphrodite.

A Hymn to Christ, at the Author's Last Going into Germany

In what torn ship soever I embark,
That ship shall be my emblem of Thy ark;
What sea soever swallow me, that flood
Shall be to me an emblem of Thy blood;
Though Thou with clouds of anger do disguise
Thy face, yet through that mask I know those eyes,
    Which, though they turn away sometimes,
        They never will despise.

    I sacrifice this island unto Thee,
    And all whom I loved there, and who loved me;   10
    When I have put our seas 'twixt them and me,
    Put Thou Thy sea betwixt my sins and Thee.
    As the tree's sap doth seek the root below
    In winter, in my winter now I go
       Where none but Thee, th'eternal root
         Of true love I may know.

    Nor Thou nor Thy religion dost control
    The amorousness of an harmonious soul,
    But Thou would'st have that love Thyself: as Thou
    Art jealous, Lord, so I am jealous now;   20
    Thou lov'st not, till from loving more, Thou free
    My soul: whoever gives, takes liberty:
       O, if Thou car'st not whom I love,
         Alas, Thou lov'st not me.

    Seal then this bill of my divorce to all
    On whom those fainter beams of love did fall;
    Marry those loves, which in youth scattered be
    On fame, wit, hopes (false mistresses), to Thee.
    Churches are best for prayer that have least light:
    To see God only, I go out of sight,   30
       And to 'scape stormy days, I choose
         An everlasting night.

Hymn to God my God, in my Sickness

Since I am coming to that holy room
    Where, with Thy choir of saints for evermore,
I shall be made Thy music, as I come
    I tune the instrument here at the door,
    And what I must do then, think here before.

Whil'st my physicians by their love are grown
    Cosmographers, and I their map, who lie
Flat on this bed, that by them may be shown
    That this is my South-west discovery
10   Per fretum febris, by these straits to die,

I joy, that in these straits I see my West;
    For, though their currents yield return to none,
What shall my West hurt me? As West and East
    In all flat maps (and I am one) are one,
      So death doth touch the resurrection.

Is the Pacific Sea my home? Or are
    The Eastern riches? Is Jerusalem?
Anyan, and Magellan, and Gibraltar,
    All straits, and none but straits, are ways to them,
20   Whether where Japhet dwelt, or Cham, or Shem.

We think that paradise and calvary,
    Christ's cross, and Adam's tree, stood in one place;
Look, Lord, and find both Adams met in me;
    As the first Adam's sweat surrounds my face,
      May the last Adam's blood my soul embrace.

So, in His purple wrapped receive me Lord,
    By these His thorns, give me, His other crown;
And as to others' souls I preached Thy word,
    Be this my text, my sermon to mine own,
30   Therefore that He may raise the Lord throws down.

A Hymn to God the Father

I

Wilt Thou forgive that sin where I begun,
　　Which was my sin, though it were done before?
Wilt Thou forgive that sin through which I run,
　　And do run still, though still I do deplore?
　　　　When Thou hast done, Thou hast not done,
　　　　　　For I have more.

II

Wilt Thou forgive that sin by which I won
　　Others to sin, and made my sin their door?
Wilt Thou forgive that sin which I did shun
　　A year or two, but wallowed in a score?　　　10
　　　　When Thou hast done, Thou hast not done,
　　　　　　For I have more.

III

I have a sin of fear, that when I've spun
　　My last thread, I shall perish on the shore;
Swear by Thyself, that at my death Thy sun
　　Shall shine as he shines now, and heretofore;
　　　　And, having done that, Thou hast done,
　　　　　　I have no more.

To Mr George Herbert, with One of my Seals, of the Anchor and Christ

Qui prius assuetus Serpentum fasce Tabellas
　　Signare, (haec nostrae symbola parva Domus)
Adscitus domui Domini, patrióque relicto
　　Stemmate, nanciscor stemmata jure nova.
Hinc mihi Crux primo quae fronte impressa lavacro,
　　Finibus extensis, anchora facta patet.

Anchorae in effigiem, Crux tandem desinit ipsam,
    Anchora fit tandem Crux tolerata diu.
Hoc tamen ut fiat, Christo vegetatur ab ipso
10   Crux, et ab Affixo, est Anchora facta, Iesu.
Nec Natalitiis penitus serpentibus orbor,
    Non ita dat Deus, ut auferat ante data.
Quâ sapiens, Dos est; Quâ terram lambit et ambit,
    Pestis; At in nostra fit Medicina Cruce,
Serpens; fixa Cruci si sit Natura; Crucíque
    A fixo, nobis, Gratia tota fluat.
Omnia cum Crux sint, Crux Anchora fixa, sigillum
    Non tam dicendum hoc, quam Catechismus erit.
Mitto, nec exigua, exiguâ sub imagine, dona,
20   Pignora amicitiae, et munera; Vota, preces.
Plura tibi accumulet, sanctus cognominis, Ille
    Regia qui flavo Dona sigillat Equo.

A sheaf of snakes used heretofore to be
My seal, the crest of our poor family.
Adopted in God's family, and so
Our old coat lost, unto new arms I go.
The cross (my seal at baptism) spread below,
Does, by that form, into an anchor grow.
Crosses grow anchors; bear, as thou should'st do
Thy cross, and that cross grows an anchor too.
But He, that makes our crosses anchors thus,
10 Is Christ, who there is crucified for us.
Yet may I, with this, my first serpents hold,
God gives new blessings, and yet leaves the old;
The Serpent may, as wise, my pattern be;
My poison, as he feeds on dust, that's me.
And as he rounds the earth to murder sure,
My death he is, but on the cross, my cure.
Crucify nature then, and then implore
All grace from Him, crucified there before;
When all is cross, and that cross anchor grown,
20 This seal's a catechism, not a seal alone.

Under that little seal great gifts I send,
Works, and prayers, pawns, and fruits of a friend.
And may that saint which rides in our great seal,
To you, who bear his name, great bounties deal.

Notes

The copy-text is 1633 unless noted otherwise. For information on Text Notes, see A Note on the Texts, p. xli.

The Good Morrow

1. *troth*: Honesty, loyalty, with a possible allusion to a pledge-troth or engagement to marry.
3. *country*: Rustic, common; a common sexual pun on 'cunt'ry'.
4. *snorted*: Snored, slumbered.
   seven sleepers: Seven legendary Christian youths hid in a cave to escape religious persecution. When their exit was blocked, they fell into a deep sleep, awakening two hundred years later after Christianity had triumphed.
19. *Whatever dies was not mixed equally*: Refers to the alchemical belief that a substance made of equal parts would remain permanently mixed and the medical belief that male and female seed must be equally mixed for conception to occur; the sexual pun on 'dies' refers to the popular belief that orgasm shortened one's life.

Text note: 13 others *ms*] other *1633*

Song: ('Go and catch a falling star')

2. *mandrake*: A poisonous and narcotic plant; the forked shape of its root was said to resemble the human body; the fruit was thought to increase women's fertility.
4. *cleft the Devil's foot*: The Devil, associated with Pan, the god of nature, and goats, was traditionally represented as cloven-hoofed.

5. *mermaids singing*: Mermaids' singing, like the mythic Sirens'
    song, was said to lure sailors to their death.
9. *honest*: Honourable, worthy of holding a respectable position.
27. *False*: Unfaithful; deceptive.

Woman's Constancy

1–2. *Now thou . . . say*: The lovers are probably about to spend their
    first night together.
9. *those*: True marriages.
14. *Vain*: Futile.
    lunatic: Changeable, fickle; under the influence of the moon
    (Luna), who was traditionally female, suggesting that the speaker
    could be a woman who demands equal freedom of choice and
    action.
    'scapes: Escapes; breaches of chastity; subterfuges.
17. *I may think so too*: I may want our relationship to end as well.

The Undertaking

2. *Worthies*: Nine historical figures who embody the chivalric ideal,
    all the facets of the perfect warrior.
6. *specular stone*: Selenite, a stone so rare that the art of cutting it
    was of little use.
15. *colour*: Outward appearances; a show or semblance that conceals
    the truth.
16. *oldest clothes*: Their outer appearance; his earliest and thus oldest
    impression of them.
19. *dare love that*: Dare love virtue; dare make love to that woman.
20. *forget the he and she*: Forget the differences between sexes; forget
    sex or intercourse.
22. *profane*: Common.

Text note: title The Undertaking *1635 and ms*] untitled *1633*,
Platonic Love *ms*

The Sun Rising

7. *the King will ride*: Often used erroneously to date the poem after
    Queen Elizabeth's death in 1603; the title 'king' was used by
    both male and female monarchs, including Elizabeth, who was
    as fond of hunting as her successor, James I.

8.   *offices*: Tasks.
17.   *both the Indias of spice and mine*: The East Indies, a source
      of spices, and the West Indies, known for precious metals and
      stones.
30.   *sphere*: Medieval astronomers envisaged a set of transparent
      hollow globes revolving round the earth and carrying with them
      the sun, moon, planets and fixed stars; the apparent outward
      limit of space.

The Indifferent

2.   *whom want betrays*: Whose poverty has forced her to choose a
      wealthy husband or lover.
3.   *who masks*: Who hides her true character behind an outward
      show; who takes part in courtly entertainments known as
      masques.
5.   *tries*: Tries to believe; puts things to the test.
11.   *do*: Copulate.
15.   *know*: In the biblical sense – have sexual intercourse with.
17.   *travail*: Labour; travel.
      thorough: Through; but also thoroughly.
      travail thorough: Travel through as in a one-night affair; labour
      thoroughly during intercourse.

Love's Usury

5.   *let my body reign*: Let passion and sexual impulses govern my
      behaviour.
6.   *snatch*: Have a passing sexual encounter; slang for the female
      genitalia.
      have: Possess sexually.
      forget: Forget the nights of debauchery or forget his lover.
7.   *relict*: Former lover.
10.   *at next nine*: At 9:00 p.m., after intercepting a letter to his lover
      from his rival.
11–12. *mistake by the way ... delay*: Pretend that the maid whom
      he meets en route to the rendezvous is his lady-love, seduce the
      maid and lie about it to his lover.
14.   *country grass*: Rural woman, with a pun on 'cunt'ry'.
      comfitures: Sweetmeats (with sexual allusion).
15.   *quelque-choses*: Dainties; insubstantial trifles (sexually sug-
      gestive).

21. *then*: When I am old.
22. *fruit of love*: Children.

The Canonization

title *Canonization*: Placing a pious person in the canon or calendar of saints; the lovers are canonized as saints of love.
5. *course*: Course of action or career path.
   place: Position, often at court.
7. *the King's real, or his stamped face*: The King's real face or his face stamped on a *real*, a Spanish coin; the pun dissolves the apparent distinction between courtiership and financial advancement.
15. *plaguy bill*: List of plague victims.
20. *fly*: A moth or a taper fly, which burns itself when attracted to a flame, often thought to be hermaphroditic and capable of resurrection.
21. *die*: Both 'expire' and 'reach sexual climax', since orgasm was thought to shorten one's life.
22. *the'eagle and the dove*: Symbols of strength and gentleness, bringing masculine and feminine traits together in one new being, the reborn phoenix (l. 23).
23. *phoenix*: A mythical creature thought to contain both sexes since, after consuming itself in flames, it is reborn from its own ashes; a common symbol for Christ.
26. *the same*: Either the same as before or the same as each other.
32. *sonnets*: Love poems.
   pretty rooms: Subtle pun on 'stanza', the Italian word for 'room'.

Text notes: 30 legend *ms*] legends *1633*;   44 from *Grierson*] frow *1633*;   45 your *1669 and ms*] our *1633–54 and ms*

The Triple Fool

6–7. *th'earths . . . away*: It was believed that seawater passed through the earth in underground tunnels.
10. *numbers*: Verses with a given number of syllables per line.
14. *set*: Set to music.

Lovers' Infiniteness

21-2. *The ground . . . all*: When land was sold, crops already growing
        on the land belonged to the new owner.
30.   *thou with losing savest it*: 'For whosoever will save his life shall
        lose it; but whosoever shall lose his life for my sake and the
        gospel's, the same shall save it' (Mark 8:35).
31.   *liberal*: Abundant, bountiful, generous; open-minded.

> *Text notes*: title Lovers' *1633–69*] Love's *Grierson and most
> modern editors*; 20 it *1635*] is *1633*

Song: ('Sweetest love, I do not go')

8.   *by feigned deaths to die*: Grow accustomed to parting by imagin-
       ing our deaths or, as the pun on 'die' suggests, by having sexual
       intercourse.
28.   *My life's blood doth decay*: Tears and sighs were said to shorten
       life by using up drops of blood.

The Legacy

16.   *cozen*: Cheat, deceive.
18.   *colours*: Various hues; the insignia of a knight or lady; figurat-
       ively, outward appearances; shows or semblances that conceal
       the truth; specifically, in law, apparent or prima-facie rights.
       corners: Angles; tight or secluded places.
        Hence, either the heart is imperfect because it is spotted and
       not perfectly round like a circle, or the heart has been altered by
       actions done in a corner, secretly or covertly, or the heart belongs
       to a person whose title gives him an apparent or prima-facie right
       to it.
20.   *entire to none*: Not solely possessed by any one person.
21.   *art*: Either her artfulness and deceptiveness or his attempts to
       court and remake her through poetry.
24.   *no man . . . thine*: Either the heart is hers because she gave it to
       him and no man (neither the speaker nor her father) could hold
       it because the choice of a lover is hers alone, or the heart is his
       but he can no longer hold on to it because he is so in love with
       her that it flies to her.

A Fever

8.   *vapours*: Rises or ascends; is emitted or diffused in the form of a vapour.

13–14. *wrangling schools ... world*: Theologians argued about the origin and nature of the fire that would, as the Book of Revelation stipulated, consume the earth on Judgement Day.

24.   *unchangeable firmament*: The arch or vault of heaven, which was not subject to decay.

Air and Angels

6.   *glorious nothing*: Something with the bodily form of an angel, but made of air.

9.   *subtle*: Rarefied, airy.

15.   *ballast*: Weigh down, balance a ship.

18.   *pinnace*: Small vessel bringing provisions to larger ships; a prostitute or mistress; possible pun on 'penis'.
      overfraught: Too heavily freighted or laden.

22.   *scatt'ring bright*: Suggesting something angelic or ethereal.
      inhere: Remain in mystical union with something or someone.

26.   *disparity*: Inequality; dissimilarity.

Break of Day

11–12. *heart ... him*: The lines reveal that the speaker is a woman who has entrusted her clandestine lover with her 'heart and honour', her love and her reputation for virtue.

13.   *business*: Official or professional duties; busyness; care, solicitude, anxiety.

18.   *Such wrong*: As much wrong.

The Anniversary

11.   *Two graves ... thine and my corpse*: Because the speaker and his lover are not married.

18.   *inmates*: Temporary residents.

21.   *throughly*: Thoroughly.

23–4. *Here ... subjects be*: On earth, in a patriarchal society where the king rules over his subjects as the husband rules over his wife, their love is unique because they are both princes and kings, and neither rules over the other.

30. *threescore*: Sixty years.

Text note: 22 we *ms*] now *1633*

A Valediction of My Name in the Window

title *Valediction*: A bidding farewell.
4.   *that which graved it*: A diamond, which engraved his name on the window.
6.   *diamonds of either rock*: Oriental diamonds were divided into two kinds, depending on whether they came from an old or a newly discovered mine.
9.   *'Tis more*: A possible allusion to Donne's fiancée, Anne More.
21. *death's head*: A memento mori or reminder of mortality.
24. *ruinous anatomy*: Decayed skeleton.
25. *all my souls*: The rational, vegetative (having the faculty of growth, but devoid of sensation or thought) and sensory faculties of the soul.
28. *rafters of my body*: Skeleton.
31. *repair*: Revive, recreate; reinstate.
32. *so*: By following the pattern of his love.
36. *have supremacy*: Are in ascendance.
48. *genius*: Protective spirit.
49–50. *melted . . . page*: The maid is 'melted': weakened by the tempting riches of her mistress's new suitor and the persuasions of his male servant.
52. *Disputed it*: Argued in favour of the new suitor's letter.
55–6. *if this treason go / To'an overt act*: If the thought of treason (which was itself illegal) progress to an overt act of treason (an even greater offence).
57. *superscribing*: Writing or addressing a letter to the poet's rival; writing one name above another.
66. *dying*: During orgasm, which was believed to shorten life.

Twicknam Garden

title *Twicknam*: From 1608 to 1617, Twickenham Park was the residence of Lucy Russell, Countess of Bedford (bap. 1581, d. 1627), to whom Donne addressed verse letters; see the notes to 'To the Countess of Bedford ("Reason is our soul's left hand")'. The title, which does not appear in some manuscripts, may be a later addition.

5.   *self traitor*: Because he, not she, is responsible for his suffering.
6.   *spider love*: Cunning, skilful and perhaps poisonous love that entraps him in its web.
      transubstantiates: Transforms from one substance to another, with an allusion to the Roman Catholic doctrine of the Eucharist.
7.   *manna*: Something beneficial or pleasing, appearing unexpectedly, opportunely or divinely (see Exodus 16); spiritual nourishment, especially the Eucharist.
      gall: A bitter substance, bile.
17.   *mandrake*: A poisonous and narcotic plant whose root was thought to groan or shriek when uprooted and to kill whoever dug it up; believed to aid conception when consumed by a woman.
22.   *mine*: Either my tears or my mistress's tears.
26.   *perverse*: Not in acceptance with standard practice; obstinate, ill-tempered; perverted, wicked.
      sex: The female sex; the act of sex.
27.   *truth*: Honesty, faithfulness.
      kills me: Destroys me; brings me to sexual climax.

      Text notes: 17 grow *1633*] groan *ms*; 24 woman's *ms*] womens *1633–69*

Valediction of the Book

3.   *eloign*: Remove to a distance.
6.   *Sibyl*: The legendary prophetess who aided Aeneas in Book 2 of Virgil's *Aeneid* (c. 29–19 BC).
7.   *Her*: Corinna, a poetess who taught the Greek poet Pindar (?518 BC–?438 BC) to write and defeated him five times in poetry-writing competitions at Thebes.
8.   *her*: Polla Argentaria, who aided her husband Lucan (AD 39–65) in writing his poetry.
9.   *her*: Phantasia, an Egyptian prophetess, whose poem on the Trojan War was thought to be Homer's source for the *Iliad*.
13.   *subliming*: Purifying.
25.   *Vandals . . . Goths*: Barbarian groups that brought about the fall of Rome and classical civilization in the fourth and fifth centuries.
27.   *Schools*: Medieval philosophers, known as the Schoolmen.
      spheres music: The movement of celestial bodies was thought to produce music.
31.   *exhaled*: Drawn out or raised.

39. *prerogative*: Prior or exclusive right or privilege.
42. *subsidies*: Pecuniary aid granted by Parliament to the sovereign to meet special needs, here privileges granted to male suitors by their mistresses, who have received their prerogative directly from the God of love.
43. *them*: Subsidies.
45. *chimeras*: Wild fancies; unreal, imaginary creatures.
      vain: Useless, worthless.
48. *their art*: Politics.
54. *find out*: Discover the falsity of.
56. *takes*: Measures.
59. *To take a latitude*: To measure the breadth or range of something; to find one's geographical latitude according to the position of the stars.
61. *At their brightest*: At their highest point in the sky.
62. *longitudes*: Lengths or durations. The only method of measuring geographical longitude was by observing the time of a marked celestial event from two different points and then comparing them; thus presence, or being together (l. 57), can show the breadth or extent of their love, but absence, or separation (l. 58), reveals its duration.

Text notes: title of the Book *ms*] to his Book *1633*; 53 their nothing *1635*] there something *1633*

Community

title *Community*: Common character; social intercourse, fellowship; a body of people.
3.   *these*: Women.
12. *rests*: Remains.
14. *as visible as green*: God has imbued all plant life with green, making it obvious which things on earth are alive. If women were inherently good, it would be equally apparent.
17. *waste*: Destroy.
22. *meat*: Nutmeat; nourishment.

Text notes: title Community *1635*] *untitled 1633*; 3 these *1633*] there *ms*

Love's Growth

4. *grass*: 'All flesh is grass, and all the goodliness thereof is as the flower of the field' (Isaiah 40:6).
8. *quintessence*: The pure essence of natural bodies, reputed to cure all ills.
13. *elemented*: Composed of mixed elements, not pure.
14. *sometimes do*: By making love.
18. *Stars ... shown*: Stars only appear to grow larger as they reflect the sun.
19–20. *Gentle love ... now*: Possibly alluding to lovemaking or pregnancy.
24. *concentric*: Having a common centre, like the heavenly spheres believed to revolve around the earth.

Text note: 23 to *ms*] so *1633*

Love's Exchange

2. *given*: Particular; given to the Devil.
4. *play*: Gambling.
11. *non obstante*: Literally, not in the way; notwithstanding; a dispensation by a monarch to act contrary to the law.
25. *by war's law condition not*: According to the law of war, a town that holds out against a siege until conquered cannot set the conditions of surrender.
32. *vowed men*: Those who have taken a vow of celibacy.
42. *Racked carcasses*: Bodies tortured on the rack.
    anatomies: Corpses used for dissection; anatomical textbooks or drawings.

Text notes: 4 and *ms*] or *1633*; 5 who *ms*] which *1633*; 20 pain *ms*] pains *1633*

Confined Love

6. *One might but one man know*: One woman might only 'know', or have sex with, one man.
12. *jointures*: Property held jointly by a husband and wife for life, retained by the widow after her husband's death unless she remarried.

14. *we are made worse than those*: Revealing that the speaker is a woman.
16. *deal*: Trade. A docked ship was a common place of prostitution, or sexual 'trading'.
    withal: In addition; at the same time; therewith.
21. *waste*: Waste away.

Text note: title Confined Love *1635*] *untitled 1633*

The Dream

16. *beyond an angel's art*: According to St Thomas Aquinas (*c.* 1224–74), only God, not angels, could read man's thoughts.
21. *showed thee, thee*: Showed you to be yourself.
22. *doubt*: Suspect.
29. *goest to come*: Leaves in order to come back and reach sexual climax.
30. *but else would die*: But otherwise, if I didn't think you were coming back, I would die of disappointment; but otherwise I would prefer to 'die', that is, to reach sexual climax.

A Valediction of Weeping

3. *coins them*: Causes them.
8. *that thou falls which it bore*: The image of you reflected in that tear falls (and breaks apart).
13. *make that, which was nothing, all*: A globemaker, by placing maps on the bare surface of an unmarked sphere, creates the entire world.
15. *Which thee doth wear*: Which reflects your image.
19. *more than Moon*: She is more powerful than the moon because she has the power to protect him as well as to destroy him.
27. *hastes the other's death*: Sighs, tears and sexual intercourse were all thought to shorten one's life.

Text note: 8 falls *ms*] falst *1633*

Love's Alchemy

2. *centric*: Central; alluding to the female genitalia, which were often referred to as a woman's 'centre'.
7. *chemic*: Alchemist.

elixir: A much-sought-after alchemical preparation that would supposedly transform base metal into gold or prolong life indefinitely.

13. *thrift*: Success, prosperity, good fortune.

14. *vain bubble's shadow*: Something as fruitless and insubstantial as the shadow of a bubble.

15. *my man*: My manservant.

17. *Endure ... play*: Brave the brief period of indignity associated with being a bridegroom.

22. *that day's*: The wedding day's.

24. *wit*: Understanding, intellect, reason.

mummy: Flesh; a medicinal substance prepared from mummified flesh; a pun on 'mammy', a common colloquial term for 'mother'. Hence (ll. 23–4), at their best, women are sweetness and wit; once possessed sexually, they are mere flesh, or mothers, too burdened by bodily concerns to exercise their minds.

The Flea

1. *Mark but this flea*: A possible parody of sermonizing.

3. *sucked*: A visual pun, since the letters *s* and *f* looked similar.

4. *bloods mingled*: It was thought that both sexual intercourse and pregnancy involved the mingling of blood.

6. *maidenhead*: Virginity.

7. *enjoys*: Experiences pleasure or possesses sexually.

15. *jet*: A dense, semi-precious black form of coal polished to a shiny brilliance.

16. *use*: Custom or habit, often with sexual innuendo; the distinctive ritual or liturgy that prevailed in a given Church; the act of holding land or property so as to derive revenue.

kill: Destroy; bring to sexual climax.

18. *sacrilege*: Because the flea is a temple where their love has been consecrated.

26. *honour*: Reputation; virginity or the female genitalia.

27. *waste*: Be consumed; be destroyed or annihilated as something immaterial.

The Curse

2. *mistress*: A woman who is courted by a man; a woman who has power or control over someone else.

3. *purse*: Money bag and its contents; slang for 'scrotum'.

3–5. *His only ... foes*: May his one and only purse, and only his purse, attract a woman to him who later gives herself freely to his enemies.

8.   *With fear ... torn*: Torn between fear of losing his love and shame of being loved by such a woman.

16. *incestuously*: Also, loosely, adulterous.

14–16. *In early ... begot*: Changed in 1635–69 to read:

> Or may he for her virtue reverence
> One, that hates him only for impotence
> And equal traitors be, she and his sense.

24. *circumcised*: Cut short (with an allusion to circumcision).
     bread: Ordinary food, means of subsistence.

25. *gamesters*: Those addicted to amorous sport.
     gall: Painful swelling, pustule.
     gamesters' gall: Venereal disease.

30. *schedules*: Supplementary papers.

31. *for*: Introducing the grounds or reason for something previously said.
     it: That man whom I have just cursed; also, there.

32. *Nature*: Innate disposition or character; sexual drive; the regulative physical power controlling the material world.
     beforehand: Already, before I began cursing.
     outcursed: Completely or thoroughly cursed; defeated or got the better of in a cursing contest.

31–2. *for if it ... me*: The final couplet can be read in various ways: if the person being cursed is a she, a woman, she is already more cursed than all my curses can make her seem; if there is a woman, i.e. if I indeed have a mistress, then nature has already cursed that man who 'guesses, thinks, or dreams he knows / Who is my mistress' more than all my preceding curses; if there is a she, if I indeed have a mistress, then nature has cursed me more than I have cursed the man who thinks he guessed my mistress's identity.

Text note: 27 mines *ms*] mine *1633–69*

The Message

4.   *fashions*: Behaviours.
23. *That will none*: That will have none of you.

Text note: title The Message *1635] untitled 1633*

A Nocturnal upon St Lucy's Day, Being the Shortest Day

title *Nocturnal*: Nocturne, a musical composition suggestive of the
      night.
      St Lucy's Day: The poem was allegedly written on 12 December,
      the night before St Lucy's Day, the shortest night of the year (the
      winter solstice) in the old calendar. St Lucy was the patron saint
      of the blind, and her name associates her with the Latin *lux,
      lucis*, 'light'.
3.   *flasks*: Powder flasks, referring to stars reputed to store the sun's
      light.
4.   *squibs*: Explosions.
6.   *balm*: Rain or any other life-giving substance.
      hydroptic: Thirsty.
7.   *bed's-feet*: The soul was said to shrink to the foot of the bed
      moments before death.
14.   *express*: Extract.
15.   *quintessence*: The purest or most perfect form of some quality;
      the pure essence of heavenly bodies, supposedly latent in all
      things, whose extraction was the great aim of alchemy since it
      was reputed to cure all ills.
15–18. *A quintessence ... are not*: Love extracted a quintessence
      from my grief and re-created me out of nothingness.
21.   *limbeck*: An alembic or distiller used in alchemy.
29.   *the first nothing*: The nothingness out of which God created the
      world.
32–4. *If I were ... invest*: Even animals, plants and stones are
      composed of something and can experience life (as Donne's ser-
      mons explain).
37.   *my sun*: My beloved.
      renew: Return.
38.   *lesser sun*: The natural sun.
39–40. *At this time ... lust*: Capricorn, the zodiacal sign of the goat,
      began at the same time as the winter solstice in the old calendar.
      Goats were considered lustful.

44.   *Vigil*: The night of prayer before a Church feast or the vigil beside a departed body.

Witchcraft by a Picture

6.   *By pictures . . . to kill*: It was believed that witches could kill by creating a picture of someone and then destroying it.
14.   *Being . . . from all malice free*: Because the picture is in your heart, you cannot destroy it without killing yourself.

The Bait

This is one of many responses to Christopher Marlowe's enormously popular song, 'The Passionate Shepherd to his Love', which was printed in *The Passionate Pilgrim* (1599) and *England's Helicon* (1600).

17.   *reeds*: Rods made from reeds.
23.   *sleave-silk flies*: Fishing lures made of silk.

Text notes: title The Bait *1635*] *untitled 1633*; 18 with *1635*] which *1633*; 23 sleave-silk *1635*] sleavesicke *1633*

The Apparition

5.   *vestal*: A virgin serving the Roman goddess Vesta.
      worse arms: Arms of another, less worthy, man.
11.   *aspen*: Quivering.
12.   *quicksilver*: Mercury; a quicksilver sweat bath was a common treatment for syphilis.

Text note: 12 in a *ms*] in in a *1633*

The Broken Heart

13.   *Love*: Cupid, the Roman god of love.
15.   *chained shot*: Cannon balls chained together.
      ranks: Battalions.
16.   *fry*: Small fish consumed by larger ones.
25.   *Nothing can to nothing fall*: Matter can never be completely annihilated.
26.   *Nor any place be empty quite*: A complete vacuum cannot exist.
29.   *glasses*: Mirrors.

A Valediction Forbidding Mourning

5.   *melt*: Dissolve by parting, but perhaps also by having intercourse.

7.   *profanation*: Desecration.

8.   *laity*: Laymen, those who are uninitiated in the mysteries of our clandestine love affair.

9.   *Moving of th'earth*: Earthquakes, seen as ominous portents of worldly disaster.

11–12. *trepidation of the spheres . . . innocent*: According to medieval astronomy, movement of the celestial spheres had no ill effects on earth.

13.   *sublunary*: Beneath the moon and subject to its changes; earthly, mundane.

14.   *sense*: Reliant on sensuality.

19.   *Inter-assurèd*: Equally certain of the other's regard and fidelity.

24.   *gold*: The chemical symbol for gold was a circle inscribed around a point, the same mark made by the compass in ll. 26–36.

26.   *twin compasses*: The two legs of a compass used to draw a circle, the symbol of perfection.

32.   *erect*: The sexual connotation alludes to the recent rediscovery of the clitoris.

34.   *obliquely*: Not in a straight line.

Text note: 20 and *ms*] *omitted 1633*

The Ecstasy

title *Ecstasy*: Rapture, transport; intense or rapturous delight; standing outside or beside oneself.

6.   *fast*: Firmly or closely knit together.
      balm: Oil or resin; figuratively, sweat.

7.   *eye-beams twisted*: Eyes were thought to send out invisible beams that carried an image back to the viewer; the entanglement of these beams unites the lovers.

9.   *to'intergraft*: To unite; to breed a plant species by inserting a shoot into another root or stem.

27.   *concoction*: Purification by heat to refine metals.

32.   *We see . . . move*: We see the source of our love that we did not see before.

33.   *several*: Separate.

42.   *Interanimates*: Gives joint life to; animates, also in the sense of instilling *anima*, 'soul'.

47. *th'atomies*: The atoms.
51–2. *we . . . the spheres*: Angels were thought to control the move-
       ments of the heavenly spheres as the lovers' souls animate their
       bodies.
56. *dross*: Impurity discarded in refining metals.
     allay: Alloy.
57–8. *On man . . . the air*: Stars were thought to control man
       indirectly by manipulating the air.
60. *repair*: Return.
62. *Spirits*: Vapours or ethereal liquids within the blood that gov-
       erned the body according to the soul.
66. *faculties*: The various powers of the mind – will, reason, memory,
       etc.; physical capabilities or functions; financial resources, pos-
       sessions or property.

     Text note: 51 though they're not *ms*] though not *1633*

Love's Deity

3.   *loved most*: Loved most intensely; loved most women.
6.   *vice-nature, custom*: Custom or social convention, which acts as
       the deputy or representative of nature.
12. *Actives to passives*: Men traditionally took the active role in
       courtship, women the passive role.
     Correspondency: Agreement, compliance; communication, inter-
       course.
18. *purlieu*: Domain subject to divine or royal authority.
25. *love me too*: Love me back; love me in addition to someone else.
26. *loves before*: Already loves me though she does not admit it;
       already has another lover.
27–8. *and that . . . love me*: That would make me a liar since she
       already loves me, and I said she does not; that would make her
       a liar since she loves me although she says she does not; that
       would make her false to her former lover.

Love's Diet

6.   *discretion*: Discrimination; liberty or power of deciding and act-
       ing according to one's own judgement.
8.   *fortune*: Bad luck; position or standing in life; position as deter-
       mined by wealth.
     faults: Deficiencies, imperfections or misdeeds.

had part: Also received some sighs.

13. *brined*: Salted with tears, preserved.

17. *meat*: Food; here, her sighs.

22. *title*: Appellation of power.

24. *the fortieth name in an entail*: Fortieth in line of succession to inherit an estate; here, the fortieth suitor.

25. *redeemed*: Liberated from captivity.

buzzard: Senseless, stupid, blind.

28. *use*: Do.

29. *spring*: Cause to appear or to rise to view, as a falconer releases a bird for the falcon to hunt.

Text note: 21 that that *1633*] if that *ms*

The Will

3. *Argus*: Mythological monster with a hundred eyes.

4. *Love ... thee*: Cupid, the god of love, is often represented as blind.

5. *Fame*: Rumour.

12. *ingenuity*: Openness, candour; high intellectual capacity.

13. *Jesuits*: Roman Catholic priests, known for their intellectual rigour, forced by English law to practise their religion furtively.

15. *Capuchin*: A Franciscan monk who took a vow of poverty.

19–27. Omitted in most manuscripts.

19. *Roman Catholics*: Religious dissidents whose allegiance to Rome and whose belief that good works contributed to salvation kept them from accepting the Church of England as required by law.

20. *schismatics*: Calvinists, many of whom lived in Amsterdam, who believed in salvation through faith alone, and who broke from the Church of England because it placed too much emphasis on church ceremony.

22. *courtship*: The art of courtiership, valuable at court but inappropriate at a university.

23. *bare*: Naked, a particularly immodest state in early modern England, where nakedness, even in the most intimate circumstances, was extremely rare.

26. *disparity*: Inequality, dissimilarity.

30. *schoolmen*: Medieval scholastic philosophers.

31. *excess*: Overindulgence, considered a cause of illness.

38. *physic books*: Medical books.

39. *Bedlam*: An insane asylum in London; synonymous with madness.
40. *brazen medals*: Antique coins that could not be spent.
44. *portion*: The part of an estate given to an heir; marriage portion or dowry.
45. *disproportion*: Render out of due proportion.

The Funeral

9. *sinewy thread*: Nervous system.
14. *except*: Unless.
17. *by me*: Next to me.

Text note: 3 crowns *Grierson*] crown *1633*

The Blossom

12. *forbidden or forbidding*: Forbidden because his courtship is prohibited, presumably by her family, and forbidding because his beloved is currently rejecting his advances.
15. *that sun*: The woman.
20. *business*: A particular matter demanding attention; duty, occupation as opposed to pleasure.
22. *content*: Gratification.

Text notes: 23 tongue *ms*] taste *1633*; 24 you a *ms*] your *1633*

The Primrose

3. *several*: Separate.
8. *true love*: Lover; another name for the primrose.
12. *a six or four*: Primroses usually possess five petals; six or four petals were a favourable sign for lovers.
17. *not to love*: Not to make love.
25. *Ten is the farthest number*: Ten, the perfect number of Pythagorean theory, is the highest number, since all subsequent numbers contain the numbers preceding ten.
28. *turn*: A common circumlocution for intercourse.
29–30. *Numbers ... us all*: Odd and even numbers, represented by three and two, are both contained within the number five; the speaker argues either that women are entitled to the whole of man or that women are entitled to all men.

The Relic

2.   *Some second guest to entertain*: Digging up graves for multiple burials was a common practice.

3.   *woman-head*: Womanhood, possible pun on 'maidenhead' – virginity.

6.   *bracelet of bright hair about the bone*: Lock of shiny hair, worn as a bracelet on an arm that is nothing but bone.

10. *the last busy day*: Judgement Day, when souls will be reunited with resurrected bodies.

16. *relics*: Bones of saints, cherished as objects of devotion by Roman Catholics but attacked as fraudulent by Protestant reformers.

17. *Mary Magdalen*: Follower of Christ and reformed sinner (prostitute), later canonized.

18. *A something else thereby*: Some kind of a saint.

23. *Yet*: But; still or until that time.

25–6. *Difference ... angels do*: Angels supposedly made love by mingling their essences, as John Milton (1608–1674) explains in *Paradise Lost* (1667), VIII, 620ff.

27–8. *coming and going ... kiss*: Kissing was socially acceptable upon arrival and departure.

28. *those meals*: Those kisses that nourished our souls.

29. *seals*: Tokens or symbols of a covenant; that which seals their lips, their vows of silence; colloquialism for genitalia.

32. *pass*: Surpass.

The Damp

5.   *damp*: Harmful vapour or gas; also a dazed or stupefied condition.

7–8. *prefer ... massacre*: Elevate your murder of me to a massacre of all those who look upon your picture.

21. *Kill, die*: Experience sexual orgasm.

23–4. *Your ... any man*: Your passivity makes you more powerful than any man.

Text note: 24 In that *1633*] Naked *1635*

The Dissolution

title *Dissolution*: The poem plays on various meanings of the word 'dissolution': death; separation into constituent elements; excess or extravagance; the action of bringing to an end; weakening, enfeeblement; dissolving of a connection, union or bond; sexual gratification.

1. *dead*: Devoid of life; benumbed, insensible; inactive, ineffectual.

9–10. *My fire . . . despair*: Alludes to the four traditional elements: fire, air, water and earth.

13. *repair*: Replenish.

20. *store*: Sufficient or abundant supply of something; a person's accumulated goods and money.

21. *use*: Expenditure, with a possible connotation of sexual activity.

24. *more*: A possible allusion to Anne More.

A Jet Ring Sent

title *Jet*: A dense, semi-precious black form of coal polished to a shiny brilliance.

1. *black*: The colour black; clouded with sorrow.

7. *Figure*: Symbolize.

10. *Circle . . . thumb*: Thumb rings were common among the wealthy.

Negative Love

3. *seldom*: Rarely stooped.

7. *silly*: Simple, ignorant.

8. *miss*: Fail to obtain what I want, a woman.

12. *negatives*: The mystical tradition of the *via negativa* defined God not by what He is, but rather by what He is not.

18. *speed*: Meet with success or good fortune.

The Prohibition

3. *repair*: Restore to good condition by making up for previous loss or waste; restore to a previous state, reinstate; make amends for harm done.

5. *then*: When I die.

11. *officer*: Agent of justice and revenge.

19. *die the gentler way*: Die from your love or from making love with you, rather than from your hate.

20. *great*: Proud, arrogant; distinguished, aristocratic.

21. *these two*: Love and hate.

22.   *stage*: A degree or step in a ladder; a platform on which plays
      are exhibited; a stage in a journey.
      triumph: Victory, conquest; the exultation of victory, rapturous
      delight.

      Text notes: 5 thee *1635*] me *1633*;   5 what to me *1635*] that
      which *1633*;   18 neither's *ms*] ne'r their *1633*]   22 stage *ms*] *stay*
      1633

The Expiration

2.   *vapours*: Vaporizes.
4.   *benight*: Darken or cloud.
12.   *Being double dead*: Both by departing and by bidding his love to
      go.

      Text notes: 5 asked *ms*] ask *1633*;   9 Or *1635–69*] Oh *1633*

The Computation

7.   *divide*: Distinguish.
9.   *this, long life*: The poem's computation of 2,400 years (100 years
      per hour) is short compared to immortality.
10.   *dead ... die*: Possible sexual connotation, with 'die' meaning to
      experience orgasm.

The Paradox

6.   *killed*: Donne plays on the sexual connotation of 'die' (experience
      orgasm) and 'kill' throughout.
7–8. *Love ... much cold*: Love kills more of the young with excess
      heat, while death kills the old with excess cold.
14.   *The light's life*: The sun.

      Text notes: title The Paradox *1635*] *untitled 1633*;   14 light's
      life *ms*] life's light *1633*;   17 loved *ms*] love *1633*;   20 lie *ms*] die
      1633–69

Farewell to Love

1.   *Whil'st yet to prove*: While still untested in the ways of life.
10.   *wax*: Grow.

size: Enlarge, suggesting sexual arousal.

11–12. *from late fair / His Highness*: A gingerbread figure purchased for children at a recent fair.

14. *the thing*: Lovemaking.

18. *them all*: All the senses.

22. *cocks and lions*: Reputedly the only animals that do not experience post-coital let-down.

28–30. *Because . . . posterity*: Refers to the brevity of sexual intercourse, which increases desire to encourage procreation; also a pun on 'posterity' and 'posterior'.

35. *moving beauties*: Beautiful women who arouse desire.

40. *worm-seed*: Dried heads of various plants used against intestinal worms and as an anaphrodisiac.

Lecture upon the Shadow

8. *brave*: Magnificent, courageous.

9. *whil'st . . . did grow*: During the morning, or early phase, of their love, when the lovers took care to hide their love from others.

11. *cares*: Concerns, attentions; troubles, anxieties.

16. *the first*: The first shadows, the morning shadows.

17. *these*: The afternoon shadows, which are still to come.

20–21. *To me . . . disguise*: You will disguise your actions falsely to me, and I will disguise my actions falsely to you.

Text note: Copy-text, *1635*; title Lecture upon the Shadow *1650*] Song *1635*; 26 first *ms*] short *1635–69*

Hero and Leander

title *Hero and Leander*: Mythical lovers who lived on opposite sides of the strait separating Europe and Asia. Each night Leander would swim across the strait, but one night he drowned in a storm. When she found his body washed up on shore, Hero drowned herself.

1–2. *air . . . water*: Referring to the four traditional elements: fire, air, water and earth.

2. *fire*: Burning passion.

Pyramus and Thisbe

title *Pyramus and Thisbe*: Mythical clandestine lovers who had arranged a tryst. Pyramus arrived and, believing Thisbe had been eaten by a lion, killed himself. When Thisbe returned and found him dead, she killed herself.

2. *parting*: Dying.
    joined: Combined, united physically; linked or united in marriage.

Niobe

title *Niobe*: Mythical queen of Thebes who believed she was superior to the goddess Leto because she had more children. As punishment, Leto's children, Apollo and Diana, killed Niobe's children, and Niobe was turned to stone. Yet she continued to cry.

Text note: 1 birth *ms*] births *1633*

A Lame Beggar

2. *lies*: Either is prostrate or speaks falsely.

A Self Accuser

1. *mistress*: Either a lover or a wife. A woman was considered responsible for her husband's morality, and so she would be blamed if he cheated on her.
    taxeth: Reproves, blames or accuses.

A Licentious Person

2. *thy hairs do fall*: Hair loss is a symptom of syphilis. Also, 'hairs' is a possible pun on 'heirs' and 'whores'.

Disinherited

2. *title*: Either an appellation indicating high rank or that which justifies a claim.

Phryne

title   *Phryne*: A courtesan who posed for the famous, erotic sculpture *Aphrodite of Knidos* by the ancient Greek sculptor Praxiteles (flourished 370–330 BC).

An Obscure Writer

1.   *Philo*: A prefix meaning 'love of' something.

Raderus

title   *Raderus*: Matthew Rader (1561–1634), a German Jesuit who edited and published Martial's works in 1602.
1.   *Martial*: A first-century Roman poet, considered the 'Father of the Epigram'.
3.   *Katherine*: Possibly Catherine Parr (1512–48), sixth wife of Henry VIII.
    stews: Brothels.

Mercurius Gallo-Belgicus

title   *Mercurius Gallo-Belgicus*: An annual published at Cologne beginning in 1594, notorious for its poor Latin and false reports.
1.   *Aesop's fellow-slaves*: Aesop, the legendary author of a collection of Greek fables, was supposedly once a slave. While being auctioned, he and his fellow slaves were asked what they could do. Two pompously replied 'Everything,' but Aesop answered 'Nothing.'
    Mercury: Roman god, patron of thieves.
5.   *credit . . . credit*: Credulousness . . . trustworthiness.
8.   *liest like a Greek*: Greeks were traditionally believed to be dishonest.

Ralphius

1.   *compassion*: Suffering together with another.
2.   *Ralphius*: The name Ralph was often given to members of the lower classes.
    broker: Pawnbroker.
    keeps: Both 'holds on to' and 'stays in'.

Text note: title Ralphius *ms] untitled 1633*

Sir John Wingefield

title *Sir John Wingefield*: Colonel in the Earl of Essex's expedition to
Cadiz, in south-west Spain, where he died and was buried in 1596.
1. *pillars*: The cliffs at the mouth of the Strait of Gibraltar, called
the 'Pillars of Hercules', were regarded as the limits of the old
world.
3. *fitter pillar*: Wingefield; also a phallic image, with sexual double
entendre.
our Earl: Robert Devereux, 2nd Earl of Essex (1565–1601).
4. *late island*: Because Cadiz is so far to the west, the sun sets later
there. (Cadiz stands not on an island, but on a narrow peninsula.)
Possible sexual puns on *travailed, pillar, know, go*.

Text note: Copy-text, Westmoreland ms

The Liar

3. *Nebuchadnezzar*: Biblical king of Babylon (*c.* 605–562 BC), who
went mad and ate grass as the oxen did (Daniel 4:33).
4. *Spanish dieting*: The English disapproved of the Spanish diet,
which was rich in leek-like vegetables.

Text note: Copy-text, Westmoreland ms

Cales and Guiana

title *Cales and Guiana*: 'Cales' refers to Cadiz, a city in south-west
Spain, sacked by the English in 1596. Many, including Donne,
believed an attack on the Spanish at Guiana, in South America,
should be next.
1. *you*: Probably addressed to the courtier, explorer and author Sir
Walter Ralegh (1554–1618), who allegedly favoured an
expedition to Guiana.
spoil: The action of pillaging or plundering.
th'old world's farthest end: Cadiz is located to the west of Gibral-
tar, regarded as the limit of the old world.

Text note: Copy-text, Westmoreland ms

Klockius

title *Klockius*: Probably from the Dutch *kloek*, 'a sly person'.
1.   *come*: Both to enter and to experience sexual orgasm.

Text note: title Klockius *ms*] *untitled 1633*

The Juggler

Text note: Copy-text, Westmoreland ms; title The Juggler
modern editors] *untitled Westmoreland ms*

Faustus

title *Faustus*: A magician who reputedly sold his soul to the Devil.

Text notes: Copy-text, Hawthornden ms; title Faustus *modern
editors*] *untitled Hawthornden ms*

Elegy: The Anagram

5.   *light*: Light-coloured; frivolous, promiscuous.
8.   *maidenhead*: Virginity; also a pun, for if he gives her his hair,
     she will have a proper maiden's head.
14. *musk and amber*: Odoriferous substances, obtained from musk
     deer and sperm whales respectively, used to make perfume.
     where: Where they came from.
19. *gamut*: The complete series of recognized notes.
30. *those which fell to worse*: The 'fallen' angels who were cast into
     hell following the battle in heaven (Revelation 12:7–9).
35. *barren*: Childless.
     husbands: Both husbandmen or farmers and married men.
37. *sovereign plaster*: Extremely potent curative, applied externally.
40. *marmoset*: Literally, a small monkey; figuratively, a grotesque
     figure.
41–2. *When Belgia's cities ... town*: When the dykes are opened,
     foul water floods the countryside, protecting the cities and towns
     of Belgium from attack.
46. *Moors*: Muslims from north-west Africa.
50. *tympany*: Swelling, tumour.
53. *dildoes, bedstaves, and her velvet glass*: Artificial penises,

bedboards and her velvet-backed mirror, all tools of female masturbation.

54. *as loath . . . Joseph was*: When his master's wife asked him to lie with her, Joseph refused (Genesis 39:7–12).
56. *wear*: Possess and enjoy as one's own.

Text notes: title Elegy: The Epigram *1635*] Elegy II *1633*; 49 childbirth's *ms*] childbed's *1633*

Elegy: Change

3. *apostasy*: Abandonment of moral allegiance.
6. *unknown*: Both undiscovered and not known carnally.
11. *foxes and goats*: Traditional symbols of cunning and lechery.
15. *clogs*: Hindrances.
24. *like*: Alike.
25. *it*: This liberty (see l. 21).

Text notes: 23 then if so thou do *ms*] and if that thou so *1633*; 32 worse *ms*] more *1633*

Elegy: The Perfume

2. *escapes*: Breaches of chastity.
3. *at bar*: In court.
6. *hydroptic*: Having an insatiable thirst.
7. *glazed*: Staring intently or wearing glasses.
8. *cockatrice*: A basilisk; a monster believed to have the power to kill with its glance; also a whore.
10–11. *beauty's beauty . . . hope of his goods*: The speaker's lover's greatest attraction is her inheritance.
20. *swoll'n*: Pregnant.
21. *To try . . . strange meats*: Names strange foods to see if she has the cravings associated with pregnancy.
23. *politicly*: Shrewdly, artfully.
29. *ingled*: Fondled or caressed (with suggestion of sexual perversity).
34. *Rhodian Colossus*: A huge statue of Apollo once stood in the Greek city of Rhodes, supposedly with one foot on either side of the harbour.
41. *loud*: Powerful.
57. *excrement*: Product, excreted substance.

59. *thee*: Perfume.
     seely: Silly, simple.
61. *man's estate*: Manhood.

Text notes: title Elegy: The Perfume *1635*] Elegy IV *1633*; 7–8 omitted from *1633*; 37 for *ms*] to *1633*

Elegy: His Picture

10. *powder*: Gunpowder.
20. *disused*: Unaccustomed.

Text notes: title Elegy: His Picture *1635*] Elegy V *1633*; 8 hoariness *ms*] storms being *1633*

Elegy: O, let me not serve so

2.   *honour's smokes*: The illusion of gaining honours.
6.   *styles*: Titles.
7.   *tribute*: Payment by one state to another in acknowledgement of submission or as the price of security.
9.   *dead names*: Empty titles.
10. *Favourite in ordinary*: A regular servant, as opposed to a temporary one.
24. *channel's bosom*: River bed.
25. *brows*: Projecting edges.
42. *Rome*: The Roman Catholic Church.
45. *recusant*: One, most often a Roman Catholic, who refused to attend Church of England services.

Text notes: title Elegy: O, let me not serve so *1635*] Elegy VII *1633*; 6 with *ms*] which *1633*

Elegy: Nature's Lay Idiot

title *Nature's lay idiot*: One unlearned in Nature's law.
1.   *thee*: The speaker's mistress.
9–10. *the alphabet / Of flowers*: How flowers may be arranged to convey secret love messages.
13, 15, 17. *since*: When.
14.   *I*: Also aye or yes.
      friends: Kinfolk.

19. *sentences*: Sayings.
21. *from the'world's common*: From society.
22. *Inlaid*: Confined.
23. *As mine*: As you are mine.
26. *knowledge and life's tree*: The Tree of Knowledge and the Tree of Life stood in the Garden of Eden (Genesis 3); here they are mentioned with sexual innuendo.
28. *Frame ... in glass*: Make an enamelled, gilded goblet only to drink from glass.
29. *chafe*: Heat.
    seals: Also, slang for 'genitalia'; the subsequent sexual innuendoes follow from that.

Text note: title Elegy VIII *1633*

Elegy: The Comparison

The poem alternates between descriptions of the speaker's mistress (1–6, 15–18, 23–4, 27–8, 35–8, 49–52) and descriptions of his interlocutor's mistress (7–14, 19–22, 25–6, 29–34, 39–48).

2. *that which ... trill*: Secretions of musk deer, used to make perfume.
3. *balm of ... East*: The balm of Gilead, a tree resin known for its fragrance.
6. *carcanets*: Ornamental collars or necklaces.
8. *issue*: Discharge.
   menstruous: Corrupt, polluted, unclean. The references to sperm and menstrual fluid imply genital sores.
10. *Sanserra*: In 1573 the Protestants in Sanserra, near Bourges in France, suffered widespread starvation while resisting the Catholic army of Charles IX of France (r. 1560–74).
12. *sovereign*: Potent.
13. *vile stones*: Paltry, cheap jewels.
    saffroned tin: Tin dyed yellow-orange to imitate gold.
14. *wheals*: pimples, pustules.
16. *the fatal ball ... on Ide*: In Greek myth, Paris, son of the king of Troy, who was tending flocks on Mount Ida, was asked to decide which of three goddesses should receive a golden apple inscribed 'For the fairest'. Aphrodite's successful attempt to bribe him with Helen, the wife of the king of Sparta, sparked the Trojan War.
17. *that*: The forbidden apple from the Tree of Knowledge in the

Garden of Eden that Eve ate, causing the Fall of Man (Genesis 3).
jealousy: Anger, wrath.

18. *ravishing*: Plundering.
21. *first Chaos*: The formless void of primordial matter from which God created heaven and earth, according to Genesis 1:1–2.
22. *Cynthia*: The moon.
23. *Proserpina's ... chest*: Venus, the goddess of love, ordered Psyche, a beautiful maiden, the personification of the human soul, to bring her some of the beauty of Proserpina (the wife of Pluto, the ruler of the underworld) in a chest.
24. *best fortune's urn*: Jove had two urns, one of good and one of ill fortune.
28. *woodbine*: A vine.
31. *quarters*: Criminals' corpses, quartered into four sections, each containing a limb, were frequently hung in public areas.
35. *chemic*: Chemist, druggist.
36. *limbeck*: Distilling apparatus.
38. *best loved part*: Genitals.
41. *Etna*: An active volcano in Sicily.
47. *last act*: Intercourse.
49. *turtles*: Turtle doves, symbols of conjugal affection and constancy.
51. *nice*: Delicate, precise.

Text notes: 4 on *ms*] of *1633*; 6 carcanets *ms*] coronets [small crowns] *1633*; 14 they hang *ms*] it hangs *1633*; 37 dirt *ms*] part *1633*; 43 kissings *ms*] kisses *1633*

Elegy: The Autumnal

7. *Golden Age*: The first of four supposed ages of history (Gold, Silver, Bronze and Iron) symbolizing a lost paradise.
13. *graves*: Wrinkles as deep engravings on the skin.
16. *anachorite*: An anchorite or religious recluse.
17. *hers*: Her death.
20. *progress*: A monarch's stately journey through the countryside. *standing house*: Permanent residence.
25. *under-wood*: Underbrush; in contrast to 'timber', older, sturdier wood.
29. *Xerxes' ... tree*: On his march into Greece in 480 BC the Persian king Xerxes found a plane tree in Lydia and ornamented its stately beauty with gold. The barren tree bore no fruit.

41. *several*: Different.
42. *To vex ... Resurrection*: On Judgement Day the soul will be reunited with the resurrected parts of its earthly body.
43. *death's-heads*: Skulls; memento mori.
47. *natural lation*: Intrinsic motion.

Text notes: 8 she's *ms*] they're *1633*; 10 habitable *ms*] tolerable *1633*; 43 death's heads *ms*] death heads *1633*; 47 natural lation *ms*] motion natural *1633*, natural station *1635*; 50 on *ms*] out *1633*

Elegy: *Image of her whom I love*

1.   *Image*: Idealized mental picture.
3.   *medal*: Stamped metal disk, used as an ornament.
8.   *the more*: The stronger the image's impression.
11. *meaner*: More moderate; more common.
24. *For even ... snuff*: Even at its start, life is like a candle already burnt to the wick.

Text notes: title Elegy X: The Dream *1635*] Elegy *1633*. Some modern editors divide the poem into stanzas and place it among the Songs and Sonnets because its rhyme scheme differs from the Elegies' rhyming couplets.

Elegy: *The Bracelet*

9.   *angels*: Dual meaning throughout of spirits and English gold coins stamped with the archangel Michael slaying a dragon.
10. *leaven*: Admixture.
23. *crowns*: French gold coins bearing a crown on one side.
24. *natural country's rot*: Syphilis, particularly attributed to France, the coins' native country.
28. *Their crowns are circumcised*: Trimmed coins were worthless.
     Jewishly: Like Jewish men, for whom circumcision is a sign of their covenant with God.
30. *Catholic*: Also universal.
31. *unlicked bear-whelps*: Bear cubs were thought to be licked into shape at birth by their mothers.
     pistolets: Small firearms; also irregularly shaped Spanish coins.
42. *seventeen-headed Belgia*: The seventeen provinces of the Low-

lands (Belgium and the Netherlands), which were fighting for independence from Spain.

55. *crier*: Town crier.

56. *groat*: An old silver coin.

61. *divided heaven in tenements*: Astrologers divided the heavens into houses of the zodiac.

62. *rents*: Fees, revenues.

71. *fallen angels*: Angels expelled from heaven and confined to hell after joining Satan's rebellion against God (Revelation 12:7–9).

78. *Virtues, Powers, and Principalities*: Orders of angels.

112. *Gold is restorative*: Gold was thought to cure diseases, especially of the heart.

114. *cordial*: Belonging to or reviving the heart.

Text notes: Copy-text, *1635*; title The Bracelet *ms*] Upon the loss . . . *1639*] Elegy XII *1635*; 6 are tied *ms*] were knit *1635*; 8 luck's *ms*] luck *1635*; 11 taint *ms*] way *1635*; 24 them, their natural country's *ms*] these, their country's natural *1635*; 26 So lean, so pale, so lame *ms*] So pale, so lame, so lean *1635*; 36 as *ms*] so *1635*; 55 O *ms*] And *1635*; 58 they *ms*] he *1635*; 60 Which *ms*] That *1635*; 60 schemes *ms*] scenes *1635*; 65 And *ms*] But *1635*; 66 O *ms*] Yet *1635*; 98 that *ms*] it *1635*; 113 Or *ms*] But *1635*; 113 with *ms*] from *1633*

Elegy: His Parting from Her

7. *Cynthia*: The moon.
    Venus: The morning or evening star.

15. *thyself art blind*: Cupid, the god of love, was conventionally depicted as blind.

17. *break . . . on the wheel*: A form of torture.

18. *old Chaos*: Either the void from which God created heaven and earth (Genesis 1:1) or the oldest of the Greek gods.

26. *golden fruit*: The golden fruit, always just beyond the reach of Tantalus in Hades, the mythic underworld.
    rapt: Carried away by force.

30. *dove-like*: Gentle, innocent, loving.
    amiss: Error.

31–2. *expiate / Thy wrath*: Extinguish Love's wrath by suffering it to the full.

39. *hazard*: Endanger.

42. *towered*: Standing in a tower, looking down; confined in a tower; hovering above, ready to swoop like a hawk; rising to a high emotional pitch.

   over all the towered husbands or *over all thy husbands*: A famously enigmatic line, further complicated by the textual alternatives: (1) *over all the husbands* or the men who wished to marry her, she having chosen and remained faithful to the speaker; (2) Venus's husband, Vulcan, watches over all as the goddess of love tries to separate the lovers; (3) the speaker's mistress's husband watches as they try to conceal their love.

46. *correspondence*: Intercourse or relations of a secret or illicit nature.

49. *shadowed with negligence*: Hid (their feelings) with the appearance of negligence.

   respects: Love, as in to send one's respects.

51. *becks*: Gestures of assent.

   under-boards: Both literally under tables and, figuratively, secretly or deceptively.

54. *thy pale ... heart*: Her pale appearance conceals her panting heart within.

56. *vulgar*: Common, ordinary.

58. *grow to*: Grow together.

61. *rive*: Sever, cleave.

68. *strokes*: Blows.

72. *shifts*: Ingenious devices for effecting some purpose.

75-6. *air ... fire ... Waters ... earth*: The four traditional elements.

76. *clear*: Serene, cheerful.

   sure: Steadfast, faithful.

77. *loose our passages*: Break off our amorous relationships.

86. *Phoebus*: The sun.

87. *like*: Equal.

90. *win on*: Subdue, take possession of.

97. *poles*: The North and South Poles, which are fixed.

Text notes: Copy-text, *1669*; first printed *1635*; title Elegy: His Parting from Her *1635*] Elegy XIII *1669*; 5–44 *omitted 1635*; 6 Thou and *ms*] And that *1669*; 9 thee *ms*] them *1669*; 11 felt want *ms*] self-want *1669*; 25 now sooner *ms*] sooner now *1669*; 34 followers *ms*] favourites *1669*; 36 informing *ms*] inflaming *1669*; 37 glow *ms*] blow *1669*; 42 all the towered husbands eyes *ms*] all thy husbands towering eyes *1669*; 43 That flamed with oily *ms*] Inflamed with th'ugly *1669*; 44 with *ms*] in *1669*;

54 thy pale colours inward as thy heart *ms*] thy pale inwards,
and thy panting heart *1635*; 57–66 *omitted 1635*; 61–2 rive us
with the deed, / Strain her eyes open; and it' *ms*] ruin us with the
deed, / Strain his eyes open, and yet *1669*; 66 shame *ms*] name
1669; 83–94 *omitted 1635*; 96 words *ms*] deeds *1669*

Elegy: The Expostulation

title *Expostulation*: Remonstrance, protest, reproof.
1.   *doubt*: Apprehension, fear.
19. *draw*: Draw a veil over something to conceal it; bring together;
     influence in a desired direction; draw up a legal document.
     bonds: The forces by which a union is maintained, as in the
     bonds of matrimony; deeds obliging one to pay a certain sum.
21. *the wrong way*: By taking the reverse of what you say.
22. *would*: Who would.
23. *profane*: Abuse what ought to be held in reverence.
25–6. *though . . . inconstancy*: Although perverse jealousy and exter-
     nal conditions might allege your inconstancy.
34. *counsels*: Secret plans.
36. *cast*: Think.
40. *Cain*: Eldest son of Adam and Eve; having murdered his brother,
     Abel, he was sent into exile (Genesis 4:1–16).
42. *witty*: Skilful, especially in contriving evil.
45. *deny God thrice*: St Peter denied Christ three times at the court
     of the High Priest (Matthew 26:69–75).
46. *not . . . soul's price*: Not be trusted any more on the value of his
     soul.
51. *carrion*: Rotten, vile.
58. *Delight . . . make*: Delight not in the product but in the process.
61. *masks*: Also courtly entertainments or masques.
64. *officious*: Eager to please.
70. *art*: Skill that results from knowledge and practice; human work-
     manship as opposed to nature; action that attains its ends by
     covert means; poetry.

Elegy: To His Mistress Going to Bed

4.   *standing*: With a bawdy pun, continued with 'upright' in l. 24.
7.   *breastplate*: Jewelled bodice.
8.   *busy*: Prying, meddlesome.
11. *busk*: Corset.

14. *meads*: Meadows.

21. *Mahomet's paradise*: Islamic paradise, filled with sensual pleasures; pronounciation 'Máh(o)met's'.

23. *these angels*: Women.

29. *empery*: Territory ruled by an emperor.

30. *discovering*: Also uncovering.

32. *seal*: Heraldic device impressed in wax; also colloquial expression for genitals.

36. *Atlanta's balls*: Distracted by the golden apples thrown in her path, Atalanta, a legendary huntress of Greek myth, lost a race against one of her suitors; here the sex roles are reversed.

Text notes: Copy-text, *1669*; 5 zones glistering *ms*] zone glittering *1669*; 14 from *ms*] through *1669*; 14 shadow *ms*] shadows *1669*; 17 safely *ms*] softly *1669*; 20 Received by *ms*] Revealed to *1669*; 26 Behind, before, above, between, *ms*] Before, behind, above, between *1669*; 30 How blest am I in this *ms*] How am I blessed in thus *1669*; 38 covet theirs *ms*] court that *1669*; 41 only we *ms*] we only *1669*; 46 much less *ms*] due to *1669*

Elegy: Love's Progress

4.   *whelp*: Cub.

14. *from fire ever free*: Gold was believed to be unaffected by fire.

16. *our new nature (use)*: The act of employing gold for profit has become so common as to seem natural.

26. *hers*: Her qualities; her family and connections.

29. *infernal*: Belonging to the underworld.

30. *Pluto*: Roman god of the underworld.

36. *the centric part*: The central part, her genitals.

42. *springes*: Nooses.

52. *Canaries*: The Canary Islands.
     ambrosial: Divine, celestial – from ambrosia, the food of the gods.

55. *sirens*: Mythological sea nymphs whose singing was said to lure sailors to destruction.

56. *Delphic oracles*: The oracle of Apollo, god of prophecy, archery, music and healing, located on Mount Parnassus near Delphi in Greece.

58. *remora*: A sucking fish thought to have the power of staying the course of any ship to which it attached itself.

60. *Hellespont*: The Dardanelles, the strait separating Europe and Asia.
61. *Sestos and Abydos*: An ancient fortress and a village located on opposite sides of the Hellespont, the homes of the lovers Hero and Leander (see l. 62).
65. *India*: Figurative source of wealth.
68. *embayed*: Enveloped, surrounded.
69. *another forest*: Pubic hair.
74. *symmetry*: Correspondence.
78. *the Devil never can change his*: The Devil can take various forms, but can never change his cloven feet.
92. *purses*: Pouches; also genitals.
      aversely: In the opposite direction.
94. *exchequer*: Treasury.
96. *clyster*: Enema.
      meat: Food.

Text notes: Copy-text, 1669; 5 strange *ms*] strong *1669*; 18 and *ms*] but *1669*; 25 beauty'is *ms*] beauties no *1669*; 47 first *ms*] sweet *1669*; 57 There *ms*] Then *1669*; 60 O'er past, and the straight *ms*] Being past the straights of *1669*; 67 thence *ms*] there *1669*; 67 thy *ms*] the *1669*; 68 would'st *ms*] should'st *1669*; 70 some do *ms*] many *1669*; 90 elements *ms*] enemies *1669*; 96 clyster gave *ms*] glister gives *1669*

Elegy: On His Mistress

1.   *fatal interview*: Fated meeting.
3.   *remorse*: Pity.
8.   *divorcement*: Complete separation.
9.   *conjure*: Entreat.
14. *my feigned page*: Disguised as my young male servant.
17. *before*: Before I return.
21–3. *Boreas's harshness ... Orithea*: Donne alters the story of Boreas, the god of the North Wind, who kidnapped the mortal princess Orithyia and made her his immortal wife, to suggest that Boreas raped and destroyed her.
24. *to have proved / Dangers unurged*: To have tested dangers not thrust upon one.
27. *Dissemble*: Disguise.
30. *discovering grace*: Revealing beauty.
33. *Men of France*: Proverbially amorous.

34.   *spitals of diseases*: Low-class hospitals.
35.   *Love's fuellers*: Aphrodisiacs.
37.   *know*: Also carnally.
       alas: Pun on 'a lass'.
38.   *indifferent*: Ready to make love to a man or woman.
41.   *Lot's fair guests*: The citizens of Sodom, mired in vice, demanded
       that Lot present two visiting angels to them (Genesis 18–19).
42.   *hydroptic*: Swollen with water, because Holland is so wet; having
       an insatiable thirst.
44.   *gallery*: Colonnade or walkway.
46.   *Our greatest King*: God.

Text notes: Copy-text, *1635*; 28 minds *ms*] mind *1635*

An Epithalamion, or Marriage Song, on the Lady Elizabeth and Count Palatine

title *Lady Elizabeth and Count Palatine*: Written for the marriage of
       Princess Elizabeth (1596–1662), daughter of James I, to Fred-
       erick, Elector of the Palatine (1596–1632), on 14 February 1613.
       Donne was part of the embassy sent to negotiate the marriage
       settlement the previous year.
7.   *neglects . . . for love*: The sparrow was believed to have a shorter
       lifespan as a result of his sexual passion.
8.   *red stomacher*: Red waistcoat, here the robin's breast.
10.   *halcyon*: Kingfisher, a symbol of serenity.
11.   *straight*: Soon.
18–22. *two phoenixes . . . not contain*: Only one of the mythic birds
       could exist at any one time, which is why it could not have
       been on Noah's ark. The legendary bird was hermaphroditic and
       immortal, being reborn from its own ashes.
27.   *courage*: Sexual desire.
37–8. *blazing . . . not die*: Falling stars were believed to foretell a
       prince's death.
52.   *his way*: The bishop unites the lovers spiritually in the sacrament
       of marriage, contrasting with their own emotional and sexual
       union.
67.   *maskers*: Guests taking part in a masquerade or masque, a courtly
       entertainment.
80.   *yet*: Still.
85.   *she Sun . . . he Moon*: The gender roles are reversed; usually the

sun, Apollo, was considered male, the moon, Diana or Cynthia, female.

93. *debt*: Conventional term for spouses' sexual and legal obligation to one another.

94. *acquittances*: Proof of paid debts.

98. *turtles*: Turtle doves, representing true love.

105. *Waiting*: Attending upon the newly-weds the morning after their marriage, as was customary.

108. *at which side*: Of the curtained bed.

112. *enlarge*: Prolong.

Text notes: 46 grow *ms*] go *1633*; 56 of *ms*] O *1633*; 60 stars *ms, 1635–69*] store *1633*; 94 acquittances *ms*] acquittance *1633*

Epithalamion Made at Lincoln's Inn

title *Lincoln's Inn*: One of the Inns of Court, where Donne studied law from 1592 to 1595 or 1596.

4–5. *your body's print . . . dint*: Your body makes a mark or impression on the down feather bed.

14. *mines*: Also with a sexual connotation.
     furnished: Stocked; accoutred, dressed; covered with flesh.

16. *angels*: Gold coins (for their dowries) stamped with the archangel Michael slaying a dragon.

19. *Conceitedly*: Fancifully, whimsically.

21. *for love fit fuel*: Something that inflames passion.

22. *Flora*: Goddess of flowers.
     Ind: India.

23. *lame*: Imperfect, with a physical connotation.

29. *fellowships*: Groups of students at Lincoln's Inn.

30. *hermaphrodites*: Unions of opposite attributes or qualities, containing characteristics of both sexes; here, the union of study, a masculine occupation, and play, socializing with women.

43. *elder claims*: Prior claims on the lovers' affections.

55. *He flies . . . stands still*: Referring to winter's shortened days and summer's long light.

56. *shadows turn*: After noon, shadows fall in the opposite direction.

58. *But*: In case they.

61. *amorous evening star*: The planet Venus, named after the goddess of love.

70. *labours*: Both in intercourse and in childbirth.

71. *turn*: Return, with a sexual connotation.
86. *this life ... spent*: It was believed that one's earthly life should be piously spent in pursuit of heaven, and also that sexual intercourse shortened one's lifespan.
87. *style*: Title; rank.
89-90. *Like ... t'embowel her*: The husband will break her hymen as tenderly as if he were an Old Testament priest disembowelling a sacrificial lamb.
93. *This sun*: The bride.
94. *want*: Lack.
95. *maim*: Damage to or loss of some bodily part. Paradoxically, losing her hymen makes the bride all the more perfect.

Text notes: 23 fair, rich, glad *ms*] fair and rich *1633*; 26 Sons *1635*] Some *1633*; 49 O *ms*] omitted *1633*; 59 run *ms*] come *1633*; 60 put *ms*] but *1633*

Eclogue

Written for the marriage of Robert Carr (1585/6–1645), a favourite of King James I who became Earl of Somerset in 1613, and Frances Howard (1590–1632), on 26 December 1613. The marriage took place shortly after Howard's divorce from Robert Devereux, 3rd Earl of Essex. Somerset and Howard were convicted in 1616 of the murder of Sir Thomas Overbury (1581–1613), who was poisoned in the Tower of London, where he had been imprisoned after opposing their marriage and threatening to publicize their premarital affair.
prologue *Allophanes*: Literally 'One Sounding Like Another', Allophanes represents Sir Robert Ker, 1st Earl of Ancram (1578–1654), a friend of Donne's and a follower of Somerset, whose name was also spelled 'Carr'.
   Idios, implying peculiarity or ignorance, probably represents Donne, who held no courtly position.
5. *courage*: Sexual desire.
8. *frieze*: Coarse woollen cloth, with a pun on 'freeze'.
21-2. *early light ... created were*: According to the Book of Genesis (1:3, 16) God created light on the first day, the sun and moon on the fourth.
27. *prevent*: Outdo.
37. *digest*: Disperse.
51. *is of the world*: Is a microcosm of the world.

54. *of courts*: An epitome of courts.
59. *East Indian fleet*: Fleet bound for the East Indies, which were known for spices and perfumes.
60. *amber*: Ambergris, a fragrant, waxy substance used to flavour food and make perfumes.
66. *heaven gild ... eye*: An alchemical belief held that sunlight can change minerals into jewels or gold.
68. *tinctures*: Spiritual qualities infused into material things; also spots or stains.
70. *use*: Employment; function; habit, custom; employment or maintenance for sexual purposes.
76. *bewray*: Reveal.
86. *pretend*: Aspire.
89. *Cupid*: The god of love, now wearing Somerset's livery.
91. *that breast*: Somerset, now a nobleman whose servants wear livery.
104. *since*: Until.
     dead and buried: See l. 97.
113. *largest circle*: During the summer solstice.
116. *Promethean*: In Greek myth, Prometheus stole fire from heaven and gave it to man.
123-4. *Be tried ... a man*: Referring to the groom's androgynous beauty.
125. *manly courage*: Conventionally masculine bravery; also sexual desire.
126. *unjust opinion*: Referring to the scandal their marriage caused.
148. *Phoebus ... Phaëton*: Phaeton, the son of the sun god Phoebus/Apollo drove his father's sun chariot so carelessly that he nearly burned the earth.
157. *the fruits of worms and dust*: Silk and gold.
169. *the Church Triumphant*: The portion of the Church that has entered into glory.
170. *the Militant*: The Church Militant, the earthly Church, still battling sin and evil.
175. *never sing*: Swans were thought to sing only once, just before death.
183. *overthwart*: Hinder, oppose; also pervert.
184. *west*: Decline.
     north: Cold.
188. *flood*: The great deluge, described in Genesis 6:12–8:19, which only the occupants of Noah's ark escaped.

189. *doctrine*: Copernicus's theory that the earth revolves around the sun, published in 1543, but still not universally accepted in Donne's day.

194. *masks*: Both facial masks and masques, dramatic courtly entertainments.

203–4. *do not set so ... depart*: The sun and moon do not set together; so the moon, the bride, must depart first.

208. *jelly*: A type of algae which appears as a jelly-like mass on dry soil after rain, supposed to be the remains of a fallen star or meteor.

218–19. *Tullia's tomb ... year*: Tullia (*c.* 79–45 BC), daughter of the Roman statesman Cicero (106–43 BC), was reportedly found in a tomb where a lamp had burned for 1,500 years.

Text notes: 12 murmur *ms*] murmurs *1633*; 29 kindle *ms*] kindles *1633*; 34 plots *ms*] places *1633*; 59 East Indian *ms*] Indian *1633*; 63 inward *ms*] inner *1633*; after 107 Epithalamion *ms*] *omitted 1633*; 129 eyes *ms*] eye *1633*; 131 singly *ms*] single *1633*; 132 Yet *ms*] *omitted 1633*; 148 Art *ms*] Are *1633*; 155 clad'st *ms*] cloudst *1633*; 181 yours *ms*] you *1633*; 234 festival *1633*] nuptial *ms*

Satire I

1. *fondling*: Foolish.
    motley: The garb of the court fool.
    humorist: A person subject to the four humours thought to determine a person's temperament (phlegmatic, sanguine, melancholy or choleric); a fanatical, whimsical or comical person.

2. *chest*: Small study; coffin.

7. *jolly*: Full of presumptuous pride; overbearing.

10. *giddy*: Dizzy, whirling with bewildering speed.
    fantastic: Existing only in the imagination; imaginative; concerned with fantasy or illusory appearances.

18. *parcel ... pay*: A parcel is a portion of the whole, suggesting that the captain, who should be a vital member of a regiment, has used the group for personal gain, appropriating 'forty dead men's pay' – pay for deceased men kept on a military company's list, often collected by the captain.

22. *blue coats*: Servants, identified by their blue uniform.

30. *broker*: Pawnbroker.
    prize: Appraise.

36. *Jointures*: Properties owned jointly by a husband and wife, often including the wife's dowry, which reverted to her if her husband died first.

45-6. *when by sin ... skin*: After the Fall, God clothed Adam and Eve in animal skins.

58. *Th'Infanta*: Probably referring to the Spanish Infanta, whom the Roman Catholics had advanced as the heir to the English throne.

59. *gulling weather-spy*: Deceitful weatherman or astrologer.

60. *heaven's scheme*: A schematic diagram of the heavenly bodies.

68-70. *creeps to the wall ... liberty*: The humorist takes the superior social position next to the wall and away from the street, where he is less likely to be splashed and sullied but where he is also less visible to wealthy passers-by.

77. *stop lowest, at highest sound*: The highest notes are obtained by stopping the strings lowest on the instrument.

78. *brave*: Finely dressed.

80-81. *wise politic horse ... ape*: Morocco, a trained performing horse and his master, Banks, became famous in the 1590s, performing with an elephant and an ape in 1594; 'heretofore' may refer to the plague's impact on their performances.

82. *King of Spain*: Philip II (r. 1556-98), whose militant Catholicism posed a political threat to England.

88. *drinking his tobacco*: Intake of tobacco was first described as 'drinking' rather than smoking.

96. *device*: The manner in which a thing is devised; an opinion; a fanciful or witty expression, a conceit.
handsoming: Making seemly or becoming; beautifying, adorning.

97. *pink*: Decorative eyelet.
panes: Cloth strips.
plight: Pleat.

98. *conceit*: Judgement or opinion; a fanciful, witty expression; an affectation of thought or style; hence a pun on 'device' in l. 96.

101. *travailed*: Laboured; travelled.

Text notes: 32 hat *1635*] hate *1633*; 39 bareness *ms*] barrenness *1633*; 50 warned *1635*] warmed *1633*; 58 Infanta *ms*] infant *1633*; 60 scheme *1635*] scenes *1633*; 61 ruffles *ms*] ruffs *1633*; 62 *witted ms*] wittied *1633*; 63 canst *ms*] can *1633*; 70 his *1635*] high *1633*; 73 them *1635*] then *1633*; 78 stoops *1635*] stoopt *1633*; 81-2 *1635*] *omitted 1633*; 95 all *1635*] s'all *1633*;

100 stop'st *1635*] stoop'st *1633*;   108 lechery *1635*], liberty *1633*

Satire II

6. *Spaniards*: England, as a Protestant country, was under constant threat from Catholic Spain.

10. *papists*: Roman Catholics, persecuted increasingly in Britain during the last two decades of the sixteenth century.

12–13. *and cannot read, / And saves his life*: A condemned man could avoid execution by proving himself literate.

19. *Rams*: Battering rams.
    slings: Weapons for hurling stones by hand, slingshots.
    seely battery: Weak or poor artillery.

20. *Pistolets*: Both small pistols and foreign gold coins, suggesting that money has become 'the best artillery' in courtiership.

27. *Rankly*: Coarsely; foully.

32. *outdo*: In sexual acts.
    out-usure Jews: Jews were known as moneylenders, since usury was prohibited among Christians.

35. *confessors*: Priests that hear confessions, banned by the Protestant Reformation.

36. *new tenements in hell*: Scholars and philosophers believed each sin had its own region of hell.

37. *canonists*: Lawyers skilled in canon or ecclesiastical law.

40. *Coscus*: A name Donne gives to the lawyer who fancies himself a poet, used by the anonymous author of *Zepheria* (1594), a collection of conventional sonnets that included legal conceits.
    my just offence: My justified sense of disgust.

41. *makes blotches pox*: Makes boils reveal themselves as signs of syphilis.

44. *scarce a poet*: Barely a poet.
    jollier: Prouder.

46. *lime-twigs*: Twigs covered in a sticky substance used as a snare for small birds.

48. *the pleas and bench*: The Court of Common Pleas and the Queen's Bench, the highest court.

50. *tricesimo of the Queen*: The thirtieth year of Elizabeth's reign, 1588.

51. *Continual claims*: Legal claims reintroduced at regular intervals to keep them on the court docket.

51–3. *injunctions ... Proceed*: Court orders have been obtained to prevent his rival's claims going forward.

53. *Hilary term*: First term of the courts at Westminster.

54. *size*: Assize, court session.

55. *remitter*: The principle whereby someone who successfully claims an estate by the later or more defective of two titles is adjudged to hold it by the earlier or more valid one. Coscus is entitled to the woman based on the right of first possession, since his love originated before his rival's.

59. *Sclavonians*: Slavs, whose speech was considered harsh in tone.

62–4. *men ... prostitute*: Men who practise law for mere gain demean the law worse than prostitutes in a brothel degrade themselves.

66. *bill*: Both a weapon, the halberd, and a legal document.

68. *suretyship*: Taking on the debt of another.

71. *Like a wedge ... bar*: Like a splitting wedge in a block of wood, wrestle his way through a crowded courtroom to the bar, the barrier or wooden rail where plaintiffs faced the judge.

72. *Bearing like asses*: Carrying like donkeys; also a hint of bribery, since 'bearing' could mean bringing forth, and 'asses' were Roman coins bearing the image of a two-faced god.

73. *carted whores*: Women accused of prostitution were paraded through the streets in carts before being brought to trial.

78. *From Scots ... to Dover Strand*: From Scotland in the north to the Isle of Wight off the southern coast, and from St Michael's Mount in the west to Dover beach in the east.

86. *Wringing*: Wrestling.
    pulling prime: Drawing the winning cards in a primero game.

88. *Assurances*: Legal documents transferring ownership of a property.

94–6. *Short Pater nosters ... clause*: The paternoster prayer, 'Our Father, which art in heaven ...', was later lengthened by the Protestants to include the clause 'For thine is the kingdom and the power and the glory'.

98. *ses heires*: French for 'his heirs', omitted from the deed so that the lawyer can claim the land for himself.

101. *controverters*: Controversialists.

104–5. *Where ... door*: The lawyer has cut and sold the spreading woodlands for profit.

106. *Carthusian*: Order of monks known for their austerity.

107. *means*: Moderation.

108. *hecatombs*: Sacrifices of many animals.

110. *Good works*: Unlike the Church of England, the Roman Catholic
     Church held that good works contributed to salvation.

Text notes: 6 dearths *ms*] 'dearth' *1633*; 32 dildoes *ms*] *omitted*
1633; 33 Litany *ms*] *omitted 1633*; 69–70 *1635*] *dashes 1633*;
74–5 *1635*] *dashes 1633*; 77 our *ms*] the *1633*; 84 Relique-like
ms] Reliquely *1633*; 87 parchments *ms*] parchment *1633*; 105
In great halls *ms*] Great halls *1633*

Satire III

1. *Kind*: Natural, innate; benevolent.
    spleen: The supposed source of laughter and melancholy.
7. *first blinded age*: Pre-Christian times were 'blind' because man
    had not yet seen the light of God.
9. *them*: Those of the pre-Christian era whose goodness enabled
    them to reach heaven even without knowing Christ and the Bible.
17. *mutinous Dutch*: England was aiding the Dutch Protestants in
    their revolt against Spain.
22. *frozen Northern discoveries*: The attempts to find a north-west
    passage to the Pacific.
23. *salamanders*: Lizard-like creatures believed to be so cold-blooded
    that they could survive fire.
24. *Children in th'oven*: The three Jews who remained unharmed
    after King Nebuchadnezzar of Babylon cast them into a furnace
    for refusing to worship his golden idol (Daniel 3:12–28).
    fires of Spain: The burning of heretics during the Spanish Inquis-
    ition.
    the line: The warm climate at the Equator.
27. *draw*: Draw his sword in a duel.
43. *Mirreus*: Fictive character representing Roman Catholicism.
44. *here*: In England, where Roman Catholicism was prohibited by
    law.
48. *statecloth*: Canopy over the chair of state.
49. *Crants*: Fictive character representing Calvinists in Switzerland.
55. *Graius*: Fictive character representing the Church of England.
62. *Pay values*: Wards who did not marry according to their guar-
    dian's wishes were expected to pay the amount the guardian
    could have made from an arranged marriage.
    Phrygius: Fictive character who rejects all religions.
65. *Gracchus*: Fictive character who accepts all religions.
76. *To'adore . . . protest*: Catholics adore images of Christ and the

saints that Protestants scorn; Protestants protest about abuses in the Roman Catholic Church.

81. *about must ... go*: To reach the pinnacle of truth one must circle the mountain repeatedly, ascending indirectly rather than straight up the most impenetrable face.

92. *vicars*: Persons acting as parish priests in place of the real rector.

95. *last day*: Judgement Day.
    boot: Avail.

96–7. *a Philip ... a Martin*: Referring to the Catholics Philip II of Spain (1527–98) and Pope Gregory XIII (1502–85) and the Protestants Henry VIII (1491–1547) and Martin Luther (1483–1546).

98. *mere contraries*: Direct opposites.

Text notes: 7 to *1635*] in *1633*; 40 itself's *ms*] it self *1633*; 44 here *1635*] her *1633*; 47 her *ms*] the *1633*; 57 bid *ms*] bids *1633*

Satire V

2–3. *he which ... courtiers*: Baldassare Castiglione (1478–1529), in *The Courtier* (1528).

11. *same elements*: All things were thought to be comprised of four principal elements: earth, wind, fire and water.

16. *self*: Same.

20. *lust*: Avarice.

27. *wittols*: Husbands who condone their wife's adultery.

28. *Empress*: Queen Elizabeth (r. 1558–1603).

31. *You, Sir*: Donne's employer, Sir Thomas Egerton (1540–1617), Lord Keeper of England, who began to investigate legal misconduct in 1597.

35. *O age of rusty iron*: Last of the four proverbial ages of history, Gold, Silver, Bronze and Iron, symbolizing humanity's corruption.

37. *The Iron Age ... sold*: Inverted syntax, meaning 'That was the Iron Age when...'

39. *gamesters*: Gamblers.

41. *controverted lands*: Lands whose ownership was disputed.

42. *Angelica*: The heroine of Ludovico Ariosto's *Orlando furioso* (1516) who escaped from two knights while they fought over her.

44. *letter or fee*: Letter from an influential person or bribe.

46. *first main head*: Queen Elizabeth.
    these: Lower courts under her.
50. *when upwards*: When you try to appeal to a higher authority.
59. *angels*: Also English gold coins, stamped with the archangel
    Michael slaying a dragon, used here as a bribe.
60–61. *to Dominations, / Powers, Cherubim*: Orders of angels.
65. *pursuivant*: A heraldic officer who searched out Roman Catholics
    during Elizabeth's reign, looking for signs that they were practis-
    ing their religion in secret.
66. *primers*: Roman Catholic prayer books.
67. *mistake*: Wrongly confiscate.
73. *chairs*: Seats in high offices.
79. *barest*: By removing one's hat in respect, with a bawdy innu-
    endo.
83. *Urim and Thummim*: Jewels that enabled their bearer to reveal
    God's will; also Hebrew for 'light' and 'perfection' (Exodus
    28:30).
84. *paper*: Both legal documents and wrapping paper.
85. *the great carrack*: The *Madre de Dios*, a Portuguese ship carrying
    pepper, captured by the English in 1592.
86. *lease*: Lose.
87. *Haman*: Offered to pay his agents to exterminate the Jews in the
    Book of Esther.
90. *the swimming dog*: The dog in Aesop's fable who lost the bone
    in his mouth when he grabbed for its reflection on the water.

Text notes: 12 implies *1635*] employs *1633*; 61 courts *ms*] court
1633; 68 ask *ms*] lack *1633*; 72 but *ms*] *omitted 1633*; 76
th'extremities *ms*] extremities *1633*; 80 erst *1635*] *omitted 1633*

The Storm

In 1597 an English fleet sailed to the Azores to intercept a Spanish
fleet carrying silver. Donne, who joined the expedition as a volunteer,
records a storm experienced during the voyage.

title *Christopher Brooke*: Brooke (*c.* 1570–1628), a friend of
    Donne's, was the legal witness to Donne's clandestine marriage
    in 1601; his brother performed the ceremony.
4. *Hilliard*: Nicholas Hilliard (1537–1619) was the first English-
    man to paint miniatures.
    is worth a history: Is worth more than a large historical painting
    by someone else.

13. *sighed a wind*: Winds were understood to be the earth's exhalations.

14. *middle marble room*: The 'middle air' was believed to be the source of storms.

18. *lie but for fees*: Remain in prison because they lack funds to bribe the jailer.

22. *Sara'her swelling*: Sarah, the wife of the Hebrew patriarch Abraham, was overjoyed when, in her old age, she became pregnant with their first child, Isaac (Genesis 17:15–21, 21:1–3).

32. *anon*: Instantly.

33. *Jonah*: God sent a tempest to punish Jonah for disobedience. When his shipmates learned that he was responsible for their suffering, they threw him overboard at his instruction (Jonah 1:4–16).

48. *last day*: Judgement Day.

54. *waist*: The middle part of the upper deck of a ship.

55. *tacklings*: Ship's rigging.

59. *ordnance*: Instruments of war, artillery.

66. *the'Bermudas*: Widely known as a tempestuous area.

67. *light's elder brother*: Darkness existed before God created light (Genesis 1:2–4).

70. *forms*: Ideal things of beauty.

72. *Fiat*: Fiat lux (Latin), 'Let there be light' (Genesis 1:3).

74. *I wish not thee*: I don't wish for your presence here.

Text notes: Some manuscripts and later editions use the title 'To Mr Christopher Brooke from the Island voyage with the Earl of Essex. The Storm'. 11 soothsay *1649*] southsay *1633*; 21 swelled *ms*] swole *1633*; 47 graves *ms*] grave *1633*; 50 As *1635*] Like *1633*; 57 tattered *ms*] tottered *1633*; 66 the'Bermudas *1635*] and the'Bermuda *1633*; 67 elder *ms*] eldest *1633*; 68 claims *ms*] claimed *1633*

The Calm

Donne wrote this poem, along with 'The Storm', during his voyage to the Azores in *1597*.

2. *'suage*: Assuage.

3–4. *fable . . . block . . . stork*: In Aesop's fable a population of frogs petitioned Jove for a king. He first sent a log, but they were dissatisfied and demanded a king that would rule with authority. In reply Jove sent a stork, which ate all the frogs.

12. *lead*: Used in the roofing of churches.

14. *courts removing*: Leaving the palace.

15. *fighting place*: The platform where rigging for the upper mast was placed.

16. *tackling*: Ship's rigging.
    frippery: Old clothes; tawdry finery; a trifle.

17. *No use of lanterns*: Lanterns, hung from the mast, allowed ships in a fleet to keep each other in view.

19. *Earth's hollownesses . . . lungs are*: Wind was believed to be the exhalation of the earth.

20. *th'upper vault of air*: The upper layer of air, believed to be completely calm.

21. *lost friends*: Donne's ship became separated from the main fleet early in the voyage.

23. *calenture*: A disease, affecting sailors in the tropics, which caused delirious sailors to leap into the sea.

26. *sacrifice*: Burnt offering.

28. *walkers in hot ovens*: King Nebuchadnezzar of Babylon had three Jews cast into a furnace for refusing to worship his golden idol. God enabled them to walk out unharmed (Daniel 3:12–28).

33. *Bajazet*: Beyazid I (1347–1403), Turkish monarch, who was captured and imprisoned in a cage by his rival, Tamerlane (1336–1405).

36. *ants . . . invade*: The snake of the Roman Emperor Tiberius (42 BC–AD 37) was eaten by ants, a classic illustration of strength in numbers.

37. *crawling . . . chips*: Either a reference to the many insects that invade different parts of a ship or a description of how the boat is slowly moved by oars rather than wind.

45–6. *Stag . . . dies*: A deer, which flies from death, is rewarded with life, whereas a dog, which flies towards death, is either rewarded with its prey or dies in the process.

Text notes: 37 gaols *editors*] goals *1633*; 38 pinnaces *ms*] Venices *1633*

To Mr Henry Wotton ('Here's no more news than virtue')

title *Henry Wotton*: Wotton (1568–1639) was a fellow student of Donne's at Hart Hall, Oxford, and a member of the Cadiz and Azores expeditions of 1596–7; he became a respected lawyer, courtier and ambassador to Venice. Wotton served Robert Devereux, 2nd Earl of Essex, who, at the time this exchange between Wotton and Donne probably began in 1598, was out of favour with Queen Elizabeth.

2. *Calis*: Cadiz, a reference to the 1596 military expedition.
    St Michael's: The Azores, the destination of Essex's expedition of 1597.
4. *stomachs*: Appetite.
6. *but*: Except.
11. *commissary*: Deputy.
12. *marshal*: Arrange or draw up for fighting.
    state: Rank or status; moral, spiritual or physical condition.
13. *seely*: Innocent, pitiable, frail.
14. *neat*: Pure.
15. *Like ... hosts*: The Spanish conquistadors were notorious for mistreating natives.
22. *antics*: Performers playing comical grotesque roles.
23. *deepest*: Most solemn, weighty; most heinous; most influential; most sly or crafty.
    projects: Plans, ideas, schemes.
    egregious: Prominent; remarkably good or bad.
    gests: Exploits; stages on a journey, especially a royal progress through the countryside.
27. *At Court*: Written while at court.
    From Court: Away from the court.

    Text note: title Mr *ms*] Sir *1633*

To Mr Henry Wotton ('Sir, more than kisses, letters mingle souls')

This verse letter is Donne's reply to Wotton's response to 'Here's no more news'.

1. *more ... souls*: In *The Book of The Courtier* (1528, London: Penguin, 1967, p. 336), Baldassare Castiglione (1478–1529) asserts that, when lovers kiss, 'this bond opens the way for their souls which ... each pour themselves into the other's body in turn and so mingle that each possesses two souls.'
4. *ideate*: Imagine, conceive an idea.
6. *bottle*: Bundle.
    lock: Handful, armful or bundle.

8. *remoras*: Sucking fish believed to have the power of staying the course of any ship to which they attached themselves.
11. *even line*: The Equator.
18. *scorpion*: Its flesh was said to cure its own sting.
    torpedo: An electric ray fish or that which has a benumbing influence.
21. *sepulchres*: Tombs; also used figuratively in biblical language for hypocrites, whose outward semblance conceals inward corruption.
24. *clay*: According to Genesis 2:7, God formed man from the dust of the ground.
28. *blocks*: Blockheads.
    lewd: Lay, not clerical; also lascivious.
29. *first Chaos*: The formless void out of which God created the earth (Genesis 1:1–2).
30. *Each element*: Each of the four traditional elements: earth, air, fire, water.
31. *covetise*: Excessive desire for wealth.
34. *denizened*: Naturalized.
35. *flinty*: Hard, impenetrable.
42. *white*: Spotless, innocent.
46. *Italian*: Italians were proverbially corrupt.
48. *Inn*: Lodge oneself.
59. *Galenist*: One who believed in the four humours.
62. *chemics*: Followers of Paracelsus (1493–1541), who believed diseases could be purged with antagonistic remedies.

Text notes: title Mr *ms*] Sir *1633*; 11 even *ms*] raging *1633*; 12 poles *ms*] *pole 1633*; 17 or *ms*] and *1633*; 22 there *ms*] they *1633*; 44 for *ms*] in *1633–69*; 52 gail *1635*] goal *1633*

To Mr Rowland Woodward ('Like one who'in her third widowhood')

title *Rowland Woodward*: Woodward (1573–1636/7) was a friend and fellow student of Donne's at Lincoln's Inn; he later accompanied their mutual friend Sir Henry Wotton to Venice as one of his secretaries.
2. *retiredness*: Seclusion, reserve.
3. *fallowness*: Idleness.
11. *scales*: Of divine justice.

17. *Wise, valiant, sober, just*: The four cardinal virtues were prudence, fortitude, temperance and justice.
21. *crystal glass*: Magnifying glass.
26. *souls of simples*: Essences of medicinal herbs.
31. *termers*: Those who resorted to London either for business at a court of law or for amusements, intrigues or dishonest practices. Some editors choose the variant 'farmer' because it fits the agricultural metaphor.
32. *uplay*: Store up.
34. *Manure*: Cultivate, fertilize; also take charge or possession of.

Text note: termers *1633*] farmers *1635*

To Mr T. W. ('All hail sweet poet')

title *T. W.*: Most likely Thomas Woodward (b. 1576), brother of Rowland Woodward (see the notes to 'To Mr Rowland Woodward').
7. *stay*: Support.
20. *surquedry*: Arrogance, presumption.
22. *resound*: Proclaim, celebrate.
30. *zany*: Imitator or mimic.
32. *Lyon*: Lion; also a pun on the title of the chief herald in Scotland.

Text notes: title T. W. *ms*] I. W. *1633*; 15 Before thy *ms*] Before by thy *1633*

To Mr T. W. ('Haste thee harsh verse')

1. *lame*: Halting, metrically defective, with a pun on 'crippled'.
4. *Feet*: Both divisions of verse and means of locomotion.
12. *Infections*: The plague was particularly virulent in London at the time.
13–14. *Live I . . . testament*: If Donne lives, T. W. acts as his security deposit (pawns); if he dies, T. W. will be his will (testament).

Text notes: title Mr *ms*] M *1633*; 5–6 *ms*] omitted *1633*

To Mr T. W. ('Pregnant again with th'old twins)

Text note: 5 and *ms*] or *1633*

To Mr T. W. ('At once, from hence')

2–3. *I ... of art*: He walks to foster (nurse) his art. His lines go to
T. W. (his heart), who has been born of art.
9.   *that*: T. W.
12. *sacrament*: The Church of England defined the sacrament as an
outward sign of an invisible presence.

Text note: In many manuscripts and in *1633* this poem is
included as a continuation of the preceding poem, 'Pregnant
again with th'old twins'.

To Mr R. W. ('Zealously my muse doth salute all thee')

title *R. W.*: Rowland Woodward (see the notes to 'To Mr Rowland
Woodward').
6.   *travailed*: Troubled, harassed.
8.   *vanity*: Futility.
12. *barren*: Fruitless.

Text note: Copy-text, Westmoreland ms, in the hand of Rowland
Woodward

To Mr R. W. ('Muse not that by thy mind thy body'is led')

2.   *distempered*: Disturbed in mood, vexed.
4.   *swoll'n*: Puffed up, proud.
11. *Wright*: Probably a misspelling of 'write', but also a possible
pun, meaning 'repair' or 'mend'.
12. *sovereign*: Surpassing all others.

Text note: Copy-text, Westmoreland ms

To Mr C. B.

This poem was probably written when John Donne and Anne More were separated after her father, Sir George More, learned of their clandestine courtship.

title *C. B.*: Christopher Brooke (see the notes to 'The Storm') was a witness at the secret marriage of Donne and Anne More in December 1601.

1. *deserts*: Good deeds or qualities.
11. *won*: Dwell.
12. *martyr*: Torture.

Text note: 10 fairer *ms*] fair *1633*

To Mr R. W. ('If, as mine is, thy life a slumber be')

3. *Morpheus nor his brother*: Morpheus, the Greek god of dreams, and his brother, Phantasus, both had the ability to metamorphose into different shapes.
7. *deed of gift*: Means of conveying property while alive.
8. *will*: Means of conveying property after death.
13. *patient*: Sufferer.
17. *gospel*: Glad tidings.
18. *Guiana*: In July 1597 the English were prevented from placing their flag in Guiana in South America.
20. *Jew's guide*: Moses, who was allowed to see the promised land beyond Jordan but not to enter it (Deuteronomy 3:25, 27).
23. *Spanish business*: The attacks on Spain and its fleets in the Cadiz and Azores voyages.
27. *all th'All*: The entire universe.
28. *India*: A source of wealth, a mine.
29. *If men be worlds*: If men are microcosms of the universe.

Text note: 22 O *ms*] Our *1633*

To Mr R. W. ('Kindly I envy thy song's perfection')

2. *all th'elements*: The four traditional elements, fire, air, water and earth.
14. *recreated*: Either to be refreshed by some agreeable object or impression or to be re-created.

Text note: Copy-text, Westmoreland ms

H. W. in Hiber. Belligeranti

title   *H. W. . . . Belligeranti*: 'Henry Wotton fighting in Ireland'.
Wotton (see the notes to 'To Mr Henry Wotton ("Here's no
more news than virtue")') fought in Ireland under Robert
Devereux, 2nd Earl of Essex, from April to September 1559.

3.   *respective*: Respectful.
9.   *skeins*: Irish daggers.
14.   *stilled*: Distilled.
19.   *dishonest carriage*: Fraudulent, underhanded or thievish convey-
ance from one place to another.
seer: Both a diviner or magician and someone who secretly
unseals and reads a private letter addressed to someone else.

Text notes: Copy-text, Burley ms, Wotton's commonplace book;
11 attack Grierson] *Burley reads* attach; 12 arrest] *emended by
Grierson from* crest

To Sir H. W. at His Going Ambassador to Venice

title   *Sir H. W. . . . Venice*: Henry Wotton was knighted by King James
on 8 July 1604, five days before leaving for Venice.
5.   *taper*: A thing that gives a feeble light, a wax candle; a wick.
30.   *last furnace*: Most severe test or trial; the final forging step needed
to solidify Wotton's 'spirits'.
39.   *stairs*: Jacob dreamed that a ladder connected heaven and earth
(Genesis 28:10–12).

To Sir Henry Goodyere

title   *Sir Henry Goodyere*: Sir Henry (1571–1628) was Donne's inti-
mate friend and frequent correspondent. Although known to be
extravagant, he was a respected member of the Privy Council
under James I.
4.   *pair*: String.
17.   *diet*: Way of eating, living or thinking.
19.   *garners*: Storehouses for grain or salt.
20.   *sports*: Amusements.
22.   *outlandish*: Foreign.
28.   *prescribe*: Assert a right or claim.

30. *sink*: Receptacle or gathering place.
31. *travail*: Labour, toil; also a pun on 'travel'.
33. *to spare*: To refrain from excess.
42. *froward*: Perverse, ungovernable.
44. *tables*: Tablets bearing inscriptions or rhetorical devices.
    trenchers: Platters, often decorated with short moral sayings.
48. *Mitcham*: Donne's residence from 1606 to 1611.

To the Countess of Huntingdon ('That unripe side of earth')

title *Countess of Huntingdon*: Elizabeth Stanley (bap. 1587, d. 1633), stepdaughter of Donne's employer, Sir Thomas Egerton.
1–3. *That unripe side . . . ate*: America, where the natives went naked like Adam before the Fall.
16. *atomi*: Smallest particles, atoms.
22. *cross-armed*: The conventional pose of an unrequited lover.
24. *white-livered*: Cowardly.
57. *sueth*: Pursues, both legally and romantically.
83. *curious hit*: Skilfully imitated.
85. *what is more*: God.
87. *next*: Shortest.
92. *zanies*: Imitators or mimics.
100. *large*: Free.

Text notes: Copy-text, *1635*; 69 sigh *ms*] sin *1635*; 74 and *ms*] I *1635*; 107 dares *ms*] dare *1635*; 121 men *ms*] man *1635*; 123 Their *ms*] There *1635*; 125 violent *ms*] valiant *1635*; 128 feigned *ms*] fancied *1635*; 128 which only tempts man's appetite *ms*] omitted *1635*; 130 contract in *ms*] contracted *1635*

To Mrs M. H.

title *M. H.*: Magdalen Herbert (d. 1627), an intimate friend of Donne's and mother of the poets Sir Edward Herbert (1582?–1648) and George Herbert (1593–1633).
1. *Mad*: Either senseless or fervent with poetic inspiration.
2. *suns*: Spelled 'sonnes' in *1633*, a pun on 'sun' and 'son', which were spelled interchangeably.
4. *rags*: Paper was made of rags.
12. *they*: Princes.
15. *die*: Pine away with desire.
19. *saple*: Sapling.

20. *creature*: Creation; one who owes his position and fortune to a patron; an instrument or puppet.
37. *any*: Any writings.
39. *revolves*: Both to read and to ponder.
    his: Probably refers to Sir John Danvers (1584/5–1655), whom Herbert married in 1608.
52. *fain*: Gladly, willingly.

To the Countess of Bedford ('Reason is our soul's left hand')

title *Countess of Bedford*: Lucy Harington Russell (bap. 1581, d. 1627), one of Donne's most valued patrons. She served as a lady-in-waiting to Queen Elizabeth, and was also a scholar and a poet. She had a close relation with Donne for a number of years, and in 1608 gave him permission to name his daughter Lucy. Residing at Twickenham Park, she became the patron of many scholars and poets.
5. *squint*: Characterized by obliquity of action.
   left-handedness: Underhandedness.
6. *want*: Lack.
10. *election*: Chosen by God to be saved.
11. *accesses, and restraints*: Permitting and withholding favour or access.
12. *devise*: Invent, imagine, by writing her own poetry.
15. *implicit faith*: Trusting in the authority of another without doubt or inquiry.
16. *catholic*: Universal.
22. *balsamum*: Balm; balsam.
27. *mithridate*: Universal antidote to poison.
29. *physic*: Medicine.
34. *factor*: Agent.
35. *return home*: Return to heaven.

Text notes: 16 voice *ms*] faith *1633*; 36 This *ms*] Thy *1633*

To the Countess of Bedford ('Honour is so sublime perfection')

4–6. *elements ... head*: The four traditional elements: earth, water ('these which we tread'), fire and air ('those ... above our head').
12. *dung*: Manure, which generates heat.

18. *Sicil Isle*: Sicily, where the active volcano Mount Etna is located.
22. *clay*: According to Genesis 2:7, God formed man of the dust of the ground.
26. *quick*: Living, animate.
29. *specular stone*: Transparent stone, once used as glass in mirrors.
34–5. *souls of growth . . . reason's soul*: According to the philosopher Aristotle (384–322 BC) the soul of man was threefold: the vegetative soul ('souls of growth') and sensible soul ('souls of sense') were believed to have existed in the body before the rational soul ('our reason's soul') was breathed into man.
44. *wit*: Reason, intellect.
46. *types*: Emblems.

> *Text notes*: 13 praisers *ms*] praises *1633*; 27 your heart's *ms*] our heart's *1633*; 31 so and of such *ms*] so and such *1633*; 48 all ways *ms*] always *1633*

To the Countess of Bedford ('You have refined me')

4. *circumstanced*: Placed in relation to other things.
11. *dark*: Obscure.
12. *usher*: Introduce.
13. *this place*: Twickenham Park, the Countess's residence.
23. *loathly*: Reluctantly.
25. *antipodes*: Those who dwell directly opposite to each other on the globe.
37. *Rome*: The seat of the papacy and Roman Catholicism.
40. *invest*: Dress or adorn.
41. *schools*: Theological disputants.
48. *th'Escuriall*: The Escorial, the sixteenth-century monastery in Castile, which became a powerful political centre during the reign of Philip II (r. 1556–98).
61. *nice*: Foolish.
69. *magazine*: Storehouse.
      commonweal: Either the public welfare or the body politic.

> *Text notes*: 52 all prophecy *ms*] and prophecy *1633*; 60 thing *ms*] things *1633*

To the Countess of Bedford ('T'have written then, when you writ')

5–6. *this . . . that*: Not to have written . . . to have written.

14. *Peter . . . fane*: It was said that St Peter's Basilica in Rome was built on the site of an ancient *fane* (temple) to Jove, and that St Paul's Cathedral in London was built on a temple of Diana.

17. *denizened*: Naturalized.

19. *bravely*: Excellently.

23. *fitness*: Propriety.

25–6. *Your . . . preserves*: Lucy's virtue 'ransoms' (redeems) the female sex, and her presence preserves the Jacobean court from corruption.

32. *stoop*: Humble yourself.

37. *new philosophy*: The heliocentric theory of Nicolaus Copernicus (1473–1543), which placed the sun, rather than the earth, at the centre of the universe.

43. *engines*: Instruments.

47–8. *he which said, Plough / And look not back*: 'And Jesus said unto him, No man, having put his hand to the plough, and looking back, is fit for the Kingdom of God' (Luke 9:62).

50. *cockle*: Weeds.

55. *engraved*: Deeply impressed; also 'ingraved', entombed.

56. *caskets*: Small, often richly ornamented boxes for valuables.

64. *stones . . . seen*: Physicians claimed to have removed such objects from their patients' bodies.

68. *Two new stars*: The astronomer Johannes Kepler (1571–1630) reported two new constellations, Cygnus and Sepentarius; Donne is probably alluding to the deaths of Bridget Harington, Lady Markham (Lucy's first cousin), who died at Twickenham on 4 May 1609, and Cecilia Boulstred, who also died at Twickenham, on 4 August 1609.

81. *aspersion*: Sprinkling.

82. *complexion*: Temperament.

85. *thralls*: Enslaves.

90. *cordial*: Restorative, reviving, especially to the heart.

Text notes: 5 debt *ms*] doubt *1633*; 7 nothings *ms*] nothing *1633*; 14 hath *ms*] have *1633*; 20 all it; you *ms*] all, in you *1633*; 30 is *ms*] it *1633*; 32 Stoop *ms*] Stop *1633*; 60 vice *1635*] it *1633*; 75 you *ms*] your *1633*

To the Countess of Bedford, on New Year's Day

1.   *two years*: One beginning, one ending.
3.   *meteor*: Any atmospheric or meteorological phenomenon.
     perplexed: Entangled.
16. *tincture*: The quintessence of a thing, which may be imbued into material things.
28. *corn*: Particle.
44. *disport*: Amusement.
45. *comport*: Agree with, accord with; suit.
47. *ingress*: Enter, invade; specifically 'go in to' carnally.
60. *state*: Financial status.
63–4. *dis-enrol / Your name*: Remove your name from the Book of Life, which lists the names of the redeemed.

Text notes: 10 times *ms*] time *1633*; 18 spirits *ms*] spirit *1633*; 35 praiser *ms*] prayer *1633*; 47 which *ms*] with *1633*

To Sir Edward Herbert, at Juliers

title *Sir Edward Herbert, at Juliers*: Herbert (1582?–1648) was the son of Magdalen Herbert (see the notes to 'To Mrs M. H.') and the elder brother of the poet George Herbert. A poet himself, Edward was also a philosopher, soldier and ambassador to France. In 1610 he travelled to Juliers, a duchy in the Lowlands besieged by Protestants at the beginning of the Thirty Years War. He was knighted in 1603, and made Lord Herbert of Cherbury in 1629.
1.   *kneaded*: Reduced to a common mass.
2.   *ark*: Place of refuge; an allusion to Noah's ark, which preserved all of the world's species during the great flood (Genesis 6:13–8:19).
3.   *jar*: Discord.
8.   *couple*: Come together sexually.
10. *disaforested*: Stripped of privilege; reduced to ordinary standards.
11. *impaled*: Fenced in.
15–17. *Else man ... worse*: Coming upon two men possessed by demons, Jesus cast the demons out into a herd of swine, which caused the herd to run suddenly into the sea (Matthew 8:28–32).
24. *Hemlock*: A plant, poisonous to man, but food to birds ('chickens').

31. *his pleasure*: His own pleasure.
    his rod: His own punishment, by living sinfully.
43-4. *For knowledge . . . opium*: In some men, knowledge causes a delirious fever ('calentures'), while in others it acts as a cooling sedative ('opium').
45. *brave*: Excellent.
    profession: Declaration.
50. *mart*: Any public place for buying and selling; originally any of various international book fairs central to the publishing trade of early modern Europe, including one held twice a year in Frankfurt until 1749.

To the Countess of Huntingdon ('Man to God's image')

1-2. *Man . . . in her*: God created man in his own image (Genesis 1:27). Eve was created from a rib of man (Genesis 2:21-3). The Bible is ambiguous as to whether she too was created in God's image. The Bible specifically states that God breathed a soul into man (Genesis 2:7), but does not indicate that He did the same for woman.
3. *canons*: Canon law.
4. *prefer*: Advance in status or rank.
13. *Magi*: The three wise men who were guided to Christ's manger by the Star of Bethlehem (Matthew 2:1-12).
17-18. *If . . . doth bend*: Many believed that the sun was nearer the earth than in the past, and this was taken as a sign that the earth was dying.
22. *She fled to heaven*: Possibly a reference to Astraea, goddess of justice, who fled to the heavens because she was so disgusted with man's corruption.
26. *informed*: Shaped, fashioned.
    transubstantiates: Transforms, transmutes.
38. *Crab and Bull*: Cancer and Taurus.
41. *one*: Her husband, Henry Hastings, 5th Earl of Huntingdon (1586-1643).
58. *long ago*: Donne had met her many years before, when she was twelve, and her mother married his employer, Sir Thomas Egerton.

Text notes: 13 the *ms*] which *1633*; 47 do so *ms*] to you *1633*; 66 and *ms*] or *1633*

A Letter to the Lady Carey, and Mistress Essex Rich,
from Amiens

title *Lady Carey, and Mistress Essex Rich*: In late 1611, while Donne
was in Amiens with Sir Robert Drury (1575–1615), Sir Robert
Rich (1587–1658) passed through and probably persuaded
Donne to write this verse letter to his sisters, whom Donne may
never have met. They were the children of Penelope Devereux
(the heroine of Sir Philip Sidney's *Astrophel and Stella* (*c.* 1582)),
who left Robert Rich (1559?–1619), 3rd Lord Rich and later 1st
Earl of Warwick, to live with Charles Blount, 8th Baron Mount-
joy (1563–1606). Lettice Rich, the eldest daughter, married Sir
George Carey of Cockington, Devon. Essex Rich later married
Sir Thomas Cheke of Pirgo. Although their father was probably
Lord Rich, their mother's notoriety cast doubts on their
parentage.

7.   *convertite*: Convert.

9.   *Pardons*: The Protestant Reformation criticized the Roman
Catholic Church for selling indulgences.

12.   *faith alone*: The Church of England believed in justification by
faith alone, while the Roman Catholic Church maintained that
good works were also necessary for salvation.

18.   *their humours*: Their temperaments, as determined by their pre-
dominant humour – phlegmatic, sanguine, melancholy, or
choleric.

21.   *phlegm*: Equanimity, one of the four humours.

31.   *parcel-gilt*: Partially gilded.

32.   *complexion*: The particular combination of the four humours
thought to determine a person's temperament.

34.   *aguish*: Fitful.
      several: Separate, distinct, various.

40.   *that part of you*: Your body.

Text notes: This is the only known poem in Donne's hand-
writing, with his punctuation which is followed in the text. 13
are *1635*] is *1633*; 30 this *1635*] their *1633*; 31 gold *ms*] golds
1633

Sappho to Philænis

title *Sappho*: Greek woman poet from the island of Lesbos, who composed love poetry about both men and women around 600 BC.
      Philænis: Literally 'Female Friend'.

3.   *draws*: Copies, emulates.

11.   *it*: Both Philænis's image and Sappho's heart.

19.   *silly*: Ordinary; frail.

20.   *A little world*: It was believed that man is a microcosm of the universe.

25.   *Phao*: A handsome ferryman whom Sappho loved unrequitedly.

31.   *wants*: Is lacking.

36.   *unmanured*: Uncultivated.

39.   *that which their sin shows*: Illegitimate children.

55.   *glass*: Mirror.

Text notes: 58 thee *ms*] she *1633*; 59–60 *1633*] cf. 'So may thy cheeks outwear all scarlet dye/May bliss and thee be one eternally' *ms*

The First Anniversary. An Anatomy of the World

'The First Anniversary' commemorates the death of Elizabeth Drury, the daughter of Donne's patron Sir Robert Drury. She died on 17 December 1610 at the age of fourteen. The first edition of 1611 was entitled *An Anatomy of the World. Wherein, by the occasion of the untimely death of Mistress Elizabeth Drury the frailty and decay of the whole world is represented.*

title *Anniversary*: The yearly commemoration of a saint's death-day.
      Anatomy: Dissection of a body; a detailed examination or analysis.

4.   *see, and judge, and follow*: Corresponding to the faculties of the rational soul – memory, understanding and will.

6.   *inmate*: Poor, temporary lodger.

7.   *that queen*: Elizabeth Drury, but probably also Queen Elizabeth.
      progress: A monarch's stately journey through the countryside.

8.   *standing house*: Permanent home.

13.   *vital spirits*: Elements in the blood that were believed to unite body and soul.

19.   *consumption*: Wasting of the body by a disease.

21. *agues physic are*: Agues, or violent fevers, were thought to be curative.
24. *in a lethargy*: Near death.
31. *thy name thou hadst*: The name that you had.
32. *o'erpast*: Passed over, forgotten.
33. *font*: The baptismal font.
36. *her coming*: Elizabeth Drury's birth.
41–2. *none / Offers . . . that's gone*: Since no one has celebrated her death in verse.
48. *A strong example . . . law*: An example equal in status to law.
50. *resolved*: Dissolved.
52. *our weakness*: The weakness of those left in the world after her death.
57. *intrinsic balm*: Restorative substance, necessary for life.
68. *inanimate*: Animate, infuse life into.
76. *new world*: Paradise within man.
82. *weedless paradises*: Like the Garden of Eden before the Fall.
98. *precipitation*: A witty pun, drawing on the root meaning, 'to fall head first'.
99. *witty*: Wise, ingenious.
102. *For man's relief*: Eve was created as Adam's helpmate (Genesis 2:20–23).
105. *that first marriage was our funeral*: By eating the apple, Eve condemned mankind to death.
107–10. *And singly . . . our kind*: These lines pun on the words 'death' and 'dying', which had a sexual double meaning since it was believed that orgasm shortened one's life.
111. *yet*: If.
       we do not that: Because our offspring are less than men.
112–26. *There is not now . . . direct*: Before the Fall, man was immortal. There were giants upon the earth in those days, in the time of the biblical patriarchs (Genesis 6:4).
116. *in minority*: While a minor.
128. *Methusalem*: Methuselah, the biblical patriarch who was a symbol of longevity because he lived 969 years (Genesis 5:25–7).
134. *three lives*: Ninety-nine years, the traditional length of a lease.
136. *span*: Unit of measurement representing the distance from the tip of the thumb to the tip of the little finger or forefinger – approximately nine inches.
148–9. *to gold / Their silver*: Adam and Eve were thought to have lived in the Golden Age, the biblical patriarchs in the Silver Age.

151. *damped*: Stifled, choked, extinguished, deadened.

159. *new diseases*: Probably syphilis and influenza.

167, 169. *This man*: Christ.

173. *depart*: Part.

176. *they called virtues by the name of she*: In Greek and Latin the words for virtues are feminine, as are most abstract nouns.

178. *alloy*: An admixture of an alien element that lowers the value or character, or detracts from the purity of, the original element.

180. *poisonous tincture*: Donne poisons the alchemical meaning of 'tincture' (a purifying spiritual principle) by equating it with original sin.

203–4. *And now ... after fifty be*: 'They that be born in the strength of youth are of one fashion, and they that are born in the time of age, when the womb faileth, are otherwise ... ye are less of stature than those that were before you. And so are they that come after you less than ye, as born of creature which now beginneth to be old, and is past the strength of youth' (2 Esdras 5:53–5).

205. *new philosophy*: New discoveries in science and astronomy, especially Galileo's (1564–1642) telescopic observation that the earth revolved around the sun, which challenged the traditional view of the earth as the centre of the universe.

206. *The element ... out*: 'All the other three elements, earth, and water, and air abound with elements proper to each of them, only the fire produces nothing' (John Donne, *Sermons*, ed. George R. Potter and Evelyn M. Simpson, 10 vols. (Berkeley: University of California Press, 1953–62), VII, 184).

211. *so many new*: New planets and stars, discovered by astronomers in the sixteenth and early seventeenth centuries.

212. *atomies*: Atoms, motes; also anatomies.

214. *just supply*: Rightful support or succour.

230. *Gild ... the East*: The West Indies were known for precious metal, and the East Indies for spices and perfumes.

234. *single money*: Small coins.

248. *age's darts*: The missiles, spears or arrows thrown by age.

255. *eccentric parts*: Deviations from the regular, circular movement of the heavenly spheres.

263–7. *zodiac ... run*: Capricorn (the Goat) and Cancer (the Crab), two of the twelve signs of the zodiac, known as the tropics, were thought to check the sun's movement toward the poles.

278. *meridians and parallels*: Longitudes and latitudes of the sky.

286. *Tenerife*: A volcanic peak on the island of Tenerife in the Canary Islands.

295. *vault infernal*: Medieval theologians thought hell was at the centre of the earth.

296. *except that*: Unless.

314. *resultances*: Emanations, reflections.

319. *type*: A person, object or event from the Old Testament that prefigures something in the New Testament.

338. *Wicked is not much worse than indiscreet*: Because discretion was the ability to distinguish between good and evil.

343–4. *compassionate turquoise . . . well*: Turquoise, it was believed, turned pale if its wearer was unwell, losing colour completely if the wearer died.

347. *the first week*: According to Genesis 1:1–2:2, God created the earth in one week.

352. *various rainbow*: The rainbow, in all its varied colours, the sign of God's covenant with Noah (Genesis 9:8–17).

364. *verdure*: The green of new vegetation.

368. *to her*: Compared to her.

376. *colours*: Cosmetics.
     elude: Trick, deceive.

380. *father . . . mother*: Traditionally, the sky and the earth.

387. *meteors*: Atmospheric phenomena, especially comets, considered ominous and portentous.

389. *worms*: Serpents.

390. *Egyptian mages*: The Egyptian magicians who turned their rods into serpents in Exodus 7:10–12.

391. *artist*: Alchemist.

392. *constellate*: Construct a charm under a particular constellation.

396. *correspondence*: Active communication; concordant or sympathetic response; similarity, agreement.

400. *embarred*: Prevented.

407. *one dying swan*: It was thought that swans sang only once, on the verge of death.

417–18. *transubstantiate / All states to gold*: Alchemists sought an elixir capable of transforming base metal to gold.

422. *stay*: Support.

426. *our age was iron*: The Iron Age, which came after the ages of Gold, Silver, and Bronze, was a period of the world's decline.

432. *travail*: Toil; trouble, hardship, suffering.

440. *punctual*: Exact, proceeding point by point.

452. *Be got*: Pun on 'begot'.
     but then: Only then.
456. *concoction*: Ripening, bringing to a state of perfection.
465. *The law, the prophets, and the history*: Referring to various books of the Bible.
467. *in due measure*: Both 'with due reverence' and 'in verse'.
474. *enrolls*: Records with honor, celebrates.

Text notes: Copy-text, 1611; title The First Anniversary 1612; marginal notes added in 1612; 144 scarce *1612 errata*] scarsc *1611*; 153 close-weaving *1633*] close-weaning *1611–25*; 217 there *1612 errata*] then *1611–69*; 259 there *1612 errata*] then *1611–69*; 262 towns *1612 errata*] towers *1611–69*; 273 reeling *1621*] recling *1611*; 474 fame *1612 errata, 1633*] same *1611–25*

Epitaph on Himself. To the Countess of Bedford

title *Epitaph on Himself*: This poem may have been written in 1608, when Donne was seriously ill.
1.   *cabinet*: Private apartment.
2.   *fame*: Reputation.
7.   *this custom*: That of giving, rather than receiving, legacies upon one's death.
12–13. *clay . . . earth*: According to Genesis 2:7, God formed man of the dust of the ground.
14.   *glass*: Made by heating and refining sand.
      grow gold: Referring to the gradual alchemical transmutation of base materials into gold; also a pun on 'grow old'.
20.   *trumpet's air*: According to the Bible, a trumpet will announce Judgement Day and the bodies of the just will then be raised to heaven (1 Corinthians 15:52, 1 Thessalonians 4:16).
23.   *well composed*: Well prepared for death; also a pun, since he is 'composing' lines of poetry, and after death he will 'decompose'.

Text notes: Copy-text, 1635; first printed in two parts: The introductory epistle and the following ten lines with the Funeral Elegies under the title 'Elegie'; the full epitaph, without the epistle, among the Divine Poems, under the title 'On himselfe'; appears as a single poem in some mss; 7 choice *ms*] will *1635*; 8 speechless *ms*] senseless *1635*; 10 see'st *ms*] see *1635*; 12 here *ms*] there *1635*; 22 to *ms*] for *1635*

Epitaph on Anne Donne

Donne wrote this Latin epitaph to commemorate his wife's death on 15 August 1617. It was inscribed on her tombstone at St Clement Danes Chapel, London, where she was buried with the stillborn female child whom she had given birth to seven days before her death. The fullest account of the poem, and the source of the following footnotes and translation, is M. Thomas Hester, ' "Fæminæ Lectissimæ": Reading Anne Donne', in *John Donne's 'desire of more'*, ed. Hester.

3–4. *Equit[o] . . . Aurat[o]*: Literally, gilt or golden knight, referring to Anne's father's title as Knight of the Garter; also a pun on the gilt or golden nights that John and Anne spent together; perhaps also a cross-lingual pun on the guilt of their clandestine courtship and marriage.

5. *Fæminæ Lectissimæ*: This suggests, as Hester's essay explains, that Anne was Donne's 'best reader and text'.
   Dilectissimæque: Chosen, or delight of the gods, suggesting that Anne was a type of the Virgin Mary.

8. *transactis*: The participial form of *transigo*, 'to finish' or 'to complete'; but also 'to stab' or 'to penetrate', thus alluding to the sexual union which produced the twelve children mentioned in the following line.

16. *Iohannes*: This form of the name, which Donne does not generally use, unites 'John' and 'Anne'.

18. *Secessit*: Could also mean 'he withdrew', suggesting the effects of Anne's death on Donne himself.

19. *et sui Iesu*: Like Jesus, Anne died at the age of thirty-three.

21. *Aug: xv*: The date of the Assumption of the Madonna, another Marian association.

Text note: Copy-text, Loseley ms, which may be written in Donne's own handwriting

To the Lady Magdalen Herbert, of St Mary Magdalen

title *Magdalen Herbert*: See the notes to 'To Mrs M. H.'.
   St Mary Magdalen: The sister of Martha and Lazarus, Mary accompanied Christ and ministered to Him (Luke 8:2–3). During the Crucifixion she stood at the foot of the cross (Mark 15:40; Matthew 27:56; John 19:25; Luke 23:49), and then was the first witness of His resurrection (Mark 16:9; John 20:11–18). Some

believe that these texts refer to three separate women, all named
Mary (see l. 8).

2.   *Bethina ... Magdalo*: Mary Magdalen is identified with Mary
of Bethany ('Bethina'), a town near Jerusalem, and her family
estates were said to be at Magdala ('Magdalo').
   jointure: Jointly held.

6.   *Fathers*: Church Fathers.

12.   *latter half*: Both Magdalen, the latter half of her full name, and
her living devoutly, as she did after Jesus forgave the sins of her
early years.

14.   *these hymns*: The 'La Corona' sequence that follows.

Text note: Copy-text, Izaak Walton's *Life of Dr John Donne*
(1640)

La Corona

title *La Corona*: The crown; originally a wreath of flowers or leaves,
the seven sonnets of the sequence are similarly woven together,
with the last line of each becoming the first line of the next; a
reference to Christ's majesty and to the crown of thorns worn
by Him at the Crucifixion; possibly a reference to the rosary.

4.   *Ancient of Days*: A name given to God by Daniel (7:9, 13, 22).

5.   *bays*: Laurel leaves – woven into a wreath, these were a symbol
of poetic achievement.

verse 2. *Annunciation*: The Angel Gabriel visited Mary to tell her
that she would bear the Son of God.

17–18. *Which cannot sin ... but die*: Christ was born to die on the
cross to save man from original sin.

21.   *nor thou give*: Christ was conceived without sin.

24.   *thy son and brother*: Mary is the mother of Jesus, but she, like
all people, is also a child of God.

26.   *Father's*: God the Father's.

27.   *light in dark*: God is light, and Mary carries Him in her dark womb.

verse 3. *Nativity*: Mary and her husband, Joseph, were in Bethlehem
when the time came for Mary to give birth. Unable to find a
room at an inn, they were forced to spend the night in a barn.
When Christ was born, they laid him in a manger. Above the
barn a great star appeared, which guided wise men seeking to
pay homage to the Son of God (Matthew 2:1–11).

32.   *Weak enough*: God chose to come to earth as a helpless infant.

36.   *Herod's jealous general doom*: When Herod, the King of Judea,

heard that the 'King of the Jews' had been born in Bethlehem, he became jealous and ordered his soldiers to kill all the infants of Bethlehem under the age of two (Matthew 2:16).

41.   *into Egypt go*: The angel of the Lord appeared to Joseph in a dream, warning him of the danger from Herod and instructing him to flee with the child to Egypt (Matthew 2:13–14).

verse 4.   *Temple*: When Jesus was twelve he was found in the temple in Jerusalem, conversing with theologians ('doctors') about subjects very advanced for his age (Luke 2:41–50).

47.   *The Word*: Jesus Christ (John 1:14).

verse 5.   *Crucifying*: Jesus was sentenced to death as king of the Jews. A crown of thorns was placed upon his head, and he was forced to carry his own cross to the site of his crucifixion.

62.   *the'Immaculate*: Christ was without sin.

64.   *span*: Unit of measurement representing the distance from the tip of the thumb to the tip of the little finger or forefinger – approximately nine inches.

68.   *Now Thou . . . to Thee*: 'And I, if I be lifted up from the earth, will draw all men unto me' (John 12:32).

69.   *dole*: Distribution of gifts; fate; grief.

verse 6.   *Resurrection*: Christ died and was buried, and on the third day afterwards he rose again and ascended into heaven. In doing so, he defeated death and gave everlasting life to his followers.

78.   *thy little book*: The Book of Life, in which men's deeds and fate are recorded.

verse 7.   *Ascension*: Christ rose from the dead and ascended into heaven, where he took his seat at the right hand of God the Father.

86.   *sun, and Son*: A widely used pun, for Christ rose like the sun.

88.   *drossy*: Impure.
      clay: According to Genesis 2:7, God formed man of the dust of the ground.

91–2.   *Nor doth . . . way*: Jesus went before us to light the way to heaven.

93.   *Ram*: Christ is identified with Aries, the astrological sign that marks the return of spring.

94.   *Lamb*: A common symbol of Christ.

95.   *Torch*: God is light.

97.   *raise*: Exalt, inspire.

Text notes: 36 effect *ms*] effects *1633*;   64 to'a *ms*] to *1633*;   82 death's *ms*] death *1633*

Holy Sonnet I ('Thou hast made me')

5. *dim eyes*: Pun on 'demise'.
8. *weigh*: Lean, incline.
13. *wing me*: Give me wings.
    prevent: Of God's grace, to go before with spiritual guidance and help; forestall.
14. *adamant*: Lodestone, magnet.

Text notes: Copy-text, *1635*; 7 feebled *ms*] 'feeble' *1635*; 12 I can myself *ms*] myself I can *1635*

Holy Sonnet II ('As due by many titles')

1. *titles*: Appellations; legal claims.
3. *decayed*: By sin.
4. *bought*: Redeemed.
6. *still*: Always.
9. *usurp on*: Seize without right or claim.

Holy Sonnet III ('O might those sighs and tears')

5. *idolatry*: Worship of a false idol or lover.
6. *rent*: Tear apart.
7. *sufferance*: Suffering.
10. *itchy*: Because infected with venereal disease.
    self-tickling: Self-satisfied.

Holy Sonnet IV ('O my black soul!')

4. *turn*: Return.
5. *death's doom*: Judgement Day.
    read: Pun on 'read'/'red' throughout.
7. *haled*: Dragged.

Holy Sonnet V ('I am a little world')

1. *little world*: Microcosm of the universe.
2. *sprite*: Spirit.
9. *drowned no more*: God covenanted with Noah never again to destroy the earth with a flood (Genesis 9:8–11).
10. *it must be burnt*: A fire will destroy the earth instead.

14. *which doth in eating heal*: God's fire consumes and purifies.

Text notes: Copy-text, 1635; 6 lands *ms*] land *1635*

Holy Sonnet VI ('This is my play's last scene')

4. *span*: Lifespan.
7. *ever-waking part*: Undying soul.
    that face: God's face.
8. *whose fear*: Fear of which.
13. *Impute me righteous*: Due to original sin, the soul cannot be righteous; it can only be considered righteous by the merit of Christ.

Text note: 6 soul *ms*] my soul *1633*

Holy Sonnet VII ('At the round earth's imagined corners')

1. *At the ... imagined corners*: 'I saw four angels standing on the four corners of the earth, holding the four winds of the earth' (Revelation 7:1).
4. *scattered bodies*: Decayed bodies waiting to be reunited with their souls on Judgement Day.
8. *never taste death's woe*: 'But I tell you of a truth, there be some standing here which shall not taste of death, till they see the kingdom of God' (Luke 9:27).

Text note: 6 dearth *ms*] death *1633*

Holy Sonnet VIII ('If faithful souls be alike glorified')

1. *faithful souls*: Of the dead in heaven.
2. *As angels*: Angels were believed to be able to read men's minds.
5. *descried*: Disclosed.
8. *tried*: Separated; extracted; found out.
10. *conjurers*: Men who conjure spirits and pretend to perform miracles by their art.
11. *pharisaical*: Self-righteous, hypocritical.
13–14. *for He ... my breast*: God can understand my soul's grief better than anyone else because He put it into my heart when He created me.

Text notes: Copy-text, 1635; 10 vile *ms*] stile *1635*

Holy Sonnet IX ('If poisonous minerals')

1-2.   *that tree . . . immortal us*: The Tree of Knowledge in the Garden
       of Eden, which brought death into the world when Eve ate its
       fruit.
3.   *goats*: Traditionally believed to be lecherous.
       serpents: Associated with Satan.
11.   *Lethean*: Of Lethe, the river of forgetfulness in Hades, the classi-
       cal underworld.
13.   *That Thou remember*: According to Christian doctrine, God
       remembers man's sins so as to pardon them.

Holy Sonnets X ('Death be not proud')

8.   *delivery*: Deliverance from the body.
11.   *poppy*: Opium.
12.   *swell'st thou*: With pride.
14.   *death . . . no more*: 'The last enemy that shall be destroyed is
       death' (1 Corinthians 15:26).

Holy Sonnet XI ('Spit in my face, you Jews')

1-2.   *Spit . . . scoff*: 'Then they did spit in his face, and buffeted him;
       and others smote him with the palms of their hands, saying
       Prophesy unto us, thou Christ, Who is he that smote thee?'
       (Matthew 26:67-8).
3.   *He*: Christ.
5.   *satisfied*: Atoned for.
7.   *inglorious*: Obscure, humble.
11-12. *And Jacob . . . intent*: Jacob disguised himself in order to
       receive the blessing his father intended for his brother, Esau
       (Genesis 27:15-29). 'Jacob' in Hebrew means 'one who sup-
       plants or replaces'.

Holy Sonnet XII ('Why are we by all creatures')

2.   *prodigal*: Extravagantly wasteful.
3-4.   *more pure . . . corruption*: Man, composed of a mixture of the
       'prodigal elements', is more subject to corruption than the pure
       elements themselves.
5.   *brook'st*: Tolerate; endure.
6.   *sillily*: Senselessly, naively.

7.   *Dissemble*: Feign.
13. *tied*: Restricted.

Holy Sonnet XIII ('What if this present')

5.   *amazing*: Terrifying; awe-inspiring.
9.   *idolatry*: unholy love of 'profane mistresses' (l. 10).
11–12. *Beauty ... rigour*: Beauty is a manifestation of mercy; foulness is a sign of strictness or severity.
14. *piteous*: Both pious and compassionate.

Text note: 14 assures *ms*] assumes *1633*

Holy Sonnet XIV ('Batter my heart')

1.   *three-personed God*: God the Father, the Son and the Holy Spirit.
5.   *usurped*: Possessed unjustly (by Satan, but due to God).
13. *enthral*: Both 'enslave' and 'captivate'.
14. *ravish*: Fill with rapture; also seize and carry away by force; violate, rape.

Holy Sonnet XV ('Wilt thou love God')

4.   *His temple in thy breast*: 'Know ye not that ye are the temple of God, and that the Spirit of God dwelleth in you?' (1 Corinthians 3:16).
6.   *still begetting ... ne'er begun*: Because God and Christ have neither beginning nor end.
7–8. *by adoption / Coheir*: 'But ye have received the Spirit of adoption ... we are the children of God. And if children, then heirs; heirs of God, and joint-heirs with Christ; if so be that we suffer with him, that we may be also glorified together' (Romans 8:15–17).
12. *and Satan stol'n*: And whom Satan had stolen.

Holy Sonnet XVI ('Father, part of His double interest')

1.   *double interest*: Double claim, as God and as man.
3.   *jointure*: Joint-tenancy of an estate.
     knotty: Full of intellectual difficulties; entangled.
5.   *This Lamb*: Christ.
6.   *from the world's beginning slain*: 'And all that dwell upon the earth shall worship him, whose names are not written in the

book of life of the Lamb slain from the foundation of the world'
(Revelation 13:8).

7. *two wills*: The Old and the New Testament.
12. *law*: The Old Testament.
    and letter kill: '[God] hath made us able ministers of the new
    testament; not of the letter, but of the spirit: for the letter killeth,
    but the spirit giveth life' (2 Corinthians 3:6).
13. *Thy law's abridgement*: The laws of the Old Testament, short-
    ened and superseded by Christ's love.
14. *all but*: Nothing but.

Holy Sonnet XVII ('Since she whom I loved')

1. *she whom I loved*: Donne's wife, Anne More, who died in 1617
    at the age of thirty-three after the birth of their twelfth child.
2. *to hers*: Either to her good or to her human nature.
3. *ravished*: Transported.
10. *for hers off'ring all Thine*: For her love offering all Your love.
13. *jealousy*: Also zealousness.
    doubt: Fear.

Text note: Copy-text, Westmoreland ms

Holy Sonnet XVIII ('Show me, dear Christ')

1. *Thy spouse*: The true Church, devoted to her bridegroom, Christ
    (Matthew 25:1–10). Donne struggles to identify the true Church
    among competing Christian traditions.
2. *the other shore*: Continental Europe, especially Rome.
3. *richly painted*: A reference to the Roman Catholic Church.
    robbed and tore: The Lutheran Church destroyed the rich vest-
    ments, the paintings and the sculptures of Roman Catholic
    churches, claiming they were idolatrous.
4. *in Germany and here*: The Protestant Church – Lutheranism in
    Germany and Anglicanism in England.
8. *one [hill]*: Mount Moriah, on which Solomon built his temple.
    seven [hills]: Of Rome.
    no hill: In Geneva, centre of Calvinism.
10. *travail*: Journey; exert; labour in intercourse or childbirth.
12. *dove*: Symbol of God's love.
14. *open*: Accessible, welcoming, with both spiritual and erotic con-
    notations.

Text note: Copy-text, Westmoreland ms

Holy Sonnet XIX ('O, to vex me')

5. *humorous*: Changeable; influenced by the four bodily humours that were thought to shape one's temperament.
6. *profane*: Worldly.
7. *distempered*: Out of humour, vexed, troubled.
   cold and hot: Subject to melancholic and passionate humours.
13. *fantastic*: Fantastical, imaginary.

Text note: Copy-text, Westmoreland ms

The Cross

title *The Cross*: Donne plays upon the multiple meanings of 'cross' throughout: as a noun, both the physical shape and the spiritual burden; as a verb, to bless oneself by making the sign of the cross on the body and to cancel or restrain.
9–10. *no pulpit . . . withdraw*: The Puritans were reluctant to use the sign of the cross in performing sacraments.
16. *dew'd*: Wet, as in the sacrament of baptism.
20. *yard*: The long pole that crosses a ship's mast and supports the sail.
37. *alchemists do coiners prove*: Alchemists allegedly could turn base metals into gold.
46. *a snake*: Satan.
47. *the rest*: Of the senses.
49–50. *that can roam / And move*: The eye can move and observe from a distance objects that cross its path.
50. *to th'others . . . home*: The rest of the senses require close physical proximity.
56. *sutures*: Seams between cranial bones.
58. *concupiscence*: Carnal desire for the things of this world.

Text notes: 50 others *ms*] other *1633*; 52 Points *ms*] Pants *1633*; 63 That *ms*] The *1633*

The Annunciation and Passion

title *Annunciation*: The Angel Gabriel's visit to Mary to tell her that she would bear the Son of God.

Passion: The sufferings of Christ on the cross, commemorated on Good Friday. In 1608 the Feast of the Annunciation and Good Friday fell on the same day, 25 March.

1. *Tamely*: Submissively.
3. *She*: The speaker's soul.
4. *circle*: A symbol of perfection.
6. *feast or fast*: The Annunciation is celebrated with a feast; Good Friday is commemorated through fasting.
12. *Golgatha*: The site of Christ's crucifixion.
14. *almost fifty ... scarce fifteen*: Mary was fifteen at the Annunciation and fifty when Christ was crucified.
16. *her to John*: After Jesus was crucified, John took Mary into his home, as Jesus had requested (John 19:26–7).
17. *orbity*: Bereavement, especially for children.
22. *Ave*: (Latin) 'Hail', the greeting of Gabriel to Mary.
    Consummatum est: (Latin) 'It is finished', Christ's last words (John 19:30).
23. *court of faculties*: Learned church administrators.
25. *the self-fixed pole*: The North Pole.
26. *the next star*: The North Star.
31–2. *fiery pillar ... cloud*: To lead the Jews, God took the form of a pillar of cloud by day and a pillar of fire at night (Exodus 13:21).
39. *spouse*: The Church.
45. *in gross*: In general.
    uplay: Store up.
46. *retail*: Relate in detail.

Goodfriday, 1613. Riding Westward

2. *The'intelligence ... moves*: Angels were thought to determine the motion of the celestial spheres.
3–6. *And as ... obey*: The natural motion of the lower celestial spheres is east to west, but the motions of higher spheres affect those paths.
11. *sun*: Pun on 'Son'.
17. *Who sees ... must die*: 'And he said, Thou canst not see my face: for there shall no man see me, and live' (Exodus 33:20).
19–20. *It made ... wink*: Christ's crucifixion produced an earthquake and an eclipse of the sun (Matthew 27:50–51; Luke 23:44–6).

32. *Half . . . ransomed us*: In bearing Christ, Mary helped give sal-
    vation to mankind.
38. *leave*: Cease.

Text note: 22 turn *ms*] tune *1633*

Upon the Translation of the Psalms by Sir Philip Sidney and the Countess of Pembroke, His Sister

title *Translation . . . His Sister*: Translated by Sir Philip Sidney (1554–
       86) and his sister Mary Sidney, Countess of Pembroke (1561–
       1621), unpublished until 1823.
1–2. *External . . . square*: God's infinite perfection, symbolized by
      the circle, cannot be held within boundaries, here represented by
      the square.
9.   *first author*: King David.
      cloven: Split – the Psalms are sung in both human and divine
      tongues.
39.   *chambers*: Music rooms.
46.   *this Moses and this Miriam*: Miriam took up the song of her
      brother Moses (Exodus 15:1–21). The Countess completed the
      translation after Philip Sidney's death.
53.   *translated*: Moved to another place (by taking up into heaven).

Text notes: Copy-text, *1635*; 46 this *ms*] Thy *1635*; 53 these
ms] those *1635*

To Mr Tilman after He Had Taken Orders

title *Mr Tilman*: Edward Tilman, who was ordained a deacon on
       20 December 1618.
2.   *thy hand . . . plough*: 'And another also said, Lord, I will follow
      thee, but let me go first to bid them farewell, which are at home
      at my house. And Jesus said unto him, No man, having put his
      hand to the plough, and looking back, is fit for the kingdom of
      God' (Luke 9:61–2).
3.   *lay-scornings*: Attitudes towards the clergy later outlined in ll.
      26–30.
6.   *vintage*: Ripening and harvesting of grapes to be made into wine,
      here a spiritual maturation.
14.   *stamp*: Instrument for making impressions; the imprint or sign
      made by such an instrument.

23.   *purchase*: Gain or attainment; also occupation.
30.   *dressing ... compliment*: Taken from George Herbert's 'The Church Porch' (1633), ll. 80–81: 'Fly idleness, which yet thou canst not fly / By dressing, mistressing, and compliment.'
40.   *dignities*: Titles and privileges.
46.   *optics*: Telescope.
47.   *brave*: Worthy, excellent.
       engines: Ingenuity; devices.
54.   *hermaphrodite*: A person embodying opposites, here the imperfections of the flesh and the holiness of the divine.

Text notes: Copy-text, 1635; 47 engines *ms*] engine *1635*

A Hymn to Christ, at the Author's Last Going into Germany

title   *Last ... Germany*: Donne travelled to Germany in May 1619, on a diplomatic mission.
2.   *ark*: Symbol of God's providence, referring to Noah's ark and the flood (Genesis 6:12–21).
9.   *island*: England.
12.   *sea*: Christ's blood.
17–18. *Nor Thou ... soul*: God granted man free will to choose whether or not to love and follow Him.
21.   *from loving more*: A punning allusion to Donne's wife, Anne More, who had died in 1617.

Hymn to God my God, in my Sickness

9.   *South-west discovery*: Probably the Strait of Magellan.
10.   *Per fretum febris*: (Latin) Through the raging fever. *Fretum* also means 'strait'.
       straits: Also trials, sufferings.
13–15. *As West ... resurrection*: The sun sets in the west, symbolizing death, and rises in the east, suggesting resurrection.
18.   *Anyan*: A north-west passage linking the Atlantic to the Pacific Ocean.
20.   *Japhet ... Cham ... Shem*: Sons of Noah, whose descendants supposedly populated Europe, Africa and Asia.
21–2. *We think ... one place*: Referring to the common belief that the Tree of Knowledge in the Garden of Eden had stood at the site of Christ's crucifixion.
23.   *both Adams*: Both the first man and Christ.

26.   *purple*: The colour both of Christ's blood and of his garments
      when he was hailed as king of the Jews (John 19:2–5).

Text notes: Copy-text, *1635*; 12 their *ms*] those *1635*

A Hymn to God the Father

1.   *that sin where I begun*: Original sin.
2.   *done*: The pun on 'Donne' occurs throughout.
6.   *more*: A pun on Anne More, Donne's wife.
15.   *Thy sun*: A pun on the 'Son', Christ, signifying mercy.

Text notes: 7 by which I won *ms*] which I have won *1633*; 15
Swear *ms*] But swear *1633*; 18 have *ms*] fear *1633*

To Mr George Herbert, with One of my Seals, of the Anchor and Christ

The original Latin text was written by Donne. The English is an
anonymous seventeenth-century translation.
title: *the Anchor and Christ*: According to Walton's *Life of Dr John
Donne*, Donne later adopted this new seal of Christ crucified upon an
anchor, a symbol of hope, engraved it in stone and set in gold, and
sent it to his closest friends as a memento to remember him by.
11.   *my first serpents hold*: The serpents represent the death of origi-
      nal sin and Christ's death upon the cross.

Text note: Copy-text, *1650*

Index of Titles

Index of First Lines